# Equity Crowdfunding in Sports Clubs

This is the first book to focus on crowdfunding in sport. Crowdfunding is an important new financial instrument that is becoming more popular with sports organisations, and this book examines the research evidence for crowdfunding and considers how it might be successfully implemented.

Presenting international cases and data, including from European football, the book explains how crowdfunding campaigns have to be fully integrated with strategic marketing plans and require a solid understanding of the needs and motivations of potential investors, consumers, and fans. The book sets out a theoretical framework for applying strategic marketing in the context of crowdfunding in sports clubs, introduces the key characteristics of the sports crowdfunding market and funders' behaviours in the crowdfunding campaigns of sports clubs, examines the market segments of the campaigns' funders, and presents recommendations for developing marketing-mix programs to target them.

This is important reading for any researcher, advanced student, or practitioner with an interest in sport business, sport marketing, sport finance, consumer behaviour in sport, or entrepreneurship, innovation, or technology in sport.

**Szczepan Kościółek** is Assistant Professor in the Faculty of Management and Social Communication at Jagiellonian University in Kraków, Poland.

## Routledge Research in Sport Business and Management

**Digital Business Models in Sport**
*Edited by Mateusz Tomanek, Wojciech Cieśliński and Michał Polasik*

**Sport Management, Innovation and the COVID-19 Crisis**
*Edited by Gözde Ersöz and Meltem Ince Yenilmez*

**Sport in the Iberian Peninsula**
Management, Economics and Policy
*Edited by Jerónimo García-Fernández, Moisés Grimaldi-Puyana and Gonzalo A. Bravo*

**EU Antitrust Law and Sport Governance**
The Next Frontier?
*Edited by Jacob Kornbeck*

**Implementing Sport Policy**
Organisational Perspectives on the UK Sport System
*Edited by Marc Keech, Iain Lindsey and John Hayton*

**Global Sport Management Education**
Policy, Curriculum and Implementation
*Mike Rayner, Tom Webb, Ruth Sibson and Jacob K. Tingle*

**Equity Crowdfunding in Sports Clubs**
Consumer-Oriented Strategic Marketing
*Szczepan Kościółek*

For more information about this series, please visit https://www.routledge.com/Routledge-Research-in-Sport-Business-and-Management/book-series/RRSBM

# Equity Crowdfunding in Sports Clubs

## Consumer-Oriented Strategic Marketing

Szczepan Kościółek

Routledge
Taylor & Francis Group
London and New York

First published 2024
by Routledge
4 Park Square, Milton Park, Abingdon, Oxon OX14 4RN

and by Routledge
605 Third Avenue, New York, NY 10158

*Routledge is an imprint of the Taylor & Francis Group, an informa business*



*British Library Cataloguing-in-Publication Data*
A catalogue record for this book is available from the British Library

ISBN: 978-1-032-34116-3 (hbk)
ISBN: 978-1-032-34117-0 (pbk)
ISBN: 978-1-003-32062-3 (ebk)

DOI: 10.4324/9781003320623

Typeset in Sabon
by codeMantra

# Contents

# Acknowledgements

The author thanks the reviewers of the initial version of the manuscript, Prof. Miroslawa Pluta-Olearnik and Prof. Jadwiga Berbeka, whose insightful evaluations were very supportive and enabled the publication to be improved for the readers. I am also very grateful to Prof. Aleksander Panasiuk and Dr. Karolina Nessel for their comments and advice during the research process, which were very constructive and helpful.

Additionally, I would like to express my gratitude to Jagiellonian University in Kraków for funding the research project 'Crowdfunding in Sport: Consumer-Oriented Strategic Marketing' under the 'Excellence Initiative – Research University' programme.

# Introduction

Crowdfunding involves raising small contributions from a large number of people for a specific venture, usually via e-commerce platforms known as crowdfunding platforms (Schwienbacher & Larralde, 2010). Originally, it was intended to help start-ups and other risky ventures fill the equity gap when conventional sources of funding were not available (Cumming & Hornuf, 2018). As of 2022, the global crowdfunding market was valued at $13.5 billion and expected to continue its upward trend (Global Newswire, 2022). There are four main models of crowdfunding, which differ based on the form of return that participants can expect (Ahlers, Cumming, Gunter, & Schweizer, 2015). In the rewards model, participants receive a specific product as a reward for their contribution. The donation model involves unconditional transfer of funds. In the lending-based model, payments are returned in the future at a certain rate of return. Finally, the equity model, which is under the special focus in this book, involves the issuance of shares or instruments similar to shares (such as profit shares) to participants who support the project.

The advantages offered by crowdfunding – including lower cost of raising capital, faster access to market data, and increased brand awareness of the campaign originator – have made it an attractive form of support for a range of organisations beyond just innovative tech start-ups (Agrawal, Catalini, & Goldfarb, 2013; Gerber, Hui, & Kuo, 2012). Among the organisations that profit from the widespread use of crowdfunding are sports clubs. Crowdfunding has enabled amateur clubs to conduct fundraising campaigns to cover the costs of the necessary equipment, travel to competitions, as well as other goods and services that membership fees, public grants, donations, and other minor sources of revenue for non-profit sports clubs could not cover. In the case of professional clubs, facing in the European model a structural problem of a lack of profitability resulting from the focus on maximising the sporting results at the expense of maximising financial profit, crowdfunding has become another source of funding for financing selected initiatives supported by fans or simply maintaining the liquidity of the club.

In practice, in the case of both sports clubs and other organisations, the process of crowdfunding takes the form of a marketing campaign with a set

DOI: 10.4324/9781003320623-1

financial threshold and time frame. The purpose of the campaign initiator is to convince a sufficiently large number of people to contribute sufficiently large sums to raise the funds. Hence, the management of crowdfunding campaigns can actually be regarded as the management of the marketing aspects of these initiatives. This requires the appropriate use of available marketing tools, making the right decisions regarding each of the marketing-mix elements. These operational activities should stem from a marketing plan based on a strategy that takes into account the needs and motivations of potential crowdfunding participants from different market segments. The challenge is how to do it effectively.

The motivations and needs of sports clubs investors on the regulated market (as well as the management decisions in the area of strategic marketing) have been the subject of extensive research, but there was a research gap in the area of crowdfunding. The gap was filled by a series of publications written by the author of this monograph as part of a project on the motivations behind crowdfunding of sports clubs. This monograph is a synthesis of the research carried out as part of this cycle, extended further by previously unpublished descriptive analyses of selected crowdinvestment and crowdlending campaigns for sports clubs carried out in Europe, an analysis of the marketing communication of these campaigns, and a discussion of all other research in the area of sports-related crowdfunding that had been published by the end of 2022 as articles in scientific journals indexed in the Web of Science and Scopus databases.

The publication is the first monograph on sports crowdfunding, which collects and synthesises fragments of data and findings described in various empirical research papers. Its aim is to describe the specific nature of crowdfunding campaigns in the context of sports clubs, as well as to formulate assumptions for a model marketing strategy for this type of campaigns run by sports clubs under equity crowdfunding. These assumptions are founded on the motivation-based two-stage segmentation of crowdinvestors and the resulting market positioning of the campaigns in relation to each of the designated and profiled segments.

The book reviews research results related to several theoretical aspects, including:

- Verification of the need to use the concept of differentiated marketing in the context of crowdfunding campaign for a sports club;
- Identification of the categories of motivation that determine the crowdinvestment in the campaigns of sports clubs;
- Design of a motivation scale to conduct research on crowdinvestment in sports clubs;
- Determination of the number and size of segments of equity crowdfunding investors, and separation of homogeneous groups of them based on crowdinvestment motivations;

- Characterisation of segments of participants in crowdfunding campaigns conducted by sports clubs;
- Development of value propositions that meet the needs of crowdinvestors, market positioning methods, and forms of providing value to selected target groups of a sports club's crowdfunding equity campaign.

Sports managers and crowdfunding platform managers can derive the following benefits from these materials:

- They can acquire a motivation measurement scale that can be used for researching the participants of crowdfunding campaigns for sports clubs;
- The materials provide information on the market segments of sports clubs crowdinvestors, including the number, size, and profiles of these segments. This information can be effectively utilised in planning the marketing communication for a crowdfunding campaign;
- They can develop a model concept for marketing strategy for crowdfunding campaigns. This model can be directly applied by sports managers in shaping strategies and marketing plans for specific crowdfunding campaigns for sports clubs.

This book is structured as follows. The first chapter provides an introduction to marketing management, emphasising the role and material scope of marketing strategy and the importance of market segmentation in shaping it. It presents an argument for what a marketing strategy should consist of and outlines the actions required to implement its provisions effectively. Chapters 2 and 3 focus on the two main subjects of this study, namely crowdfunding campaigns and sports clubs. Chapter 2 begins with an overview of crowdfunding campaigns, followed by a presentation of their typology and an analysis of the consumer behaviour of participants in such ventures. The latter part of this chapter reviews the existing research on marketing strategies for non-sports organisations' crowdfunding campaigns. Similarly, Chapter 3 presents the essence of the functioning and financing of sports clubs. This serves as a starting point for the subsequent subchapters, which discuss research findings on the marketing strategies of sports clubs. Finally, Chapter 4 integrates these perspectives together by presenting the issues of strategic marketing management of sports clubs' equity crowdfunding campaigns. It starts from the general insights of the sports crowdfunding market, then focuses on consumer behaviour of participants of sports clubs' equity crowdfunding campaigns, and on this basis presents a background for developing marketing strategies for sports clubs' equity crowdfunding campaigns.

Taken together, the author hopes that the publication will be a valuable contribution for both researchers and practitioners of sports clubs crowdfunding, with a particular focus on the initiators of equity crowdfunding campaigns. Given that the literature review on marketing management and crowdfunding campaigns was based on publications not strictly related to sports organisations, the publication may also be useful for representatives of other industries.

## References

Agrawal, A., Catalini, C., & Goldfarb, A. (2013). Some simple economics of crowdfunding. *Natural Bureau of Economic Research, 19133*. Retrieved from http://www.nber.org/papers/w19133

Ahlers, G. K. C., Cumming, D., Gunter, C., & Schweizer, D. (2015). Signaling in equity crowdfunding. *Entrepreneurship Theory and Practice*, *39*(4), 955–980. https://doi.org/10.1111/etap.12157

Cumming, D., & Hornuf, L. (2018). Introduction. In D. Cumming & L. Hornuf (Eds.), *The Economics of Crowdfunding* (pp. 1–8). Cham: Palgrave Macmillan.

Gerber, E. M., Hui, J. S., & Kuo, P. (2012). Crowdfunding : Why people are motivated to post and fund projects on crowdfunding platforms. *Proceedings of the International Workshop on Design, Influence, and Social Technologies: Techniques, Impacts and Ethics*, 2(11), 10.

Global Newswire (2022). *Demand for Global Crowdfunding Market Size & Share to Surpass USD 28.2 Billion by 2028, Exhibit a CAGR of 11.8%*, https://www.globenewswire.com/news-release/2022/04/12/2420860/0/en/Demand-for-Global-Crowdfunding-Market-Size-Share-to-Surpass-USD-28-2-Billion-by-2028-Exhibit-a-CAGR-of-11-8-Industry-Trends-Status-Revenue-Opportunities-Segmentation-Analysis-Forec.html

Schwienbacher, A., & Larralde, B. (2010). Crowdfunding of small entrepreneurial ventures. In D. Cumming (Ed.), *The Oxford Handbook of Entrepreneurial Finance* (pp. 369–391). Oxford University Press.

Chapter 1

# Strategic marketing management

## 1.1 Fundamentals of marketing

### *1.1.1 Essence of marketing activities*

The starting point for the considerations on marketing management, including the development of a marketing strategy (which is part of this process), is the outline of the general conceptual framework for marketing activity in an enterprise. Originally, marketing was understood as the use of various factors controlled by the enterprise to increase the sales of the products on offer (Butler, De Bower, & Jones, 1914). According to Drucker (1973), the purpose of modern-day marketing, however, is no longer simply to try to persuade potential customers to purchase given products, but to get to know and understand them well enough to be able to use this knowledge to prepare an offer that evokes in the potential customer[1] the desire to purchase the product.

Marketing can be analysed at two levels: micro level (as a set of activities conducted by organisations) and macro level (as a social process) (Perreault, Cannon, & McCarthy, 2002). Kotler and Keller (2012) indicate that this classification corresponds to the social and managerial perspectives. At the macro level, the role of marketing can be described as a social process whereby individuals or groups of individuals obtain what they need and want by creating, offering, and freely exchanging products of value with others. When conducting a social analysis of marketing, the focus should, therefore, be not on the activities of individual organisations but on the mechanism of functioning of the entire marketing system in society (Perreault et al., 2002).

At the micro level, marketing is understood as a process whereby organisations operating on the market engage customers, build strong relationships with them, and create value for them in order to obtain value in return (Armstrong & Volkov, 2018). From the customer's perspective, value is understood as the difference between the benefits that he or she can obtain and the costs that he or she has to incur in order to purchase the product in question (Dobiegała-Korona & Krzepicka, 2012). For such a theoretical framework

DOI: 10.4324/9781003320623-2

of marketing, the American Marketing Association (2020) adopted the definition of marketing as a set of activities, institutions, and processes for creating, communicating, delivering, and exchanging value for customers, partners, and society as a whole.

Taking into account the described transformations in the perception of marketing in organisations, at least two approaches can be adopted with respect to the terminology:

- Narrow and broad;
- Classic and modern;

with the narrow view of marketing being closer to the classical one, while the broad view being closer to the modern one (Panasiuk, 2013b). What is stressed in the narrow approach is the need for planning, coordination, and control of the market-oriented activities of the enterprise. In turn, the broad approach assumes the integration of marketing instruments and activities as the basis for market-related decisions.

The narrow view, which corresponds to the classic approach, assumes putting the customer at the centre of the company's activities, shaping the market and influencing it through marketing instruments, and basing decision-making processes on planning in order to find optimal market solutions. The modern approach, which is similar to the broad approach, emphasises the purposefulness and sustainability of the adopted solutions, where the organisation relies on a set of multiple integrated instruments and activities, the use of which is based on market conditions, processes, and phenomena (Panasiuk, 2013b).

### *1.1.2 Marketing-oriented management*

If the aforementioned marketing activities become the management concept of the entire organisation, this means that the company has adopted the so-called marketing concept of management (or simply marketing concept) (Kotler, Keller, Brady, Goodman, & Hansen, 2016; Panasiuk, 2017; Perreault et al., 2002; Sławińska, 2015a). The latter can be analysed at two levels: the culture of the organisation and the related activities, processes, and behaviours. The manifestation of the former is the organisation's marketing orientation[2] (cultural dimension), while the expression of the latter is the organisation's marketing management (managerial dimension) (Kozielski, 2015). These two dimensions of marketing are strongly linked to each other. Assuming that marketing orientation is a reflection of organisational culture, it determines the process activities undertaken by a given organisation as part of its marketing management.

Marketing orientation is one of the five basic orientations characterising companies, mentioned in the literature (along with production, product, sales, and strategic orientation) (Armstrong & Volkov, 2018; Kotler et al., 2016). The production orientation used to be adopted at a time when demand exceeded supply on the market, customers were offered a homogeneous mass product, and competition was based on technological progress leading to qualitative development of goods. Then, the approach changed in favour of the product orientation, according to which the goal of the product offered was to satisfy the needs of consumers as much as possible. The sales orientation assumed that consumers and companies, if left alone, would not buy enough products offered; hence, they needed to be persuaded. In turn, under the marketing orientation, the organisation's resources are focused on sourcing and retaining customers (Brzustewicz, 2014; Kotler & Keller, 2012).

The evolution of the orientations adopted by companies has been driven by changes in the business environment, mainly in terms of technological advancement, globalisation, and the growing importance of social responsibility (Figure 1.1) (Kotler et al., 2016). These three factors have radically changed the market, offering new opportunities to consumers and companies and creating a stronger relationship between the buyer and the seller. Kaczmarczyk and Pałgan (2008) observed that this is due to the development of competition, the saturation of markets, changes in customer needs and demands, and the increasing liberalisation of the global economy.

By adopting the marketing orientation, companies have also adopted the 'outside-in' principle, i.e. manufacturing the products that consumers actually want (Knecht, 2008). Marketing orientation should, therefore, be perceived as focusing the company's efforts on satisfying the customers' needs by identifying those needs, and subsequently generating and delivering the highest possible value to the customers (Hult, Ketchen Jr, & Slater, 2005). Further changes in the business environment have led to the development of a higher form of marketing orientation – the strategic marketing orientation,

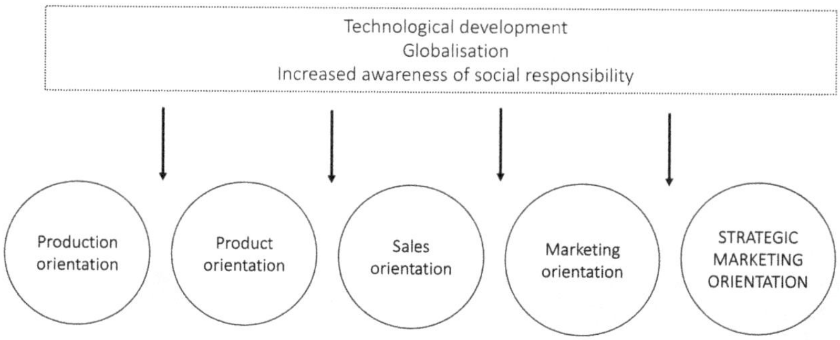


*Figure 1.1* Orientations of enterprises

Source: Based on Kotler and Keller (2012), Armstrong and Volkov (2018), Knecht (2008), Panasiuk (2013a), Sławińska (2012)

which assumes long-term strategic efforts aimed at adaptation to the changing market conditions, including primarily customer behaviour.

Due to the transformations related to the growing awareness of customers and the resulting aversion to aggressive marketing campaigns, as well as the development of environmental movements, some enterprises have adopted the so-called social orientation (otherwise known as social responsibility orientation) (Armstrong & Volkov, 2018). In this approach, the company's activities focus not only on meeting the customers' needs but also on making sure that the principles of sustainability and environmental protection are followed, enabling it to build relationships with customers who share these values. This orientation should, nevertheless, be treated as a variation of the conventional or strategic marketing orientation, rather than a fully autonomous orientation (Panasiuk, 2017).

The classification presented above is the most popular one, although not the only one describing the evolution of organisations' orientation. Alternative approaches do not either distinguish between the product phase and the production phase (as both are focused on the organisation of the production process) or replace a strategic orientation with a holistic one (based on the development, design, and implementation of integrated marketing programmes, processes, and activities) (Brzustewicz, 2014; Kotler & Keller, 2012). Taking into account the subject matter of this book, what is important is that both approaches (holistic and strategic marketing orientations) assume that marketing activities are based on a previously adopted marketing strategy.

The development of the internet and new technologies is of crucial importance for changing the way customer value is generated, as well as the nature of the interactions between the customer and the organisation (Brzustewicz, 2014). In this new market reality, customers and companies work together to develop personalised services through dialogue and interaction (Svensson & Grönroos, 2008). As a result of this, companies are adopting a specific form of marketing orientation: e-marketing orientation, the aim of which is reaching out to customers through direct communication via social media, websites, and smartphones (Eid & El-Gohary, 2013). At the same time, shaping integrated marketing communication under these conditions, maintaining the consistency of the messages sent to the audience via electronic and conventional media may be challenging (Pluta-Olearnik, 2018).

The adoption of the e-marketing orientation in an organisation entails the use of an integrated information technology and marketing concept, connecting buyers, sellers, business partners, and employees through the use of one or several of the following elements (Trainor, Rapp, Beitelspacher, & Schillewaert, 2011):

- Customer relationship management software[3];
- Extranets, including private websites created especially for the customer;
- The use of e-commerce websites.

Based on the above elements, it can be assumed that undertakings conducted exclusively in the online domain are e-marketing-oriented by definition. The crowdfunding campaigns discussed in this publication are an example of such activities.[4]

### 1.1.3 Creating customer value

Marketing-oriented organisations (including e-marketing-oriented ones) adopt a relational approach to marketing. In contrast to the conventional, transactional approach,[5] in the case of relationship marketing, marketing activities are aimed at establishing long-term relations with the company's key stakeholders, especially its customers (Doyle & Stern, 2006; Pluta-Olearnik, 2010). Depending on their perspective, one can identify three levels of relations between the company and the customers (Mitręga, 2008): financial (resulting from material incentives), social (resulting from direct contacts), and structural (resulting from the adaptation of the offer to the customer's needs).

In terms of building relationships in the structural dimension, companies target individual customers with custom offers prepared based on their previous transactions, demographics, psychographics, preferences, and other data (Hollensen, 2010). Contemporary consumers want to have influence over every part of the business system by interacting with companies, becoming *de facto* co-creators of the value generated by them (Prahalad & Ramaswamy, 2004). This type of customers are referred to as prosumers (Pluta-Olearnik, 2013). The benefits resulting from this phenomenon are recognised by company managers, who observe that customers are one of the main sources of innovation on the leisure industries market (Bednarczyk, 2006). According to Mazurek and Zach (2018), the stage of co-creation of value by the company and the customer represents the next stage, following transactional marketing and relationship marketing, in the development of the company–customer relationship. Its most advanced form is deemed to be crowdsourcing,[6] which gives customers the opportunity to become involved in the process of creation or development of products.

A tool used by customers to create value is user-generated content (Ye, Law, Gu, & Chen, 2011). It includes mainly online activities related to rating products, writing reviews, giving recommendations, and sharing information on the products consumed on social media (in the area of sports, possible examples include discussions about sports events organised by sports clubs, but also reviews of products for practising sports) (Kotler et al., 2010). The latter is also a reflection of the shift of the word-of-mouth marketing to the virtual domain, and its transformation into so-called electronic word-of-mouth marketing. In general, word-of-mouth marketing is a complex process of exchanging information between acquaintances, shaping their individual purchasing decisions and behaviour. Research on this phenomenon has shown that positive messages conveyed in this form increase the likelihood of purchasing a particular product, while negative messages have the opposite effect (Arndt, 1967; Pan & Fesenmaier, 2006). In line with described evolution, word-of-mouth marketing ceased to mean merely verbal communication between two acquaintances, but began to encompass all forms of communication between customers (Westbrook, 1987).

The aforementioned activities undertaken as part of customer value co-creation also fall within the scope of social media marketing, which is understood as the process through which companies create, communicate, and deliver their offer via social media to build and maintain relationships with stakeholders (Yadav & Rahman, 2017). These activities increase stakeholder value by facilitating interactions, sharing information, presenting personalised offers, and encouraging word-of-mouth marketing. The use of modern communication tools reinforces the effectiveness of the adopted marketing concept in the company. The implementation of marketing functions via electronic media has a positive impact on the long-term financial performance of the company (Brodie, Winklhofer, Coviello, & Johnston, 2007), due to their lower costs compared to conventional distribution and communication channels (Ciunova-Shuleska, Osakwe, & Palamidovska-Sterjadovska, 2016).

Online marketing not only generates additional value with the customers' participation but also translates into other benefits resulting from their engagement (Kopera, 2016). The greater the engagement of the customers, the greater their satisfaction with the products purchased, which leads to stronger brand loyalty (Jaakkola & Alexander, 2014). The concept of satisfaction is understood here as the overall level of satisfaction with the goods or services purchased (Johnson & Fornell, 1991). Satisfied customers are more likely to become loyal customers, who are committed to consistently purchasing their preferred products or patronising preferred companies, despite circumstances and marketing efforts on the part of competitors that attempt to change these attitudes (Oliver, 1999). Loyal customers are particularly desirable to companies as they generate repeat purchases and word-of-mouth marketing (Figure 1.2) (Evanschitzky et al., 2012; Keller, 1993; See-To & Ho, 2014).

The evolution of the customer value creation process stems from the digital revolution, which evolved from Web 1.0 to Web 2.0 to Web 3.0. Web 1.0 technologies only allowed for cognitive processes resulting from contact with the content provided. Web 2.0 technologies provide the basis for the development of communication processes through interactive platforms (e.g. social media), while Web 3.0 technologies facilitate the processes of collaboration and integration in the creation of new information and meaning (Barassi & Treré, 2012; Mazurek, 2007; O'Reilly, 2007). The marketing effects of these transformations can be described by the analogous conceptual frameworks of marketing 1.0, 2.0, and 3.0 (Brzustewicz, 2014). When shifting away from

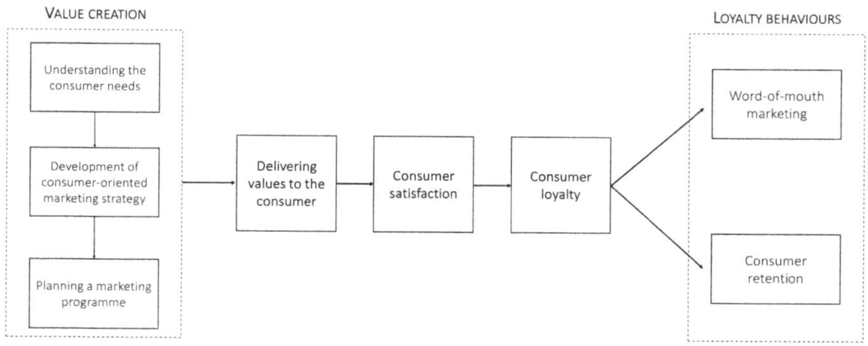


*Figure 1.2* Schematic representation of building relationships with customers

Source: Based on Armstrong and Volkov (2018); Brodie et al. (2007) and Ciunova-Shuleska et al. (2016)

the era of marketing 1.0 to marketing 2.0, in order to generate demand for products, the 'customer' replaced the 'product' at the centre of all marketing activities, including developing marketing strategies based on the market segmentation process (Kotler, Kartajaya, & Setiawan, 2010). Marketing has, thus, evolved from a purely tactical to a more strategic level, making it more effective at delivering value to the customer (Mruk, 2008).

The development of new technologies, including social media, has enabled rapid communication also between customers themselves. Customers interact and influence one another by commenting on content available online and sharing their own experiences and opinions, creating in this way virtual social networks (Kachniewska, 2013). This has forced companies to focus not only on horizontal communication but also on vertical (Brzustewicz, 2014; Kotler et al., 2010), and to take into account human feelings and values in the marketing communication. This change in approach is behind the creation of a new dimension of marketing 3.0.

## 1.2 Customer-oriented marketing management

### *1.2.1 Scope and stages of marketing management*

Activities adapting the marketing concept in an organisation fall within the field of marketing management (Kotler et al., 2016; Pomykalski, 2005). There is a relative consensus in the literature with respect to the essence of the concept of marketing management, which is understood as the process of identifying target groups, researching the needs of these groups, and then developing the product, pricing, distribution, and promotion model, and shaping an offer that meets the needs of the organisation's stakeholders

(Armstrong & Volkov, 2018; Doyle & Stern, 2006; Hollensen, 2010; Kotler & Keller, 2012; Niestrój, 2002). The presented definition of marketing management clearly implies that this process requires understanding of the value that the customers are looking and delivering it to the appropriate target group through an effective configuration of marketing-mix elements (Armstrong & Volkov, 2018).

Based on such conceptual framework of marketing management, a specific set of activities undertaken as part of this process can be identified, including (Kotler et al., 2016):

- Developing and implementing marketing strategies and plans;
- Conducting market research in order to verify product potential and sales forecasts on an ongoing basis;
- Reaching out to customers;
- Building brand awareness and positioning the brand on the market;
- Creating and delivering value in order to build long-term relationships with customers.

Marketing management, similar to any other typical management process, consists of four stages (Griffin, Rusinski, & Rozanska, 1999; Perreault et al., 2002): analysis, planning, implementation, and control (Figure 1.3). The first stage involves the analysis of the internal and external situations of the organisation, which serves as a basis for formulating marketing objectives and strategy.[7] The assumptions of the marketing strategy are used to develop a marketing plan (also referred to as a marketing programme) with specific solutions designed to deliver the expected value to the target groups.

As part of marketing planning, the company develops an integrated marketing mix composed of factors under its control. The marketing management process is concluded with a control stage, as part of which verification is carried out of the achieved marketing objectives (Armstrong & Volkov, 2018). The following sections will briefly discuss each of these elements. The marketing strategy, which is the subject of this study, and the resulting marketing plan will be presented in detail in Section 1.3.

The analysis of the internal situation mainly involves identifying the core competencies and the level of competitiveness of the company (Hollensen, 2010). The basis of the latter is the value proposition – a set of benefits that are promised to customers in order to satisfy their needs (Grabińska & Nessel, 2016). The value, as perceived by the customer, is the difference between his or her evaluation of the total benefits and costs of a particular offer against possible alternatives. The total benefit, in this case, is the perceived monetary value of a set of economic, functional, and psychological benefits that customers expect from a given offer composed of goods, services, people, and brand image.

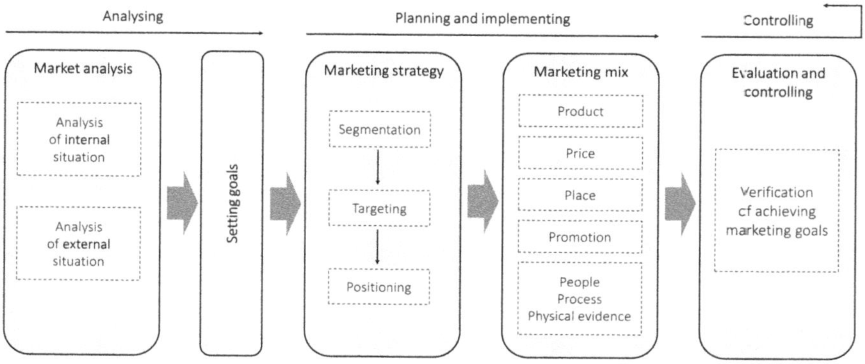


*Figure 1.3* Marketing management process in an organisation

Source: Based on Armstrong and Volkov (2018); Grabińska and Nessel (2016); Hollensen (2010); Kotler and Keller (2012); Perreault et al. (2002); Sidorkiewicz (2013).

### *1.2.2 Internal environment analysis*

Porter (1985) puts forward the concept of the value chain as a tool for identifying the sources of customer value creation. According to this model, the performance of each company is the result of the activities related to designing, producing, marketing, delivering, and providing support for its products. The conventional concept of the value chain identifies nine strategically important activities (five core and four support activities) that create value and generate costs on the part of the company. The core activities that make up the value chain include (Kotler & Keller, 2016) inbound logistics (the supply of materials to the company), operations (the processing of materials into final products), outbound logistics (the shipment of final products), marketing (including sales), and after-sales service.

For organisations offering services instead of goods, the subsequent stages of the value chain are related to the stages of solving a particular problem of the customer (Kotler & Keller, 2016): problem identification and formulation, identification of the opportunities to solve the problem, selection of the solution, implementation of the solution, and control and evaluation of the actions taken (Figure 1.4). Support activities are the area of responsibility of specialised company departments. These activities mainly include development of new technologies, human capital, and company infrastructure management (including general management, planning, finances, accounting, and legal matters).

Limitations on the effective use of material goods marketing instruments in the area of services have resulted in the need for the development of new solutions and the adaptation of existing ones (Panasiuk, 2013b). With respect

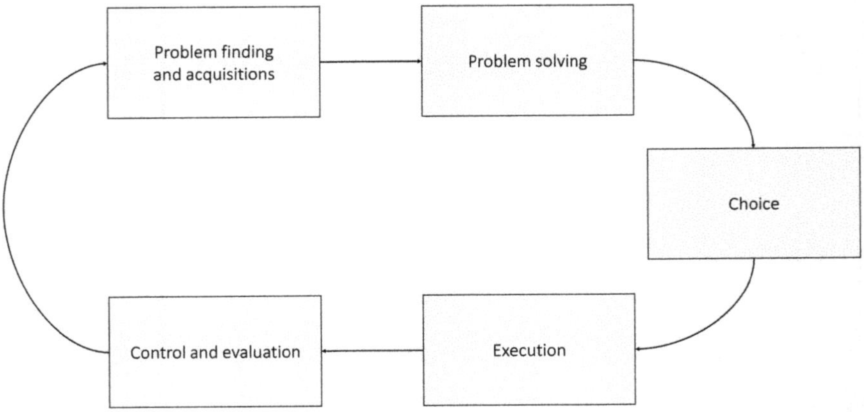


*Figure 1.4* Service value chain

Source: Hollensen (2010); Stabell and Fjeldstad (1998)

to the value chain, Stabell and Fjeldstad (1998) identified two new models: value shops and value networks. In this approach, the value chain is understood as a model for the production of goods, while the value shop is a model for solving customer problems in the services sector (service value chain). It is based on value creation through the mobilisation of resources and activities to solve a specific customer problem. In turn, the value network is understood as a collaboration of several companies, where each entity has a small stake in the overall process of holistic efforts aimed at meeting the customers' needs (Hollensen, 2010).

The basic activities that make up a service value chain include (Hollensen, 2010) problem identification (identifying, reviewing, and formulating the problem and selecting an overall approach to solving it), identification of possible options for solving the problem (coming up with and evaluating alternative solutions), selection of a solution (from among several alternatives), implementation (communicating, organising, and implementing the selected solution), control and evaluation (measuring and assessing to what extent the problem has been solved). In contrast to the conventional value chain where activities are sequential processes, the service value chain consists of cyclical processes. This means that solving customer problems in the services sector is a continuous process, and that feedback from each cycle should result in an improvement in the quality of the service provided.

In practical terms, the situation where we are dealing with purely material goods or services is almost non-existent (Panasiuk & Tokarz, 2005). Typically, material goods are supported by services or vice versa, or we are dealing with hybrids of the two. This has two important implications for marketing management:

- In the case of most products, value is generated through elements of both the conventional and the service value chain;
- The value generated for the customer is verified only when the two chains are combined and the product is delivered to the customer.[8]

The activities undertaken as part of value delivery should be systematic and consistent – both internally (with each other) and externally (in line with the organisation's operating philosophy, its mission, and its vision) (Grabińska & Nessel, 2016). The vision describes what the organisation is going to look like in the future. It constitutes the company's raison d'être and indicates what it is aiming at, whose and what needs it strives to meet, and what its social mission is (Gierszewska, 2000). It is a sort of reference point indicating the direction the organisation is pursuing. On the other hand, Obłój (2014) defines mission as the vision reformulated for the purpose of the strategy. In this sense, the mission is a brief statement of the scope of the company's activities in relation to its environment (Pomykalski, 2005).

Mission is communicated to all stakeholders of the organisation. It plays an important role in indicating the direction for further actions, sanctioning decisions made, and motivating staff to work towards the achievement of specific goals (Kotler & Keller, 2016). Mission highlights the company's main principles and values and identifies the most important areas of competition (Smoleń, 2012b). It also outlines the tasks to be fulfilled by the company at a less detailed level than the objectives and strategies formulated on its basis, but is essential to the development of the latter (Gierszewska, 2000).

The prerequisite for an organisation to adopt a customer-oriented approach is the use of the so-called S-D logic (service-dominant logic), which represents one of two ways of thinking about customer value generation. S-D logic adopts a perspective in which services are the primary object of business (Vargo & Lusch, 2008). This is contrasted with the goods-dominant logic (G-D), where the company is focused on material resources and transactions. From the point of view of the S-D logic, goods only serve as a kind of tools that enable the provision of services. The service itself, in turn, is seen as a process of using resources for the benefit of another entity (Ng & Vargo, 2018).

Under the S-D logic, customer value can only be created contextually and through collaboration (Ng & Vargo, 2018). Vargo and Lusch (2016) identified five axioms of the S-D logic: service is exchanged for another service (axiom 1), the customer is always a co-creator of value (axiom 2), all social and economic entities (manufacturers, business partners, auxiliary entities, customers, etc.) are integrators of resources (axiom 3), value is always uniquely and phenomenologically determined by the beneficiary (axiom 4), and the process of value creation is coordinated by institutions and institutional arrangements (axiom 5).

The second element of internal analysis is the identification of core competencies. The literature identifies two dominant approaches, based on which competitive advantage is built: the resource-based view (RBV) and the dynamic capabilities view (DCV). The category of marketing resources refers to the company's tangible or intangible attributes that help it deliver value that is perceived as distinctive compared to the solutions of competitors. In the DCV approach, resources can be treated as equivalent to and related to the intangible processes that help the company use marketing resources in an effective way (Mitręga, Wieczorek, Małecka, & Pfajfar, 2018).

In turn, in the RBV approach, competitive advantages arise from the development and deployment of unique, valuable, and irreplaceable resources (Barney, 1991; Day, 1994). Less critical processes are outsourced if companies can achieve better quality or lower costs in this way. What is crucial is to own and develop the resources and competencies that make up the core of the business (Hamel & Prahalad, 1990). This is known as the competence core, which is characterised by three key aspects (Day, 2011):

- It is a source of competitive advantage, as well as a significant contribution to the perceived benefits for customers;
- It is applicable across various markets;
- It is difficult for competitors to imitate.

In the DCV approach, on the other hand, the performance of the organisation depends on both the company's resources and the effectiveness in transforming them (Teece, Pisano, & Shuen, 1997). The capabilities are dynamic in the sense that they provide companies with the freedom to implement new strategies to adapt to the changing business environment (Mitręga et al., 2018). From the marketing strategy perspective, DCV implies that marketing resources or capabilities must be combined and integrated with other complementary capabilities in order to generate and maintain competitive advantage (Menguc & Auh, 2006). This approach suggests that, in the face of dynamically changing market conditions, rather than focusing on their own resources, companies should look for differences in opportunities to acquire and use resources in a better way than competitors.

### *1.2.3 External environment analysis*

This type of analysis is related to the assessment of the enviromnent outside the organisation (Hollensen, 2010). It includes both the macroenvironment and the microenvironment (Kotler & Keller, 2012; Pomykalski, 2005; Rosa, 2008; Smoleń, 2012c). Since the aim of the analysis is to formulate marketing strategy objectives, it is usually conducted using strategic management techniques[9]. The complexity associated with this type of analysis is reflected in the characteristics of the company's environment, which can be summarised as 4Ds: difficult to predict, dangerous, dynamic, and diverse (Pilarczyk, 2015a).

The macroenvironment represents the operating conditions, which the company does not control, but which have a strong impact on it (Gierszewska, 2000). This means that the company has to interpret these external circumstances and actively react to them. The elements of the macroenvironment usually include political, economic, social, technological, environmental, and legal factors (Hollensen, 2010; Pomykalski, 2005; Rosa, 2008; Smoleń, 2012c). These forces influence and moderate the behaviour of all market actors, including the company's competitors, suppliers, distributors, and customers. The analysis of the aforementioned factors is most often conducted using the PESTEL technique[10], which assists in identifying the impact of these variables on the company's situation (Grabińska & Nessel, 2016).

The microenvironment consists of stakeholders that have direct relations with the organisation. Unlike the macroenvironment, the microenvironment consists of entities whose actions the company can influence. These mainly include customers, competitors, suppliers, business partners, and employees (Armstrong & Volkov, 2018; Pomykalski, 2005; Smoleń, 2012c). In terms of the marketing management process, the analysis of customers and the competitive environment has the greatest importance among the aforementioned elements of the immediate environment (Armstrong & Volkov, 2018; Grabińska & Nessel, 2016; Kotler et al., 2016; Perreault et al., 2002).

A tool used for incorporating elements of the microenvironment to competitive analysis is the five forces model proposed by M.E. Porter (2001). This model identifies five determinants of internal long-term market attractiveness, including industry rivalry, threat of new entrants, threat of substitutes, bargaining power of buyers, and bargaining power of suppliers (Figure 1.5).

For each of the five forces in Porter's model, a number of criteria influencing the company's competitive environment can be identified (Pilarczyk, 2015b; Pomykalski, 2005). Synthesising these criteria, two universal rules can be adopted:

- The lower the concentration of the sector of buyers or suppliers, the greater the competitive level of the company (and vice versa);
- The lower the probability of new entrants or substitutes on the market, the more favourable the competitive position of the firm (and vice versa).

There are two main categories of customers: companies (institutional customers; B2B – business-to-business) and individuals (individual customers; B2C – business-to-customer) (Hollensen, 2010; Smoleń, 2012c). On the consumer market (which is the area of interest of crowdfunding campaigns), customer behaviour is influenced by two main categories of external factors:

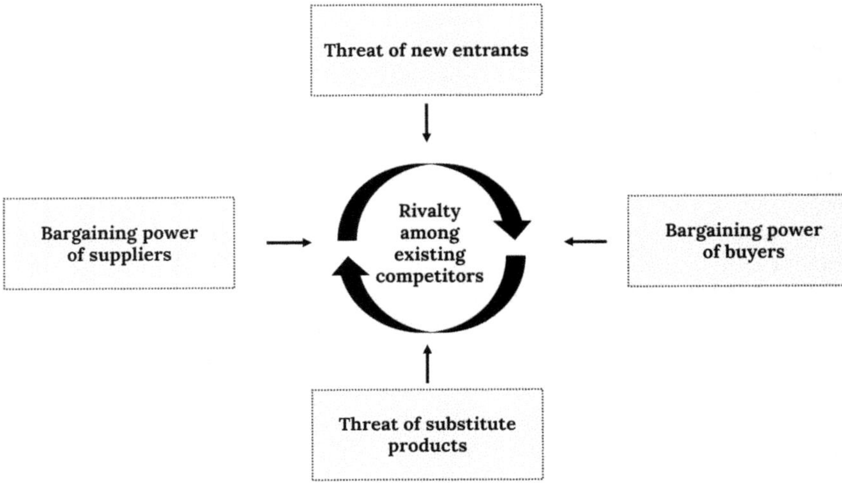


*Figure 1.5* Porter's five forces model

Source: Porter (2008)

marketing stimulants (issued by the organisation) and other stimulants, related to the contextual environment (e.g. economic, technological, cultural, and political issues) (Kotler & Keller, 2016). In terms of intrinsic factors, consumers make purchase decisions based on cultural, social, and psychological factors, which mainly include accompanying buyer motivations, perception, memory, and learning ability. This means that the key challenge when developing a marketing strategy is to learn both the buyer's explicitly expressed needs and their intrinsic, covert purchase motivations (Berbeka, 2003).

Elements of the macro- and microenvironments can be analysed by establishing the so-called marketing intelligence system, understood as a set of procedures involving tracking trends, important changes in the organisational environment, and associated opportunities and threats (Kotler & Keller, 2016). This system typically consists of three elements: an internal record-keeping system containing information on payments, orders, and sales; a marketing intelligence system consisting of a set of procedures and sources used by managers to obtain information on important changes in the marketing environment on an ongoing basis; and a marketing research system enabling systematic design, collection, analysis, and reporting of data related to specific marketing circumstances.

The presented stage of analysis (the first stage of marketing management) serves as a basis for formulating the strategic objectives of the company and the objectives of the marketing strategy as such. Based on the assessment of the internal and external situations of the organisation, four model strategies can be identified (Pilarczyk, 2015b): aggressive (focused on strengthening the market position), conservative (focused on exploiting the company's strengths in order to expand into new markets), competitive (focused on exploiting market opportunities), and defensive (focused on survival).

In turn, in terms of the product–market relationship, two strategic development directions can be identified: growth and consolidation, with the growth strategy being further subdivided into (Sidorkiewicz, 2013):

- Market penetration – maintaining existing products on the markets which the company currently operates within;
- Product development – offering new or modified products on the markets which the company currently operates within;
- Market development – offering existing products on new markets;
- Diversification – launching new products on new markets.

Regardless of the strategic direction adopted, marketing objectives typically concern achieving a specific profit level, market share, turnover, growth level, or market position of a given product (Kowal, 2001). It is practically impossible to prepare these strategies without prior analysis of the environment and customer needs described in this part of the publication. This is due to the constantly changing business environment, including (Doyle & Stern, 2006) shifting customers' needs, the emergence of new technologies, and the development of competitive offers. As a result, marketing strategies adopt a time frame of several years at most, as companies that fail to adapt to changes in the environment go out of business.

## 1.3 Development of marketing strategies

### *1.3.1 Material scope of a marketing strategy*

The marketing strategy is a functional document, governed by assumptions of the corporate and business strategy (Figure 1.6) (Hollensen, 2010). Many companies, especially global ones, consist of multiple strategic business units with separate business development programmes (Armstrong & Volkov, 2018). They are all governed by a corporate strategy, which is the most general and comprehensive manifestation of the company's business concept (Pluta-Olearnik & Olearnik, 2015). This implies that the implementation of its assumptions at the functional level is expected to translate into the achievement of the strategic objectives of the entire organisation.

Functional strategies are created for the entire organisation, also for departments other than the marketing department. The provisions of all these functional strategies and the activities undertaken as part of them must be coordinated (Hollensen, 2010). The digital marketing strategy is a special type of marketing strategy. Basically, it is a channel marketing strategy, concerning a single means of communication, which must also be integrated

*Figure 1.6* Strategy hierarchy in an organisation

Source: Based on Armstrong and Volkov (2018); Chaffey and Ellis-Chadwick (2012); Hollensen (2010); Pilarczyk (2015a)

with other channels under an omnichannel marketing framework (Chaffey & Ellis-Chadwick, 2012).

Although the notion of marketing strategy has a well-established place in the concepts of strategic management and marketing management, the literature lacks consistency in terms of the terminology and definition of what should actually be classified as a marketing strategy and what should be classified as an organisation's marketing plan (programme) (Shaw, 2012). According to such researchers as Armstrong and Volkov (2018), Hollensen (2010), Kotler and Keller (2012), Piercy (2009), and Sławińska (2015a), marketing strategy determines the area of action in terms of the selection of target groups and the values generated for customers, while marketing plans translate this into specific actions related to the delivery of these values. Marketing strategy understood in this way is defined as a pattern of current and planned marketing activities, including the management of the company's resources and the interactions between the organisation, on the one hand, and customers, competitors, and other stakeholders, on the other (Hollensen, 2010).

An alternative approach is proposed by Varadarajan (2010), who defines marketing strategy as an integrated decision-making process related to products, markets, marketing activities, and resources aimed at creating, communicating, and delivering value to customers, ultimately allowing the organisation to achieve its adopted strategic objectives. Adopting this perspective, marketing strategy can be thought of as consisting of two elements (Perreault et al., 2002; Pomykalski, 2005): the definition of the target market or market segments which the company wants to reach with its offer and the development of the marketing mix and selection of specific solutions to meet the needs of the target group (Pilarczyk, 2015c). This conceptual framework of marketing strategy corresponds to the classification proposed by Morgan, Whitler, Feng, and Chari (2019) into content and process, whereby the former encompasses specific strategic assumptions, while the latter is related to decisions regarding the implementation of these assumptions.

What is considered a general marketing strategy in the first approach presented here is referred to as a 'market segmentation strategy' in the other (Hunt, 2018). The marketing-mix elements are then no longer a marketing programme developed based on the strategy, but a second pillar of the strategy. Under this concept, a marketing programme is a document that specifies the marketing strategy by defining a time frame for specific tasks along with control procedures for their implementation (Perreault et al., 2002). A marketing programme understood in this way should contain information specifying the plan of activities to be undertaken, the entities forming the target group, the resources required, the costs of individual activities, and the expected results.

In terms of the essence of marketing strategy, the element combining the two presented approaches is the classification of marketing activities into strategic and tactical (Kotler & Keller, 2012). Based on the above considerations, it can be assumed that marketing strategy can be viewed:

- In narrow terms, including only strategic decisions, i.e. the definition of values to be generated for the buyers and the selection of the target group;
- In broad terms, with both strategic and tactical decisions incorporated into the marketing strategy.

The marketing strategy of a crowdfunding campaign is, therefore, a functional strategy governed by the corporate strategy of the club initiating the campaign. Taking into account the scope of the publication, the author has adopted a narrow understanding of marketing strategy, consisting in identifying and formulating the value proposition expected to be received by specific groups of sports clubs' crowdinvestors.

### *1.3.2 Segmentation, targeting, and positioning*

In terms of the size of the target group, three model solutions can be identified (Hollensen, 2010):

- Undifferentiated marketing – all customers are treated the same way and the developed products are intended to be attractive to everyone; the company focuses on one or a few products; by streamlining production, distribution, and promotion processes, it may be possible to achieve improvements in quality and save costs taking advantage of economies of

scale; however, the standardised product may fail to meet the individual needs of the customers;
- Differentiated marketing – the company caters to several selected groups of customers, using a separate marketing mix with respect to each; the advantage of differentiated marketing is that the needs of individual segments are met in a more optimal way; the disadvantage is higher costs compared to undifferentiated marketing;
- Micromarketing – the offer is targeted at a market niche; the customers are not subdivided into smaller groups, as the niche itself forms a homogeneous market segment and target group at the same time (Toften & Hammervoll, 2009).

The fourth solution, resulting from the development of web analytics tools, is the adoption of so-called mass customisation, i.e. the creation of target groups composed of individuals (Kopera & Najda-Janoszka, 2019). Such an approach does not yet find widespread use, but seems possible in the virtual space.

The selection of one of the presented solutions with respect to the target group depends on the capabilities to cater to a given number of potential customers and diversify the products, the phase of the product life cycle (the later the phase, the more differentiated the marketing solutions), the complexity of the preferences and characteristics of the customers, and the level of competition on the market (Pilarczyk, 2015c). However, it is assumed that contemporary customers are too numerous, too dispersed, and too diverse in terms of their needs and purchase behaviours for companies to communicate with them in the same way using undifferentiated marketing (Armstrong & Volkov, 2018).

Differentiated marketing and micromarketing, by their very definition and customer-oriented approach, have shifted away from mass marketing to target marketing, aimed only at a selected group of potential customers (Armstrong & Volkov, 2018). Designing strategies that implement this concept consists of the identification of the values sought by customers and an extended STP procedure (*segmentation, targeting, and positioning*) (Figure 1.7) (Webster, 2005). Subsequent stages of this process are described further in this chapter.

In the first two steps of the STP procedure, the customers that the company will cater to are identified and selected. The starting point for this is consumer market segmentation, which consists in dividing a heterogeneous mass market into mutually exclusive and homogeneous market segments comprising subgroups of potential or existing customers characterised by common features (Armstrong & Volkov, 2018; Doyle & Stern, 2006; Hollensen, 2010; Jonas, 2012; Kotler & Keller, 2016; Piercy, 2009; Pilarczyk, 2015c). The usefulness of market segmentation lies in its benefits across three main areas: better allocation of marketing resources, development of more effective marketing programmes, and increased opportunities for new product

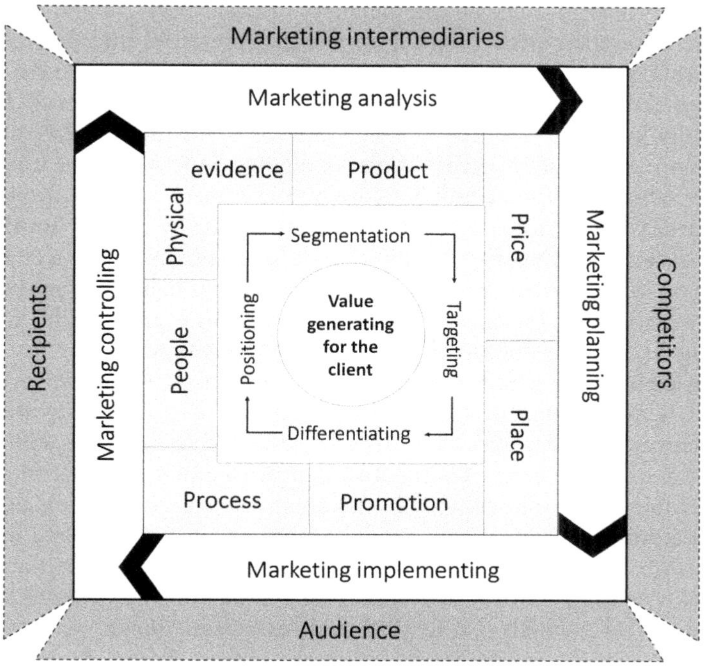


*Figure 1.7* Schematic representation of marketing strategy management

Source: Based on Armstrong and Volkov (2018); Kotler and Keller (2012)

development or the expansion of existing products. By tailoring marketing efforts to the specific needs of particular customer groups, market segmentation allows for more efficient use of resources than a generic marketing approach targeted at all potential customer.

The segments must be (Kotler & Keller, 2012; Hollensen, 2010) measurable, significant, accessible, diverse, and achievable. This means that the size and characteristics of the segments must be quantifiable (measurable), and their reach must be possible (accessible). Segments must be large enough to make their servicing profitable (significant) and distinctive enough to design a dedicated marketing programme for them (attainable). Customers grouped within a segment must differ less among themselves than from entities belonging to other segments (diversity).

From a methodological standpoint (Dolnicar, 2002; Tkaczynski, Rundle-Thiele, & Beaumont, 2010), there are two opposing approaches to market segmentation: *a priori* (also known as 'common sense') and *post hoc* (also known as 'data-driven'). In *a priori* segmentation, criteria are established before the market division process. Conversely, *a posteriori* segmentation is based on primary market research and variables that prove statistically significant in determining the homogeneity of customers groups. This means that *a priori* segmentation is based on defined categories that determine segments (e.g. segmentation based on the place of purchase), while the number of segments and the precise variables that will influence market division are not initially known in *a posteriori* segmentation. Within a *post hoc* segmentation approach, single- or two-stage segmentation can be performed, with the latter being recommended. This involves segment identification using a specific group of variables in the first stage, followed by the use of other variables to determine consumer profiles for these segments in the second stage. Profiling enables a better understanding of consumer behaviour and serves as a tool for validating the segmentation performed (i.e. the profiles of people belonging to separate market segments should be different).

The selection of a specific target group from among the identified market segments is determined by the purchasing power of the entities that make up the segment, the compatibility of the customers' preferences with the features of the offer, the level of competition in the segment in question, and the costs of catering to this group of customers (Pilarczyk, 2015c). Structural factors affecting the attractiveness of the segment in the long term must also be taken into account. The assessment of segment attractiveness is analogous to the analysis of the entire sector in Porter's model of five forces (Armstrong & Volkov, 2018), which is a helpful tool for conducting it, as it takes into account the level of competition within the sector, threat of new entrants, threat of substitutes, bargaining power of customers, and bargaining power of suppliers (Porter, 2001).

Upon the completion of the assessment of the segments, one of five tactics for selecting a target market can be adopted: single-segment concentration, selective specialisation, product specialisation, market specialisation, or full market coverage (Table 1.1) (Kotler & Keller, 2012). Instead of isolated segments, companies may also try to operate in so-called supersegments, which are segment sets that share significant similarities in key areas from the perspective of the planned marketing activities (Hollensen, 2010).

The last two steps of strategy development involve differentiating the market offer and product positioning. The differentiation step involves determining how the products available on the market are perceived, while positioning involves creating the desired image of the product against competitive solutions (Armstrong & Volkov, 2018). Positioning is, therefore, defined as the process of organising a market offer in such a way so that it occupies a distinctive, desirable place in the mind of target customers relative to competitive products (Pilarczyk, 2015c). According to Pogorzelski (2008), the aim of positioning is to compete for recognition of the product in the consumer's perception not only in terms of simply remembering it but also in terms of evoking certain desired connotations. However, it is not so much the product that is positioned as its brand, namely a set of attributes, including the name, symbolism, design, or a combination thereof, which serve to identify given goods or services and distinguish them from competitive products (Szwajca, 2009).

Based on the price–quality relationship, there are five positioning strategies that enable achieving success on the market (Armstrong & Volkov, 2018): more for more, more for the same, the same for less, less for much less, and more for less. Pilarczyk (2015b) observes that the presented relationships are, however, only one way of differentiating a product from among competitive solutions. Other aspects can be categorised into three main categories: manufacturer's characteristics (e.g. country of origin, tradition), product characteristics (e.g. quality parameters, usage, unique features), and user characteristics (e.g. celebrity endorsements, favourite choice of most customers).

*Table 1.1* Strategies for the selection of target markets

| *Strategy* | *Description* |
|---|---|
| Single-segment concentration | By focused marketing on a single segment, companies can gain in-depth knowledge of the needs of consumers who are part of that segment, as well as generate savings through the specialisation of production, distribution, and promotion. However, this strategy carries the risk of insufficient diversification of the consumer portfolio. |
| Multiple segment specialization | The company selects multiple segments. There may be few or no synergies between the segments, but each of them seems profitable on its own. The advantage of the multi-segment strategy is that it allows for greater risk diversification. |
| Product specialisation | The company produces different versions of the same product, offering it to several market segments. The advantage of this approach is its broad scope of action, while the disadvantage is the risk of the product becoming replaced within individual segments by competitive products that are better suited to the consumers' needs. |
| Market specialisation | The company focuses on meeting multiple needs of a specific group of customers. The company enjoys considerable brand recognition among this group and becomes a supplier of additional products to it. |
| Full market coverage | The company attempts to cater to all customer groups with all the products they need. Only very large companies can adopt this strategy, covering the entire market using either undifferentiated or differentiated marketing. |

Source: Based on Armstrong and Volkov (2018); Kotler et al. (2016).

### *1.3.3 Decisions related to marketing mix*

Tactical implementation of the strategy is carried out through the use of a marketing mix, which consists of a set of elements controlled by the company that influence consumers' choices (Hollensen, 2010). Initially, Borden (1964) identified 12 such elements, including: product planning, pricing, branding, channels of distribution, personal selling, advertising, promotions, packaging, displays, servicing, physical handling, and fact finding and analysis. McCarthy reduced the 12 factors proposed by Borden to four elements consisting of product, price, place (distribution), and promotion (the so-called 4Ps of marketing mix), which have become an integral part of marketing theory and marketing management (Constantinides, 2006).

Taking into account the complexity of market relationships and changes in the orientation of companies, another three decision-making areas affecting the consumers have been added to the 4Ps of marketing mix: people, processes, and physical evidence (Armstrong & Volkov, 2018). This change was derived from service marketing research, which found that the greatest role in generating customer value in a service company is attributed to its staff. This is due to the fact that by interacting with the customer and taking responsibility for the implementation of marketing plans, the organisation's staff has a direct impact on the level of overall customer satisfaction (Panasiuk, 2013b; Smoleń, 2012a). Therefore, the retention and development of human capital within an organisation is fundamental to building the competitive edge of a company operating in a knowledge-based economy (Batorski & Wszendybył-Skulska, 2016).

The other two elements of the extended marketing-mix are (Hollensen, 2010):

- Processes – understood as the procedures, mechanisms, and activities associated with the provision of services through which the product is purchased and delivered;
- Physical evidence – understood as the service provided and any material goods that facilitate its delivery.

The addition of these three extra elements has led to the formulation of the concept of the so-called 7Ps marketing mix. Its practical application in the area of service is, however, difficult. The concept that seems to work best in the marketing management of organisations operating on the leisure industry market (including sports clubs) is the five-element marketing-mix concept (5Ps – product, price, distribution, promotion, and personnel) (Panasiuk, 2013a). Hence, in the remaining part of this publication, this structure will be applied to sports clubs' equity crowdfunding campaigns.

Another reason is that, according to Lauterborn (1990), the 4Ps marketing mix is product-oriented, while an effective marketing plan must put the customer at the centre of marketing planning. The researcher proposes the 4Cs marketing-mix concept, the elements of which are formulated in such a way as to emphasise customer orientation. These include customer needs, convenience, cost, and communication. In practice, the concept only reformulates the way marketing is perceived, since the aspects that exert an impact on the customer remain unchanged. Each of the 4C elements corresponds to one of the 4Ps: customers' needs vs. product, convenience vs. place, cost vs. price, and communication vs. promotion.

In addition to details related to its implementation, the marketing plan contains information on budgets, time frames, and indicators for monitoring and evaluating the results of marketing activities (Pilarczyk, 2015a). Mruk (2002) highlights certain important principles related to the creation and implementation of a marketing strategy, being the first (or the leader), concentration of resources in key areas of activity, synergy (coordination of the coherence of the undertakings), safety (taking measures to limit the risk of unforeseeable events), and economy (spending resources on activities that yield measurable results).

In most organisations, strategic marketing planning is an annual process (Hollensen, 2010). This is due to the high variability of the environment, which forces the company to constantly modify its objectives and manners of their achievement (Pilarczyk, 2015a). The continuity of market success usually depends on the control and evaluation stage, which involves collecting feedback on the implementation of marketing programmes and revising plans for subsequent activities (Perreault et al., 2002). Marketing control consists of four stages: determining specific marketing objectives, measuring their effectiveness, assessing discrepancies between expectations and effects, and taking corrective action (Armstrong & Volkov, 2018).

Thanks to advancements in information technology, feedback from the implementation of marketing programmes can be obtained and monitored on an ongoing basis. There are two types of marketing control (Perreault et al., 2002):

- Strategic, related to the course of action to be taken in specific market conditions;
- Operational, related to the verification of the implementation of marketing plans.

These approaches correspond to the two main areas of control: control of performance, i.e. the results of operational marketing activities, and marketing audit, related to the verification of the implementation of the marketing strategy as a whole (Sławińska, 2015b).

The list of possible evaluation and control measures is essentially unlimited, with the marketing audit providing feedback on what has been achieved in both financial and non-financial terms (Hollensen, 2010). According to Pomykalski (2005), the most important evaluation and control measures include return on sales (ROS), net profit margin (NPM), return on investment (ROI), return on equity (ROE), and earnings per share (EPS).

The marketing strategy is, therefore, developed as a result of an analytical process related to the assessment of the internal and external situations of the organisation, and is used to formulate its strategic objectives. The core of the strategy is market segmentation combined with targeting and positioning. It serves as a basis for creating tactical solutions related to the delivery of specific values to individual market segments through the use of available marketing-mix tools.

## Notes

1 In some studies, the terms 'buyer', 'customer', and 'consumer' are not used synonymously. One of the classifications derived from legal sciences defines the consumer as a person who purchases a given product in order to fulfil his or her own needs and the customer as an entity who purchases the product for further distribution. In this publication, all three terms are treated synonymously and denote a person who purchases a given product.
2 Marketing orientation is also referred to as market orientation, customer orientation, or competitor orientation. Although some authors point to subtle differences between the two, these terms are often treated synonymously, including in the academic literature on the subject, and will be treated as such in this publication (Mazurek-Łopacińska, 2002).
3 The increased capabilities to use information technology to generate customer data and apply this information to relationship marketing programmes have led to the development of the concept of customer relationship management (CRM). Although both terms – relationship marketing and CRM – are often used interchangeably, it is important to note that the former refers to the strategic management of relationships with all relevant stakeholders (including not only customers but also suppliers, influencers, referral sources, internal markets, etc.), while CRM denotes the strategic management of customer relationships, involving the appropriate use of technology, which is an important supporting aspect of CRM (Sheth & Parvatiyar, 2000).
4 See more on this subject in Chapter 2.
5 Pursuant to the transactional marketing concept, marketing programmes mainly focus on persuading existing or new customers to buy a given product.
6 The conceptual framework of this concept is detailed in Section 2.1.
7 For a detailed discussion of the nature and scope of the marketing strategy, see Section 1.3.
8 This situation highlights the role of staff in the marketing management process. More on this subject is provided in Section 1.3, where the implementation of the marketing strategy is discussed.
9 For more information on the place of marketing management in the organisation's strategic management structure, see Section 1.3.
10 The name is an acronym from the first letters of the forces acting on the company (political, economic, sociological, technical, environmental, and legal factors).

## References

American Marketing Association. (2020). Definitions of Marketing. Retrieved April 24, 2020, from https://www.ama.org/the-definition-of-marketing-what-is-marketing/
Armstrong, A., & Volkov, D. (2018). *Principles of Marketing*. Melbourne: Pearson Australia.

Arndt, J. (1967). Role of Product-Related Conversations in the Diffusion of a New Product. *Journal of Marketing Research*, *4*(3), 291. https://doi.org/10.2307/3149462

Barassi, V., & Treré, E. (2012). Does Web 3.0 come after Web 2.0? Deconstructing theoretical assumptions through practice. *New Media and Society*, *14*(8), 1269–1285. https://doi.org/10.1177/1461444812445878

Barney, J. (1991). Firm resources and sustained competitive advantage. *Journal of Management*, *17*(1), 99–120. https://doi.org/10.1177/014920639101700108

Batorski, J., & Wszendybył-Skulska, E. (2016). Zmiany w kapitale ludzkim jako rezultat organizacyjnego uczenia się. *Prace Naukowe Uniwersytetu Ekonomicznego we Wrocławiu= Research Papers of Wrocław University of Economics*, *422*, 27–38. https://doi.org/10.15611/pn.2016.422.02

Bednarczyk M. (2006). *Konkurencyjność małych i średnich przedsiębiorstw na polskim rynku turystycznym*. Kraków: Wydawnictwo Uniwersytetu Jagiellońskiego.

Berbeka, J. (2003). Czynniki kształtujace zachowania konsumentow na rynku sportowym. *Marketing i Rynek*, *10*(5), 23–29.

Borden, N. H. (1964). The concept of the marketing mix. *Journal of Advertising Research*, *4*(2), 2–7.

Brodie, R. J., Winklhofer, H., Coviello, N. E., & Johnston, W. J. (2007). Is e-marketing coming of age? An examination of the penetration of e-marketing and firm performance. *Journal of Interactive Marketing*, *21*(1), 2–21.

Brzustewicz, P. (2014). Marketing 3.0 — nowe podejście do tworzenia wartości. *Marketing i Rynek*, *2*, 2–8.

Butler, R. S., De Bower, H. F., & Jones, J. G. (1914). *Marketing methods and salesmanship: Part I: Marketing methods, by Ralph Starr Butler. Part II: Selling. Part III: Sales management* (Vol. 3). Alexander Hamilton Institute: Arkose Press.

Chaffey, D., & Ellis-Chadwick, F. (2012). *Digital Marketing: Strategy, Implementation and Practice*. Essex: Pearson Education.

Ciunova-Shuleska, A., Osakwe, C. N., & Palamidovska-Sterjadovska, N. (2016). Complementary impact of capabilities and brand orientation on SMBs performance. *Journal of Business Economics and Management*, *17*(6), 1270–1285. https://doi.org/10.3846/16111699.2016.1181101

Constantinides, E. (2006). The marketing mix revisited: Towards the 21st century marketing university. *Journal of Marketing Management*, *22*, 407–438. https://doi.org/10.1017/CBO9780511616402.005

Day, G. S. (1994). The capabilities of market-driven organizations. *Journal of Marketing*, *58*(4), 37–52. https://doi.org/10.1177/002224299405800404

Day, G. S. (2011). Closing the marketing capabilities gap. *Journal of Marketing*, *75*(4), 183–195.

Dobiegała-Korona, B., & Krzepicka, A. (2012). Wartość dla klienta a społecznie odpowiedzialny marketing. *Zaszyty Naukowe Uniwersytetu Szczecińskiego*, *736*(55), 557–568.

Dolnicar, S. (2002). A review of data-driven market segmentation in tourism. *Journal of Travel & Tourism Marketing*, *12*(1), 1–22. https://doi.org/10.1300/J073v12n01_01

Doyle, P., & Stern, P. (2006). *Marketing management and strategy*. Essex: Pearson Education.

Drucker, P. F. (1973). *Management: Tasks, responsibilities, practices*. NewYork: Harper&Row.

Eid, R., & El-Gohary, H. (2013). The impact of E-marketing use on small business enterprises' marketing success. *The Service Industries Journal*, *33*(1), 31–50. https://doi.org/10.1080/02642069.2011.594878

Evanschitzky, H., Ramaseshan, B., Woisetschläger, D. M., Richelsen, V., Blut, M., & Backhaus, C. (2012). Consequences of customer loyalty to the loyalty program and to the company. *Journal of the Academy of Marketing Science*, *40*(5), 625–638. https://doi.org/10.1007/s11747-011-0272-3

Gierszewska, G. (2000). *Zarządzanie strategiczne*. Warszawa: Wydawnictwo Wyższej Szkoły Przedsiębiorczości i Zarządzania im. Leona Koźmińskiego.

Grabińska, E., & Nessel, K. (2016). Zarządzanie marketingowe w organizacji sportowej. In M. Bednarczyk & K. Nessel (Eds.), *Przedsiębiorczość w sporcie. Zasady i praktyka* (pp. 303–329). Krakow: CeDeWu.

Griffin, R. W., Rusinski, M., & Rozanska, I. (1999). *Podstawy zarzadzania organizacjami; Przekl. M. Rusinski; Konsultacja nauk. B. Glinski; Red. I. Rozanska.* Wydaw. Nauk. PWN Warszawa.

Hamel, G., & Prahalad, C. K. (1990). The core competence of the corporation. *Harvard Business Review*, *68*(3), 79–91.

Hollensen, S. (2010). *Marketing Management: A Relationship Approach*. Essex: Pearson Education.

Hult, G. T. M., Ketchen Jr, D. J., & Slater, S. F. (2005). Market orientation and performance: An integration of disparate approaches. *Strategic Management Journal*, *26*(12), 1173–1181. https://doi.org/10.1002/smj.494

Hunt, S. D. (2018). Advancing marketing strategy in the marketing discipline and beyond: From promise, to neglect, to prominence, to fragment (to promise?). *Journal of Marketing Management*, *34*(1–2), 16–51. https://doi.org/10.1080/0267257X.2017.1326973

Jaakkola, E., & Alexander, M. (2014). The role of customer engagement behavior in value co-creation: A service system perspective. *Journal of Service Research*, *17*(3), 247–261. https://doi.org/0.1177/1094670514529187

Johnson, M. D., & Fornell, C. (1991). A framework for comparing customer satisfaction across individuals and product categories. *Journal of Economic Psychology*, *12*(2), 267–286. https://doi.org/10.1016/0167-4870(91)90016-M

Jonas, A. (2012). Segmentacja rynku usług. In A. Czubała, A. Jonas, T. Smoleń, & J. W. Wiktor (Eds.), *Marketing usług* (pp. 81–109). Warszawa: Oficyna Ekonomiczna Grupa Wolters Kluwer.

Kachniewska, M. (2013). Media społecznościowe jako narzędzie nowoczesnego marketingu usług hotelarskich. In P. Dominik (Ed.), *Innowacyjne rozwiązania we współczesnym hotelarstwie* (pp. 106–121). Warszawa: Almamer Szkoła Wyższa. Wydział Turystyki i Rekreacji.

Kaczmarczyk, S., & Pałgan, R. (2008). *Marketing w przedsiębiorstwie: ujęcie zarządcze i systemowe z przykładami*. Gdańsk: Ośrodek Doradztwa i Doskonalenia Kadr.

Keller, K. L. (1993). Conceptualizing, measuring, and managing customer-based brand equity. *The Journal of Marketing*, *57*(1), 1–22. https://doi.org/10.1177/002224299305700101

Knecht, Z. (2008). *Zarządzanie marketingiem*. Warszawa: Wydawnictwo C.H. Beck.

Kopera, S. (2016). Social media challenges. In T. Byers (Ed.), *Contemporary Issues in Sport Management: A Critical Introduction* (pp. 349–362). Thousand Oaks: Sage Publications.

Kopera, S., & Najda-Janoszka, M. (2019). Rynek tradycyjny a rynek przestrzeni cyfrowej. In M. Bednarczyk, M. Najda-Janoszka, & S. Kopera (Eds.), *E-przedsiębiorczość. Zasady i praktyka* (pp. 41–68). Kraków: Wydawnictwo Uniwersytetu Jagiellońskiego.

Kotler, P., Kartajaya, H., & Setiawan, I. (2010). *Marketing 3.0. From Products to Customers to the Human Spirit.* https://doi.org/10.1007/s00403-005-0564-x

Kotler, P., & Keller, K. L. (2012). *Marketing Management.* 14e. Global ed. Essex: Pearson Education Limited.

Kotler, P., & Keller, K. L. (2016). *A Framework for Marketing Management.* Essex: Pearson Education.

Kotler, P., Keller, K. L., Brady, M., Goodman, M., & Hansen, T. (2016). *Marketing Management. 3rd edition.* https://doi.org/10.1017/CBO9781107415324.004

Kowal, W. (2001). Opracowanie strategii marketingowej. In R. Kłeczek, W. Kowal, & J. Woźniczka (Eds.), *Strategiczne planowanie marketingowe* (pp. 195–270). Warszawa: Wydawnictwo Naukowe PWN.

Kozielski, R. (2015). Możliwości biznesowe a orientacja marketingowa przedsiębiorstw. *Studia Ekonomiczne. Zeszyty Naukowe Uniwersytetu Ekonomicznego w Katowicach*, (233), 149–158.

Lauterborn, B. (1990). New marketing litany: Four Ps passe: C-words take over. *Advertising Age*, *61*(41).

Mazurek-Łopacińska, K. (2002). *Orientacja na klienta w przedsiębiorstwie.* Warszawa: Polskie Wydawnictwo Ekonomiczne.

Mazurek, G. (2007). Web 2.0 implications on marketing. *Organizacijų Vadyba: Sisteminiai Tyrimai*, *51*, 69–82. https://doi.org/10.1300/J123v53n01_15

Mazurek, G., & Zach, K. (2018). Strategia i planowanie e-marketingowe. In G. Mazurek (Ed.), *E-marketing. Planowanie, narzędzia, praktyka* (pp. 27–51). Warszawa: Wydawnictwo Poltext.

Menguc, B., & Auh, S. (2006). Creating a firm-level dynamic capability through capitalizing on market orientation and innovativeness. *Journal of the Academy of Marketing Science*, *34*(1), 63–73. https://doi.org/10.1177/0092070305281090

Mitręga, M. (2008). *Marketing relacji: teoria i praktyka.* Warszawa: CeDeWu.

Mitręga, M., Wieczorek, A., Małecka, A., & Pfajfar, G. (2018). Dynamic marketing capabilities implemented into social media. *Wydawnictwo Uniwersytetu Ekonomicznego w Katowicach*, *360*, 82–93.

Morgan, N. A., Whitler, K. A., Feng, H., & Chari, S. (2019). Research in marketing strategy. *Journal of the Academy of Marketing Science*, *47*(1), 4–29. https://doi.org/10.1007/s11747-018-0598-1

Mruk, H. (2002). *Strategie marketingowe.* Poznań: Wydawnictwo Akademii Ekonomicznej w Poznaniu.

Mruk, H. (2008). *Marketing-zagadnienia współczesne.* Poznań: Wydawnictwo Forum Naukowe.

Ng, I. C. L., & Vargo, S. L. (2018). Service-dominant (S-D) logic, service ecosystems and institutions: Bridging theory and practice. *Journal of Service Management*, *29*(4), 518–520. https://doi.org/10.1108/JOSM-07-2018-412

Niestrój, R. (2002). *Zarządzanie marketingiem: aspekty strategiczne.* Warszawa: Wydawnictwo Naukowe PWN.

O'Reilly, T. (2007). What is web 2.0?: Design patterns and business models for the next generation of software. *Communication & Strategies*, *65*, 17–37.

Obłój, K. (2014). *Strategia organizacji.* Warszawa: Polskie Wydawnictwo Ekonomiczne.

Oliver, R. L. (1999). Whence consumer loyalty? *The Journal of Marketing*, *63*(4_suppl1), 33–44.

Pan, B., & Fesenmaier, D. R. (2006). Online information search. *Annals of Tourism Research*, *33*(3), 809–832. https://doi.org/10.1016/j.annals.2006.03.006

Panasiuk, A. (2013a). Koncepcja marketingowa w turystyce i rekreacji. In A. Panasiuk (Ed.), *Marketing w turystyce i rekreacji* (pp. 81–96). Warszawa: Wydawnictwo Naukowe PWN.

Panasiuk, A. (2013b). Podstawy marketingu usług. In A. Panasiuk (Ed.), *Marketing w turystyce i rekreacji* (pp. 17–30). Warszawa: Wydawnictwo Naukowe PWN.

Panasiuk, A. (2017). Geneza i istota orientacji marketingowej. In A. Panasiuk (Ed.), *Regulacja a orientacja marketingowa touroperatorów* (pp. 20–30). Szczecin: Wydawnictwo Naukowe Uniwersytetu Szczecińskiego.

Panasiuk, A., & Tokarz, A. (2005). Specyfika i klasyfikacja usług. In S. Flejterski, A. Panasiuk, J. Perenc, & G. Rosa (Eds.), *Współczesna ekonomika usług* (pp. 41–58). Warszawa: Wydawnictwo Naukowe PWN.

Perreault, W. D., Cannon, J. P., & McCarthy, E. J. (2002). *Basic Marketing. A Marketing Strategy Planning Approach*. New York: McGraw-Hill.

Piercy, N. (2009). *Market-Led Strategic Change, Fourth Edition Transforming the Process of Going to Market*. Oxford: Elsevier.

Pilarczyk, B. (2015a). Proces tworzenia strategii marketingowej. Rodzaje strategii. In H. Mruk, B. Pilarczyk, & M. Sławińska (Eds.), *Marketing. Koncepcja - strategie - trendy* (pp. 55–85). Poznań: Wydawnictwo Uniwersytetu Ekonomicznego w Poznaniu.

Pilarczyk, B. (2015b). Przewaga konkurencyjna i strategie konkurowania. In H. Mruk, B. Pilarczyk, & M. Sławińska (Eds.), *Marketing. Koncepcja - strategie - trendy* (pp. 86–102). Poznań: Wydawnictwo Uniwersytetu Ekonomicznego w Poznaniu.

Pilarczyk, B. (2015c). Segmentacja nabywców i wybór rynku docelowego. In H. Mruk, B. Pilarczyk, & M. Sławińska (Eds.), *Marketing. Koncepcja - strategie - trendy* (pp. 126–145). Poznań: Wydawnictwo Uniwersytetu Ekonomicznego w Poznaniu.

Pluta-Olearnik, M. (2010). Zmiany strategii marketingowych w dobie społeczeństwa informacyjnego. *Prace Instytutu Lotnictwa*, *6*(208), 11–29.

Pluta-Olearnik, M. (2013). *Marketing przedsiębiorstw usługowych w procesie internacjonalizacji*. Warszawa: Polskie Wydawnictwo Ekonomiczne.

Pluta-Olearnik, M. (2018). Zintegrowana komunikacja marketingowa - koncepcje, praktyka, nowe wyzwania. *Marketing Instytucji Naukowych i Badawczych*, 2(28), 121–138. https://doi.org/10.14611/MINIB.28.06.2018.06

Pluta-Olearnik, M, & Olearnik, J. (2015). Marketing a koncepcja biznesowa. *Zeszyty Naukowe Uniwersytetu Szczecińskiego. Problemy Zarządzania, Finansów i Marketingu*, 7(37), 9–22.

Pogorzelski, J. (2008). *Pozycjonowanie produktu*. Warszawa: Polskie Wydawnictwo Ekonomiczne.

Pomykalski, A. (2005). *Zarządzanie i planowanie marketingowe*. Warszawa: Wydawnictwo Naukowe PWN.

Porter, M.E. (2008). The five competitive forces that shape strategy. *Harvard Business Review*, January, 78–93.

Porter, M. E. (1985). Creating and sustaining superior performance. *Competitive Advantage*, *167*, 167–206.

Porter, M.E. (2001). *Porter o konkurencji*, Warszawa: PWE.

Prahalad, C. K., & Ramaswamy, V. (2004). Co-creation experiences: The next practice in value creation. *Journal of Interactive Marketing*, *18*(3), 5–14. https://doi.org/10.1002/dir.20015

Rosa, G. (2008). Zarządzanie marketingowe w przedsiębiorstwach usługowych. In B. Filipiak & A. Panasiuk (Eds.), *Przedsiębiorstwo usługowe. Zarządzanie* (pp. 298–324). Warszawa: Wydawnictwo Naukowe PWN.

See-To, E. W. K., & Ho, K. K. W. (2014). Value co-creation and purchase intention in social network sites: The role of electronic word-of-mouth and trust - a theoretical analysis. *Computers in Human Behavior*, *31*(1), 182–189. https://doi.org/10.1016/j.chb.2013.10.013

Shaw, E. H. (2012). Marketing strategy: From the origin of the concept to the development of a conceptual framework. *Journal of Historical Research in Marketing*, *4*(1), 30–55. https://doi.org/10.1108/17557501211195055

Sheth, J. N., & Parvatiyar, A. (2000). The domain and conceptual foundations of relationship marketing. In J. N. Sheth, & A. Parvatiyar (Eds.), *Handbook of Relationship Marketing* (pp. 3–38). Thousand Oaks: Sage Publications.

Sidorkiewicz, M. (2013). Strategie marketingowe w turystyce i rekreacji. In A. Panasiuk (Ed.), *Marketing w turystyce i rekreacji* (pp. 338–360). Warszawa: Wydawnictwo Naukowe PWN.

Sławińska, M. (2015a). Istota i znaczenie marketingu w zarządzaniu przedsiębiorstwem. In H. Mruk, B. Pilarczyk, & M. Sławińska (Eds.), *Marketing. Koncepcja - strategie - trendy* (pp. 11–38). Poznań: Wydawnictwo Uniwersytetu Ekonomicznego w Poznaniu.

Sławińska, M. (2015b). Kontrola działalności marketingowej. In H. Mruk, B. Pilarczyk, & M. Sławińska (Eds.), *Marketing. Koncepcja - strategie - trendy* (pp. 336–350). Poznań: Wydawnictwo Uniwersytetu Ekonomicznego w Poznaniu.

Smoleń, T. (2012a). Personel jako instrument marketingu firmy usługowej. In A. Czubała, A. Jonas, T. Smoleń, & J. W. Wiktor (Eds.), *Marketing usług* (pp. 303–322). Warszawa: Oficyna Ekonomiczna Grupa Wolters Kluwer.

Smoleń, T. (2012b). Strategie marketingowe firm usługowych. In A. Czubała, A. Jonas, T. Smoleń, & J. W. Wiktor (Eds.), *Marketing usług* (pp. 42–80). Warszawa: Oficyna Ekonomiczna Grupa Wolters Kluwer.

Smoleń, T. (2012c). Zarządzanie marketingiem w firmie usługowej. In A. Czubała, A. Jonas, T. Smoleń, & J. W. Wiktor (Eds.), *Marketing usług* (pp. 42–80). Oficyna Ekonomiczna Grupa Wolters Kluwer.

Stabell, C. B., & Fjeldstad, Ø. D. (1998). Configuring value for competitive advantage: On chains, shops, and networks. *Strategic Management Journal*, *19*(5), 413–437. https://doi.org/10.1002/(SICI)1097-0266(199805)19:5<413::AID-SMJ946>3.0.CO;2-C

Svensson, G., & Grönroos, C. (2008). Service logic revisited: Who creates value? And who co-creates? *European Business Review*, *20*(4), 298–314. https://doi.org/10.1108/09555340810886585

Szwajca, D. (2009). Pozycjonowanie marki na rynku globalnym – możliwości i ograniczenia. *Ekonomia i Zarządzanie*, *1*, 44–59.

Teece, D. J., Pisano, G., & Shuen, A. (1997). Dynamic capabilities and strategic management. *Strategic Management Journal*, *18*(7), 509–533. https://doi.org/10.1002/(SICI)1097-0266(199708)18:7<509::AID-SMJ882>3.0.CO;2-Z

Tkaczynski, A., Rundle-Thiele, S., & Beaumont, N. (2010). Destination segmentation: A recommended two-step approach. *Journal of Travel Research*, *49*(2), 139–152. https://doi.org/10.1177/0047287509336470

Toften, K., & Hammervoll, T. (2009). Niche firms and marketing strategy. *European Journal of Marketing*, *43*(11/12), 1378–1391. https://doi.org/10.1108/03090560910989948

Trainor, K. J., Rapp, A., Beitelspacher, L. S., & Schillewaert, N. (2011). Integrating information technology and marketing: An examination of the drivers and outcomes of e-marketing capability. *Industrial Marketing Management*, *40*(1), 162–174. https://doi.org/10.1016/j.indmarman.2010.05.001

Varadarajan, R. (2010). Strategic marketing and marketing strategy: Domain, definition, fundamental issues and foundational premises. *Journal of the Academy of Marketing Science*, *38*(2), 119–140. https://doi.org/10.1007/s11747-009-0176-7

Vargo, S. L., & Lusch, R. F. (2008). From goods to service (s): Divergences and convergences of logics. *Industrial Marketing Management*, *37*(3), 254–259. https://doi.org/10.1016/j.indmarman.2007.07.004

Vargo, S. L., & Lusch, R. F. (2016). Institutions and axioms: An extension and update of service-dominant logic. *Journal of the Academy of Marketing Science*, *44*(1), 5–23. https://doi.org/10.1007/s11747-015-0456-3

Webster, F. E. (2005). Back to the future: Integrating marketing as tactics, strategy, and organizational culture. *Journal of Marketing*, *69*(4), 4–6.

Westbrook, R. A. (1987). Product/consumption-based affective responses and postpurchase processes. *Journal of Marketing Research*, *24*(3), 258–270. https://doi.org/10.1177/002224378702400302

Yadav, M., & Rahman, Z. (2017). Measuring consumer perception of social media marketing activities in e-commerce industry: Scale development & validation. *Telematics and Informatics*, *34*(7), 1294–1307. https://doi.org/10.1016/j.tele.2017.06.001

Ye, Q., Law, R., Gu, B., & Chen, W. (2011). The influence of user-generated content on traveler behavior: An empirical investigation on the effects of e-word-of-mouth to hotel online bookings. *Computers in Human Behavior*, *27*(2), 634–639. https://doi.org/10.1016/j.chb.2010.04.014

Chapter 2

# Crowdfunding campaigns

## 2.1 Essence of crowdfunding

### *2.1.1 Crowdfunding and crowdsourcing*

The concept of crowdfunding was identified from the broader concept of crowdsourcing. The term 'crowdsourcing' was first used by Howe (2006) to describe a situation in which 'a profit-oriented company outsources specific tasks, necessary to produce or sell a product, to the general public (the crowd) in the form of an open offer made via the Internet, with the aim of encouraging individuals to (voluntarily) contribute to the company's production process, either for free or for much less return than the contribution is worth to the company'. The relatively rapid spread of the concept of crowdsourcing entailed a dynamic evolution of its meaning, often in a disorganised and chaotic way, with different researchers drawing contradictory conclusions, at times departing entirely from the original definition of the term (Y. Zhao & Zhu, 2014).

Crowdsourcing is perceived as a versatile problem-solving method, which uses a group of participants (as large as possible and not necessarily knowing each other) who respond to a request for assistance in solving a given problem (DiPalantino & Vojnovic, 2009; Doan, Ramakrishnan, & Halevy, 2011; Kazai, 2011; Poetz & Schreier, 2012). As defined by Kopera (2019), it is a model of cooperation between an entity requesting specific resources and a community that possesses them and is willing to share them. A crucial aspect of crowdsourcing is the use of the internet. It makes it possible for a large number of people to offer solutions and the best ideas to be rewarded with prizes (Brabham, 2008; Hosseini, Phalp, Taylor, & Ali, 2014; Kopera, 2019). When defining crowdsourcing, it is important to emphasise that it refers to a form of online activity, whereby an individual, a non-profit organisation, or a company issues an open invitation to a group of individuals to voluntarily undertake a specific task (Estellés-Arolas & González-Ladrón-De-Guevara, 2012).

DOI: 10.4324/9781003320623-3

Those who decide to take part in it solve the task by providing labour, money, knowledge, and experience, which the organisation in question lacks (Kędzierska-Szczepaniak, Szopik-Depczyńska, & Łazorko, 2016; Kleemann, Voß, & Rieder, 2008; Lenart-Gansiniec & Sulkowski, 2018; Schenk & Guittard, 2011). This type of cooperation leads to mutual benefits: the initiating party receives the resources it needs, while the community supports the values that are important to it (Bederson & Quinn, 2011; Kopera, 2019; Oliveira, Ramos, & Santos, 2010). This situation also allows for co-creation of values by the organisation and the community supporting it through 'collective intelligence' which combines the potential of individuals (Buecheler, Sieg, Füchslin, & Pfeifer, 2010; Kleemann et al., 2008; Oliveira et al., 2010). At the same time, crowdsourcing is regarded as an example of open innovation, which assumes that companies can and should take advantage of both internal and external ideas (Chanal & Caron-Fasan, 2008; Sloane, 2011). Crowdsourcing can also be viewed as a method that optimises operational costs, and as a marketing tool and platform for collaboration with customers (Lenart-Gansiniec, 2017).

Crowdsourcing is essentially based on four pillars: *a crowdsourcer* who reports a problem to be solved, people responding to that demand, a task to be performed, and a crowdsourcing platform providing a space to manage the problem and the community (Hosseini et al., 2014). There are eight prerequisites that are required for a given instance of community support to be regarded as crowdsourcing (Y. Zhao & Zhu, 2014): the addressee of the campaign, the purpose of the campaign, clarification of the expectations from the community, identification of the crowdsourcer (beneficiary of the support), presentation of the forms of remuneration offered to the participants, assignment to a specific type of crowdsourcing, an open request for support, and the use of the internet for the purpose of the campaign.

In terms of the relationship between the participating problem solvers, two types of crowdsourcing can be identified (Blohm, Leimeister, & Kremar, 2013):

- Collaborative (based on cooperation), where the participants work together on a specific task and make small contributions each, which yield valuable results when a sufficiently large community is involved;
- Tournament-based (based on competition), where the crowdsourcer collects independent solutions (e.g. ideas, prototypes, business plans) from among which he or she selects one or more in exchange for financial or non-financial compensation.

Numerous attempts have been made so far to classify crowdsourcing initiatives, including mainly in terms of the processes involved in the collaboration and the type of task carried out (Sánchez, Gimilio, & Altamirano, 2015).

When it comes to the former, crowdsourcing can be divided into (Estellés-Arolas, Navarro-Giner, & González-Ladrón-de-Guevara, 2015) crowdcasting (the participant who comes up with the best solution to the problem receives a reward); crowdcollaboration (the community is collaborating to solve the problem); crowdcontent (the community independently creates the content requested); crowdopinion (the crowdsourcer is seeking opinions, ratings, and comments on a specific problem); and crowdfunding (funds are collected from community members).

On the other hand, when it comes to the classification based on the type of task to be carried out, crowdsourcing can be divided into four general categories (Geiger, Fielt, Rosemann, & Schader, 2012; Geiger & Schader, 2014): crowdsolving (solving the problem by the community), crowdcreation (co-creating complex products by the community based on a variety of user-generated content), crowdrating (collective evaluations or forecasting), and crowdprocessing (engaging the community in a large number of homogeneous activities in order to implement a specific project). From this perspective, crowdfunding should be classified under the last category – crowdprocessing – as raising funds allows for the implementation of a specific business or social project.

Sánchez, Gimilio, and Altamirano (2015) propose an integrated typology, which combines both perspectives of crowdsourcing classification. It consists of five general and eight specific problem-solving areas. These include crowdcasting, crowdcollaboration (which includes crowdstorming and crowdsupport), crowdcontent (divided into crowdproduction, crowdsearching, and crowdanalysing), crowdfunding, and crowdopinion. A detailed discussion of these is provided in Table 2.1.

In accordance with the integrated typology of crowdsourcing, crowdfunding is classified as one of its types, although some authors point out that the latter should not be considered as a form of crowdsourcing, but rather a completely separate activity (Brabham, 2013; Kozioł-Nadolna, 2015), due to the fundamental difference between the two in terms of the value delivered, which in the case of crowdsourcing is the involvement of the participants and certain work performed, while in the case of crowdfunding, it is funds contributed (Pluszyńska, 2018).

### 2.1.2 *Nature and development of crowdfunding*

In terms of the etymology of the word, crowdfunding is a combination of two words: crowd and funding. It can be analysed in broad or narrow terms. It involves collecting small amounts of money from a large number of people (communities), usually via online channels (Dziuba, 2012) (broad definition). When defining crowdfunding, some authors (Belleflamme, Lambert, & Schwienbacher, 2014; Gerber & Hui, 2013) also include information on

*Table 2.1* Integrated typology of crowdsourcing

| *Type* | *Description* |
|---|---|
| **Crowdcasting** | The participant who solves the problem first or proposes the better solution than the others receives a reward. |
| **Crowdcollaboration** | The participants that contribute their knowledge (usually free of charge) to solve the problem or come up with ideas in cooperation with other participants on how to solve it. Once the challenge is posted, the company which has published it does not communicate with the community responsible for solving the task. |
| Crowdstorming | Creative problem-solving in the form of online brainstorming, where solutions are proposed to the company, and the community comments on them, and votes on the best ones. |
| Crowdsupport | The customers are allowed to solve the problems by themselves, without the need for the company's technical support or after-sales service. |
| **Crowdcontent** | This type differs from crowdcasting in that it is not based on a competition to complete a single task, but rather compiles the work of all the participants supporting the project. |
| Crowdproduction | Projects that involve content creation with the collaboration of community members. |
| Crowdsearching | Projects that involve the participants searching for content available online to a specific end. |
| Crowdanalysing | Similar to the above, but in this case the participants are searching texts or multimedia documents. |
| **Crowdfunding** | Involves campaigns launched to raise funding from the community for a given project. |
| **Crowdopinion** (including crowdvoting) | Includes projects aimed at obtaining feedback and/or ratings from users on a given topic. When it takes the form of voting, it is referred to as crowdvoting. |

Source: Based on Sánchez et al. (2015).

some form of reward for the support (which is optional), while others (Bradford, 2012; Ryu & Kim, 2016) point out that the amounts paid are usually relatively small.

In its narrow understanding, a commonly accepted definition proposed by Schwienbacher and Larralde (2010) views crowdfunding as 'an open invitation, usually via online channels, to provide funds either in the form donation or in exchange for some kind of reward and/or voting rights, in order to support initiatives pursuing specific goals'. In contrast to more general approaches to the concept, this definition stresses the integral aspects of a campaign (public invitation and various forms of reward). Hence, it seems more appropriate than the previously mentioned ones.

Crowdfunding combines the idea of crowdsourcing and microfinance (Mollick, 2014). The main idea behind crowdfunding was to fill an equity gap in the market and provide funding for businesses at their early stage of development. Small and micro businesses, especially start-ups, find it difficult to implement their projects using conventional sources of financing, including bank loans, venture capital funds, or own funds (Bradford, 2012). The support of angel investors is aimed at filling this gap, but it is rather limited in scope. Crowdfunding is an example of co-creating access to financial resources based on co-creating a point of access (Baran, 2013).

Although the idea of conducting money collection campaigns from people predates the development of the internet, running such campaigns in the digital space made it possible to reduce the costs of connecting initiators and participants, as well as to increase the scale of impact of these undertakings (Dziuba, 2015). What has also been achieved is lower risk exposure due to smaller contributions and low communication costs, facilitating better (though far from perfect) information gathering and monitoring the progress of often geographically dispersed collection campaigns (Agrawal, Catalini, & Goldfarb, 2013).

Crowdfunding increases the availability of capital for projects that are perceived as too risky or not profitable enough to be granted a bank loan, angel investor support, or venture capital funds (Gierczak, Bretschneider, Haas, Blohm, & Leimeister, 2016). For this reason, crowdfunding is considered to be the long tail of the financial services sector.[1] Surprisingly, crowdfunding is, at the same time, a tool that may increase the possibility of obtaining funding from other sources. It was found that projects enjoying a high level of crowdfunding support were more likely to obtain additional funds in the future from venture capital (Colombo & Shafi, 2016). In addition, if a given entity has already conducted a crowdfunding campaign before, the likelihood of receiving further support increases to a considerable extent (Belleflamme, Omrani, & Peitz, 2015).

### 2.1.3 Crowdfunding platforms

The central role in the crowdfunding process is played by crowdfunding platforms, which provide a space for the two parties to the transaction to meet virtually: the beneficiaries and the participants. They define the scope of the service provided under the crowdfunding model adopted, the categories of projects (e.g. sports, art, music, technology start-ups), the geographical scope, and the settlement model (Viotto, 2015). The main business challenge for the developers of such a platform is to design them in such a way to, on the one hand, attract a sufficient number of users and, on the other hand, generate sufficient values for the participants to convince them to provide campaign initiators with funding for their projects, while maximising their own profits.

In terms of the scope of the activities, crowdfunding platforms can be divided into two categories (Baumgardner et al., 2017):

- Specialised – collecting funds for specific campaigns (e.g. sports projects);
- General-purpose – not limited in any way as to the partners they work with.

Both types of platforms have up to three main sources of revenue: commissions, transaction fees, and additional services provided (e.g. campaign handling, sharing information on previously implemented campaigns, or project diagnostics) (Belleflamme et al., 2015). The amount of the commission most often ranges[2] between 5% and 15% of the amount raised and is charged to the initiators once the funds have been disbursed (Kędzierska-Szczepaniak et al., 2016; Lissowska, 2018a).

The funds are paid out to the initiator when the campaign reaches its financial target. If this target is not reached, the allocation of funds depends on the settlement model adopted. There are two options in this respect (Gierczak et al., 2016):

- The all-or-nothing (AON) principle – the amount raised is paid to the initiator's account only if the campaign achieves its goal; this principle is based on the assumption that failure to reach the set target will not allow the company to meet its campaign goal;
- The keep-in-all (KIA) principle – the initiator receives the amount raised regardless of its relation to the pre-defined goal; this form of settlement is common in the case of projects of a social nature.

The decision to choose one of the settlement models can be left to the initiator or predetermined by the way the platform operates – the more common one being the AON principle (Cumming, Leboeuf, & Schwienbacher, 2020). From the point of view of the organisation, a more advantageous model is the KIA one. The AON option, however, is much more transparent to investors, who know that their funds will only be transferred to the beneficiary once the amount required to implement the campaign goals has been collected (Gierczak et al., 2016). This may be one of the reasons behind the greater effectiveness of the AON model, with a higher proportion of campaigns achieving their financial target (Gierczak et al., 2016; Haas, Blohm, & Leimeister, 2014). For instance, on the Idiegogo and Kickstarter platforms, campaigns based on the AON principle reach their goal in 34% of cases, while those based on the KIA principle reach their goal only in 17% of cases.

Unlike conventional intermediaries who transfer capital from its holders to the investor or consumer (based on various types of debt securities), crowdfunding platforms are not involved in the actual financing process (Figure 2.1) (Haas et al., 2014). In the crowdfunding model, intermediaries do not raise or lend money on their own account. They merely serve as an agent matching capital seekers and capital providers. Crowdfunding thus fits into the general economic concept of two-sided markets (Lissowska, 2018b). Unlike multi-sided markets, which are characterised by numerous entities acting as intermediaries in the process of providing given goods on the market (at the same time interacting and influencing one another), in the case of two-sided markets, only two groups of entities who are parties to a given transaction are interacting with each other (Rochet & Tirole, 2004).

Crowdfunding platforms, however, are responsible not only for bringing together the parties to the transaction but also for a significant part of the operational tasks involved in the campaign, including planning and implementing marketing communications (Rossi & Vismara, 2018). In cases where shares are issued,[3] in addition to financial and marketing support, the platform may also be responsible for estimating the value of the company, which serves as the basis for determining the issue price per share (Hagedorn & Pinkwart, 2016). Some platforms also offer a range of post-issue services, including assistance in conclusion of the issue process or organisation of a secondary market (Rossi & Vismara, 2018). There might also be cases when a crowdfunding platform receives shares in the company they have been assisting (Ralcheva & Roosenboom, 2019).

Due to the continuous development of crowdfunding and the still relatively small number of regulations governing this market, an increasing number of new business models of crowdfunding platforms are being developed, offering both campaign initiators and financing entities unprecedented solutions in terms of functionality (e.g. consulting, project evaluation, due diligence,[4]

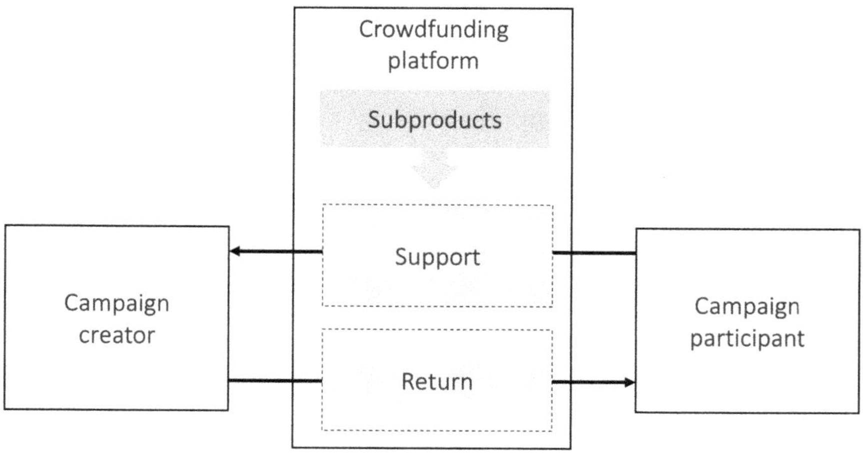


*Figure 2.1* Entities involved in the crowdfunding campaign process and the relationship between them

Source: Based on Haas et al. (2014)

community building assistance, public relations, advertising, project management, etc.), financing methods (e.g. commission-based schemes), searching for investors and intermediaries, etc. (Hemer, 2011).

Despite the important role played by crowdfunding platforms, crowdfunding can also take place without them, e.g. through the originator's own online channels (Kuti & Madarasz, 2014). On the one hand, this allows for much more personalised solutions tailored to the needs of the target group (Belleflamme et al., 2013). On the other hand, however, such a solution shifts the responsibility for the entire process of running the campaign to the initiator and deprives him or her of access to the communication channels that crowdfunding platforms offer.

## 2.2 Equity crowdfunding in comparison with other crowdfunding models

### *2.2.1 Crowdfunding classification criteria*

The most commonly used criterion for the classification of crowdfunding is the form of return that participants receive for supporting a given campaign. Such a classification is important, as it affects the legal complexity of crowdfunding operations, the degree of information asymmetry between the entities involved (funding and funded), and the behaviour of campaign participants.[5] In addition, the subject matter of the campaign determines which model will be most appropriate for a given project.

The funds provided by participants in crowdfunding campaigns can take the form of donations, sponsorship, pre-sale orders, membership fees, loans, and shares in the profit (Hemer, 2011). The participants may, therefore, either receive nothing in return for their involvement (in which case the campaign is supported out of non-material motives) or expect one of the following four forms of compensation (Bradford, 2012):

- Reward – the participant receives a product (not necessarily directly related to the campaign), which can take the form of a tangible good (e.g. a T-shirt with the logo of the sports club) or a service (e.g. a ticket to a match);
- Pre-sale order – the provided support is, in practical terms, a prepayment for the purchase of the object of the campaign;
- Interest – the support takes the form of a loan;
- Shares or share in the profits – the participant receives in return an equity interest in the project.

The most common (Adamska-Mieruszewska & Mrzygłód, 2014; Ahlers, Cumming, Günther, & Schweizer, 2015; Bradford, 2012; Collins & Pierrakis, 2012; Kędzierska-Szczepaniak, 2017; Kuti & Madarasz, 2014; Li, He, Song, Yang, & Zhou, 2018; Schwienbacher & Larralde, 2010; Viotto,

2015) and, at the same time, the most accurate classification of crowdfunding models is as follows (Ahlers et al., 2015; D. Cumming & Hornuf, 2018): donation-based crowdfunding, reward-based crowdfunding, peer-to-peer lending crowdfunding, and equity crowdfunding (Table 2.2).

These four main models can be further divided into philanthropic (donation-based and reward-based crowdfunding) and commercial crowdfunding (equity crowdfunding and lending-based crowdfunding) (Hossain & Gospel, 2017). As the reward-based, lending-based, and equity crowdfunding models differ from donation-based crowdfunding by the fact that they offer material compensation in return for the provided support, Bretschneider and Leimeister (2017) refer to these models collectively as incentive-based

*Table 2.2* Crowdfunding models depending on the form of return for the support provided

| | *Donation-based crowdfunding* | *Reward-based crowdfunding* | *Lending-based crowdfunding* | *Equity crowdfunding* |
|---|---|---|---|---|
| **Name variant** | Donation crowdfunding | Bonus crowdfunding | Crowdlending Peer-to-peer lending | Crowdinvesting Investment crowdfunding |
| **Essence of model** | Form of support without material compensation | Support rewarded with a product with a market value lower than the amount donated | Support provided on the basis of microloans and social loans | Acquisition of the company's shares or an equity-like instruments outside the regulated market (e.g. a share in the profits) |
| **Form of return** | Intangible benefits | Product | Return on investment | Return on investment, share in the profits |
| **Type of support** | Donation | Pre-sale order | Loan | Investment |
| **Financing entity** | Donor | Backer | Crowdlender | Crowdinvestor |
| **Main purpose** | Social projects | Pilot products; new products | Start-ups and small and medium enterprises | Start-ups and small and medium enterprises |

Source: Based on Collins and Pierrakis (2012); Cumming and Hornuf (2018); Dziuba (2012); Hossain and Gospel (2017); Krupa and Żołądkiewicz (2017)

crowdfunding. A separate category is the mixed (or hybrid) model, which combines elements of the four models.

### 2.2.2 *Characteristics of crowdfunding models*

In the case of donation-based crowdfunding, the participants donate resources to selected causes for which they may receive a token of gratitude in the form of a thank-you message, but no material reward (Hossain & Gospel, 2017). Ahlers et al. (2015) equate this form of support with conventional forms of philanthropy or sponsorship. However, the donation-based model is not limited to non-profit organisations (Belleflamme et al., 2015). It is the least complex model of crowdfunding in legal and organisational terms, since the relationship between the supported and the supporting entity ends with the transfer of funds to the former. For this reason, the problem of uncertainty and asymmetry of information regarding the campaign is less important than in other types of crowdfunding.

In the case of reward-based crowdfunding, the campaigns are initiated with a publication on a dedicated page of all relevant information describing the campaign, including the exact purpose of the project, the investment needs, and the time frame for its completion (Kuti & Madarasz, 2014). It is possible to establish several financial thresholds to be reached, describing the specific goals that will be implemented with the raised funds. The larger the amount donated by an individual participant, the higher the compensation he or she can expect. The rewards are often symbolic, with a market value lower than the amount donated. They can also be entirely symbolic, such as a thank-you message (a postcard with an autograph of an athlete, a T-shirt with the logo of the club, a public mention of the participant) or the opportunity to purchase the product concerned earlier (Hemer, 2011). They can also include the opportunity to benefit from certain services on preferential terms (e.g. watching a sports event from the VIP area or in the company of an athlete).

In the case of lending-based crowdfunding (otherwise known as peer-to-peer lending or crowdlending), the funds of individual participants are transferred via crowdfunding platforms to campaign initiators in the form of loans (Kuti & Madarasz, 2014) without the involvement of financial institutions and collateral. This form of support is regarded as a substitute for bank loans and entails considerable financial risk (Belleflamme et al., 2015) due to the fact that, unlike in the case of conventional bank loans, which require prior analysis of the project in question by a professional institution, this task is taken over by a group of individual amateur lenders. In contrast to other crowdfunding models, in the case of crowdlending, the only thing that is exchanged are funds (Hossain & Gospel, 2017).

The last model discussed is equity crowdfunding, also known as investment crowdfunding or simply crowdinvesting. In the case of this solution, investors receive shares in the organisation or share-like instruments (e.g. share in the profits[6]) of the supported venture (Ahlers et al., 2015). Although this model is essentially based on the sale of shares, campaign initiators often introduce other, additional rewards for the participants (Krupa & Żołądkiewicz, 2017). Compared to the other models, equity crowdfunding has the strictest requirements for companies: the initiator must submit a business plan to the crowdfunding platform and operate based on a specific legal form (Kędzierska-Szczepaniak, 2017; Motylska-Kuźma, 2018). While, in the reward-based model, campaigns are mainly initiated by private individuals, in the case of equity crowdfunding, the initiator of the campaign must be a legal entity (Colombo, Franzoni, & Rossi-Lamastra, 2015).

Other classifications of crowdfunding can be found in the literature, which are also based on the type of compensation received for the support provided, but they usually differ only in details with respect to the classification adopted. For example, reward-based crowdfunding is sometimes classified as a specific form of donation-based crowdfunding (Dziuba, 2012). Bradford (2012) makes a distinction between pre-sale crowdfunding and reward-based crowdfunding, while Belleflamme, Omrani, and Peitz (2015) identify license-based crowdfunding as a separate equity crowdfunding model. The adoption of the classification dividing crowdfunding into four main models, preferred by most researchers, seems justified to the author.

### 2.2.3 *Criteria for selecting a crowdfunding model*

Crowdfunding campaign initiators select one of the presented models, depending on the stage of development of the product that is the subject of the campaign (Leboeuf & Schwienbacher, 2018). As a rule, companies are funded in line with the so-called financial growth cycle paradigm proposed by Berger and Udell (1998), which takes into account the relationship between the dominant sources of financing and the different stages of the company's development (Figure 2.2). According to this model, at their initial stage of development, start-ups may rely on financial support from friends and family or use bootstrap financing.[7] As they move to the subsequent stages, they can benefit from venture capital funds or obtain support of angel investors. Much larger and more developed companies obtain funding through bank loans, mergers, acquisitions, and/or initial public offerings (IPOs) to expand their business.

Conventional financing sources can be replaced by an appropriate crowdfunding model at each stage of the company's development (Agrawal et al., 2013). Reward-based crowdfunding can be a substitute for financing the company from own funds, crowdlending can be a substitute for bank loans, while equity crowdfunding can be a substitute for obtaining support from angel investors, venture funds, and an IPO (Leboeuf & Schwienbacher, 2018). Donation-based crowdfunding resembles the financing model based

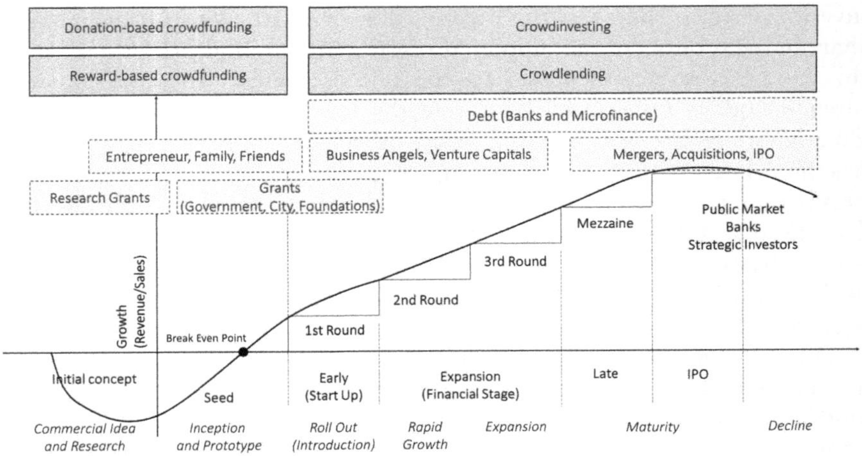


*Figure 2.2* Place of crowdfunding in the company's financial growth cycle

Source: Lasrado and Lugmayr (2013); Leboeuf and Schwienbacher (2018); Rossi and Vismara (2018).

on support from family and friends. Taking these differences into account, Leboeuf and Schwienbacher (2018) observe that crowdfunding is a particularly attractive solution for companies that are in the early stage of development and expansion.

Individual campaigns are not run in isolation from the entire crowdfunding ecosystem, which means that the success of one campaign may limit the amount of funds allocated to competitive campaigns (Hornuf & Schwienbacher, 2018). However, this mechanism, found in the reward-based crowdfunding model, is not applicable to equity crowdfunding. One of the reasons is that equity crowdfunding campaigns have an upper limit on the amount of funding. As a result, individual projects have certain restriction as to their size so as not to monopolise potential investors at the expense of other undertakings. This contrasts with the reward-based model, under which campaign initiators can accept as much capital as the market offers.

In the case of the equity crowdfunding model, the funding process consists of seven key stages (Hagedorn & Pinkwart, 2016): application, screening and selection, contracting, roadshow, subscription, holding, and exit. This path describes the issue of shares from the moment of submitting an application by the campaign initiator to the crowdfunding platform, through the publication of the invitation for support, to the shareholders' decisions. This process is illustrated in detail in Figure 2.3, with the subscription stage being of key importance, determining the chance of success. For this reason, it is also this stage that is characterised by the highest level of marketing activity, on the part of both the platform and the initiator. If the target is not reached,

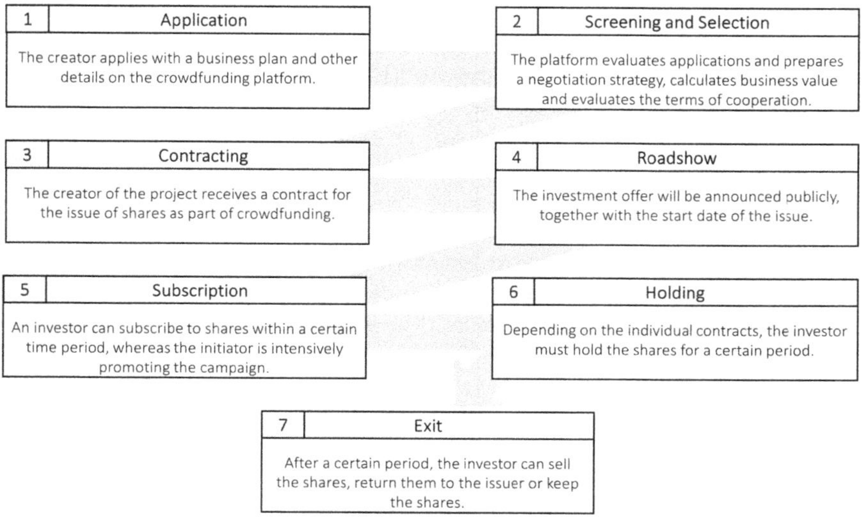


*Figure 2.3* Stages of the equity crowdfunding campaign process

Source: Based on Hagedorn and Pinkwart (2016)

the raised capital goes back to the contributors and neither the platform nor the initiator receives the funds.

Similar to the regulated market, equity crowdfunding initiators make decisions on the form of the share issue and the investment method. Based on an analysis of the German market, Hagedorn and Pinkwart (2016) present four possible forms of issue: typical and atypical silent partnerships,[8] subordinated participating profit loans, participation rights, and registered shares with restricted transferability.

The shares may be issued based on the simple subscription method or the pre-auction method (Hagedorn & Pinkwart, 2016). In the case of the latter, the value of the shares depends on investor demand. The advantage of this solution is a market-based valuation of the company. The simple subscription method, on the other hand, operates based on the first-come-first-served principle. The investment contract is concluded directly between the platform (which provides the issuing infrastructure and technical support) and the issuer. The advantage of this solution is the reduced complexity of the undertaking.

On the other hand, however, in the absence of the strict requirements in terms of governance, reporting and other formal matters which are in place on stock markets, the participants of funding equity crowdfunding campaigns are exposed to an extremely high degree of risk,[9] related to information asymmetry, which is partly limited in the case of regulated markets (Viotto, 2015). This can lead to an inappropriate selection of campaigns by participants (i.e.

choosing less profitable and riskier initiatives) and uncontrollable disloyalty of campaign initiators (spending the funds received in a manner that is not in accordance with their intended purpose) (Lissowska, 2018a).

A similar problem can be seen when comparing equity crowdfunding with other crowdfunding models (Agrawal et al., 2013). In non-equity crowdfunding models, the asymmetry risk relates to the feasibility and ability of the initiator to deliver the product. In the case of equity crowdfunding, the problem of asymmetry encompasses the above issues, as well as the ability of the initiator to generate value through the development of the company (rather than simply delivering a product as a one-off reward). In terms of measures capable of countering this phenomenon, four categories of market mechanisms can be identified which have been or can be applied to mitigate the shortcomings of the market related to information asymmetry between participants and initiators of equity crowdfunding campaigns. These include (Hagedorn & Pinkwart, 2016) signalling, industry regulations (Sadzius & Sadzius, 2017), community due diligence,[10] and a backup point mechanism.

Among those, the key mechanism for reducing information asymmetry is signalling, i.e. the public display and real-time updating of information about the campaign in question (Viotto, 2015). It also covers additional information that can be found on campaign pages, including data on the financial target, duration of the campaign, number of participants at a given point, and number of interactions between the participants (updates, comments, sharing on social media, etc.). All this allows the participants to make a better assessment of the funded projects in qualitative terms (Ahlers et al., 2015; Mollick, 2014). At the same time, signalling elements are one of the leading criteria that participants use to select campaigns they want to support.[11]

## 2.3 Behaviour of crowdfunding campaign participants

### 2.3.1 *Fundamentals of the customer's buying process*

Organisations adopting a marketing orientation in their activities aim at meeting the expectations and needs of customers. When it comes to individual clients (that is the subject of the analysis), their needs can be ordered hierarchically (in line with A. Maslow's pyramid), where physiological needs are satisfied first, followed by safety needs, love and belonging, esteem, and self-actualisation (Maslow, 1954). Products are purchased when their value exceeds their cost to the customer (Smoleń, 2012).

Depending on the object traded, the customer's purchasing decisions may be made prudently (based on a detailed analysis of the available options, which is usually the case when purchasing luxury goods), occasionally (in the case of goods already purchased before), habitually (in the case of commonly used products), or impulsively (under the influence of a marketing stimulus) (Mruk, 2015).

The buying process of an individual customer is comprised of three stages (Armstrong & Volkov, 2018; Kotler & Keller, 2016):

- Influence of the environment;
- Mechanisms of the so-called 'black box' of consumer behaviour;
- Purchase response.

The customer's environment is shaped by sociocultural factors, with culture being considered the fundamental determinant of human behaviour, shaping the social conditions in which the individual operates (Armstrong & Volkov, 2018; Hollensen, 2010). The mechanisms occurring in the customer's 'black box' are the result of individual characteristics (including age, nationality, and lifestyle) and the customer's decision-making process. The latter consists of five stages: identification of needs, searching for information, evaluation of alternatives, purchase decision, and post-purchase behaviour (Jedlińska, 2013). This shows that the buying process starts long before the actual purchase of the product and continues for a long time thereafter.

Understanding the mechanisms of the buying process has become the topic of interest to researchers, as it is indispensable for exerting an effective influence over the consumer with marketing stimuli through the use of marketing-mix tools, thus becoming an additional factor of the customer's environment, affecting his or her decisions.

The research on the behaviour of crowdfunding campaign participants focuses on three main aspects:

- The analysis of the factors influencing the preferences of the participants (e.g. the time and number of contributions made by other participants, the location of the initiator, relationship with the initiator, etc.) (Gafni, Marom, & Sade, 2018; Schwienbac her & Larralde, 2010);
- Verification of individual activities undertaken by the initiator in terms of their impact on the participants' engagement (e.g. the use of media, the number of updates, the purpose, the duration and description of the campaign) (Ahlers et al., 2015);
- Identification of the motivations behind participation in crowdfunding campaigns (Bagheri, Chitsazan, & Ebrahimi, 2019; Cholakova & Clarysse, 2015; Gerber & Hui, 2013; Y. C. Zhao & Zhu, 2014).

This section discusses in detail the factors affecting the success of crowdfunding campaigns and the motivations of their participants. The analysis of the initiators' actions, as part of the campaign's marketing strategy (in broad terms), will be presented in Section 2.4.

### 2.3.2 *Motivations of crowdfunding campaign participants*

The theoretical basis of most studies (Bagheri et al., 2019; Bretschneider & Leimeister, 2017; Bruton, Khavul, Siegel, & Wright, 2015; Cholakova & Clarysse, 2015; Choy & Schlagwein, 2016; Gerber & Hui, 2013; Zhang & Chen, 2019) focusing on the motivations of crowdfunding campaign participants is the self-determination theory (SDT), which says that people take certain actions as a result of intrinsic motivation (when they find it entertaining, challenging, or interesting) or extrinsic motivation (when they expect to obtain tangible benefits) (Ryan & Deci, 2000). Based on a review of the literature on the behaviour of crowdfunding participants, it

*Table 2.3* Extrinsic and intrinsic motivations of crowdfunding campaign participants

| *Crowdfunding* | *Donation-based* | *Reward-based* | *Lending-based* | *Equity* |
|---|---|---|---|---|
| **Intrinsic motivations** | | | | |
| Support for a given initiative | ✔ | ✔ | ✔ | ✔ |
| Be part of a community | ✔ | ✔ | ○ | ○ |
| Interest in crowdfunding | ○ | ○ | ○ | ✔ |
| Help (philanthropy) | ✔ | ✔⊗ | ⊗ | ✔⊗ |
| Self-image | ○ | ✔ | ✔ | ✔ |
| Own interests | ✔ | ✔ | ✔ | ✔ |
| Desire to be recognised | ○ | ✔ | ✔ | ✔ |
| Participation for fun | ○ | ✔ | ○ | ○ |
| **Extrinsic motivations** | | | | |
| Preferential access to products | ⊗ | ✔ | ○ | ✔ |
| Reward | ⊗ | ✔⊗ | ○ | ⊗ |
| Return on investment | ⊗ | ⊗ | ✔ | ✔ |
| New professional contacts | ○ | ○ | ○ | ✔ |

✔ – positively verified by empirical studies
⊗ – negatively verified in empirical studies (or contrary to model assumptions)
○ – not verified
Source: Based on Agrawal et al. (2013); Bagheri et al. (2019b); Bretschneider and Leimeister (2017); Cholakova and Clarysse (2015); Cox, Nguyen, and Kang (2018); Estrin et al. (2018); Gerber and Hui (2013)

can be concluded that participants are affected by both intrinsic and extrinsic motivations to support a given crowdfunding campaign (Table 2.3) (Bagheri et al., 2019; Choy & Schlagwein, 2016; Y. C. Zhao & Zhu, 2014).

SDT is a macro-theory that encompasses several minor ones, including cognitive evaluation theory (CET) and organismic integration theory (OIT) (Deci & Ryan, 2008). According to CET, intrinsic motivations stem from the desire to satisfy three categories of needs: competence (showing skills, abilities, and confidence), autonomy (doing something considered by the individual to be interesting or important), and relatedness (the sense of belonging to a community and building relationships). According to OIT, on the other hand, extrinsic motivations result from four types of regulation: external (autonomous actions motivated by rewards and punishments), introjected (autonomous actions motivated by instinctively expected outcomes), identified (self-determined choices based on beliefs about how one should act), and integrated (self-determined actions related to prevailing norms and value system) (Deci & Ryan, 1985).

The second most common theoretical framework for studying the behaviour of crowdfunding campaign participants is social exchange theory (SET) (Bagheri et al., 2019). SET emphasises the expectations of individuals with respect to the consequences of their actions as motivations driving human social behaviour. Based on this theory, Füller (2010) pointed out that decisions to participate in crowdfunding campaigns are driven by expectations of benefits in tangible (e.g. return on investment or reward) and intangible (e.g. friendship and connections) forms.

The first research paper that identified the specific motivations of crowdfunding campaign participants was authored by Gerber and Hui (2013). In this exploratory, theory-based study, the authors analysed the behaviour of participants of crowdfunding campaigns based on reward and found that participants were motivated by the desire to help others, the sense of being part of a community, and interesting rewards.

The findings presented by Gerber and Hui (2013) were in line with the earlier conceptual framework of Schwienbacher and Larralde (2010), according to which the main motivations of people supporting non-equity crowdfunding campaigns were social acceptance and self-satisfaction with one's philanthropic involvement. These findings were also corroborated in subsequent studies, where crowdfunding was described by the participants themselves as enjoyable (due to personal interest in the subject matter of the campaign), rewarding, and fulfilling (Huili, Zhenzhen, & Tao, 2016; Zhang & Chen, 2019). The participants were also motivated by their interest in new forms of support for entrepreneurial activity, as well as in the implementation of the campaign objective (Bagheri et al., 2019; Bretschneider & Leimeister, 2017; Huili et al., 2016).

Other models than donation-based crowdfunding are, by design, addressed to people expecting some tangible benefits in return for their support (extrinsic motivation). In the case of reward-based crowdfunding, the desire to receive a given product seems to be the intuitive motivation of participants. However, research results are inconclusive in this respect. On the one hand, Cholakova and Clarysse (2015), as well as Colombo et al. (2015), observe that the desire to receive tangible benefits is one of the motivations in the reward-based model of crowdfunding. However, Clauss, Breitenecker, Kraus, Brem, and Richter (2018) present results to the contrary. As noted by Zhang and Chen (2018), both rewards that are disproportionately large to the contribution made and too many rewards may discourage potential participants.

The intricacy of the role of rewards as a motivational tool for participants is further complicated by the fact that some participants willingly opt out of a material form of return (Cox et al., 2018). This points to a certain level of altruism on the part of backers, which is observed mainly among participants who are geographically close to the campaign initiator (Giudici, Guerini, & Rossi-Lamastra, 2018). Based on the existing knowledge, it can be assumed that obtaining a reward should be considered as one of the (extrinsic) motivations of the participants, but its importance should not be overestimated.

On the other hand, in addition to obtaining a reward, many participants also provide their resources partly in order to gain preferential access to the content generated by the campaign initiator (e.g. updates on products, direct communication) (Agrawal et al., 2013). The decision to provide financing, even if based on intrinsic motivations, is therefore not necessarily altruistic, but may also be dictated by self-interest stemming from selfishness (Cholakova & Clarysse, 2015; Gerber & Hui, 2013). Cox et al. (2018) hypothesised that anyone who reveals his or her identity on the campaign page is at least partly motivated by the desire to improve his or her reputation among family and friends, the campaign initiator or the crowdfunding platform community.

Based on the identified non-financial motivations of crowdfunding campaign participants, two dimensions of these motivations can be distinguished: self-oriented and other-oriented (Zhang & Chen, 2019). This orientation has been shown to vary depending on the gender of the participant, with women participating in crowdfunding campaigns more likely to be other-oriented, while men more likely to be self-oriented (Belleflamme et al., 2014; Zhang & Chen, 2019). Women also tend to support campaigns run by other women (Greenberg & Mollick, 2017). In terms of selfish and altruistic motivations, participants are usually motivated by either of these two categories (Zhang & Chen, 2019).

While reward-based campaign platforms, at least by design, are intended to attract people who participate in them for their own pleasure, the offer of equity crowdfunding platforms is aimed at people who seek a financial return on investment (Schwienbacher & Larralde, 2010). This is confirmed by the results of a study by Cholakova and Clarysse (2015), who found that non-financial motivations do not play a significant role for participants of equity crowdfunding campaigns. A later study by S. Estrin, D. Gozman, and S. Khavul (2018) found that the expected financial benefits are the primary motivation for purchasing shares.

In the equity crowdfunding model, in addition to acquiring shares or a share-like instrument, the participants also have the opportunity to receive an additional reward. While this solution is typical of reward-based crowdfunding, it is also practised in the equity model, where it can act not only as an incentive for potential participants but also as a tool to increase the value of the company's shares (Agrawal et al., 2013). Both Cholakova and Clarysse (2015), as well as Vismara (2016a), agree that offering rewards in equity crowdfunding campaigns does not increase the likelihood of achieving their financial target.

Despite this fact, investors interested in equity crowdfunding campaigns are motivated not only by financial considerations but also by intrinsic needs, such as the desire to support a given cause, the need for social engagement, and prestige (Collins & Pierrakis, 2012). Other non-financial motivations include the use of equity crowdfunding as an instrument to get acquainted with a new form of investment, the development of a network of contacts, and a sense of belonging to the community supporting the initiative in question (Estrin et al., 2018; Iwankiewicz-Rak & Mróz-Gorgoń, 2015; Schwienbacher & Larralde, 2010).

According to Lukkarinen, Wallenius, and Seppälä (2018), not just the mere fact of participating in equity crowdfunding but also the choice of a specific campaign are dictated by more than financial considerations and the commercial potential of the project. Participants also take into account:

- The description of the campaign, including, in particular, the terms and conditions of the contract and the attached materials;
- Familiarity with the initiator's company and its business;
- The scale of the venture, as measured by the investment activity and the threshold for the campaign's financial target;
- Personal acquaintance with the investor or people responsible for running the campaign.

Based on the above, it can be concluded that participants of crowdfunding campaigns are motivated by both internal and external factors of a social nature. Organisations generate value through social networks, which are one of the factors determining the success of crowdfunding campaigns. These networks reflect the social capital held, understood as the sum of the existing and potentially available resources, derived directly from one's network of relationships (Medina-Molina, Rey-Moreno, Felício, & Romano Paguillo, 2019). Social networks can influence the behaviour of campaign participants and, consequently, the achievement of its financial target in at least three ways (Belleflamme et al., 2015):

- Through personal connections with the campaign initiator;
- Through the network effect in social media groups;
- Through the use of social channels by crowdfunding platforms.

Research on crowdfunding (Choy & Schlagwein, 2016), as well as crowdsourcing (Kaufmann & Veit, 2011), has helped to expand the SDT with a new dimension to the existing classification of motivations into extrinsic and intrinsic ones – the classification of motivations into individual and social, with each having either an intrinsic or an extrinsic nature.

### 2.3.3 Factors affecting the decisions of campaign participants

The second main research area related to the behaviour of crowdfunding participants, in addition to motivation, is the analysis of factors influencing their buying decisions. What is emphasised here is the social aspect of the criteria determining participants' behaviour. In both the reward-based model and the donation-based model, shared values and regional or social ties linking the participants to the initiators of crowdfunding campaigns have a positive impact on their decisions whether to provide financial support (Bagheri et al., 2019; Clauss et al., 2018).

Supporting local initiatives (at the expense of other projects) may be partly due to the direct benefits of the implementation of the objective of the campaign in the immediate vicinity of the participant. However, it may also be the issue of trust, as the perception of a campaign as trustworthy is deemed as important in the decision-making process of potential participants (Colombo et al., 2015). The willingness to support a given campaign may be limited by the participants' concerns as to the competence of the initiator, the risk of fraud, and the overall risk of the investment in question (Agrawal et al., 2013; Estrin et al., 2018). This leads to a situation where, despite the removal of geographical barriers in crowdfunding, people are still more likely to support campaigns run in their immediate vicinity. As a result, initiatives launched in large urban centres are more likely to reach their financial targets (Adamska-Mieruszewska & Mrzygłód, 2017; Agrawal et al., 2013; Agrawal, Catalini, & Goldfarb, 2015).

In addition to the aspect of location, uncertainty of potential participants may also be reduced by contributions made in the first days after launching a given campaign. In this case, three mechanisms come into play (Colombo et al., 2015):

- Observational learning (Bikhchandani, Hirshleifer, & Welch, 1998) which takes place when the quality of the product cannot be directly observed

and individuals derive information from observing the behaviour of other people;
- Word-of-mouth marketing (Arndt, 1967), i.e. information about the campaign that its participants pass on to their friends (potential new participants);
- Feedback, which gives the initiators insight into what the customers think and prevents problems that may arise during the campaign.

Similar to the conventional funding cycle of enterprises, the very first investors on crowdfunding platforms are often family and friends (which is why it is referred to as the friend-funding phase) (Ordanini, Miceli, & Pizzetti, 2011). In view of the importance of initial contributions for building trust among potential participants, family and friends thus act not only as financing entities but also as actors increasing the credibility of the campaign. The impact of financial support provided by family and friends as a stimulus affecting the behaviour of other campaign participants has been demonstrated in numerous studies, regardless of the crowdfunding model analysed (Agrawal et al., 2015; Bagheri et al., 2019; Clauss et al., 2018; Kuppuswamy & Bayus, 2017b).

Initial contributions are indirectly promoted by the crowdfunding platforms themselves by providing better positioning on the website for those campaigns that have reached more participants (Belleflamme et al., 2014). They are important in later stages, attracting new investors and increasing the likelihood of reaching the funding target (Vismara, 2016b). The effect of initial contributions on the behaviour of other participants is compounded when these contributions are made by individuals who disclose their identity. This is true of both donation-based and equity crowdfunding models (Burtch, Ghose, & Wattal, 2015). In addition, contributions from such individuals tend to be higher than those made anonymously (Cox et al., 2018).

The high frequency of contributions in the first few days after launching the campaign is quickly followed by a decrease in interest from participants (Figure 2.4) (Kuppuswamy & Bayus, 2017a). The second key stage is the last few days before the end of the campaign. A tool that can increase support for the campaign is the marketing activity of the initiator. Large contributions made in the last days before the end of the campaign[12] have a positive impact on the behaviour of the remaining participants. This effect, however, is not as strong as in the case of the contributions made in the first few days of the campaign (Hornuf & Schwienbacher, 2018).

When the campaign moves closer to reaching its financial target, many potential participants give up on the idea of providing financial support, assuming that other users will do it in their place. Kuppuswamy and Bayus (2017b) describe this type of behaviour as a diffusion of responsibility. Lissowska (2018b) regards it as a manifestation of negative in-group effects, typical of two-sided markets. On the other hand, there are also positive

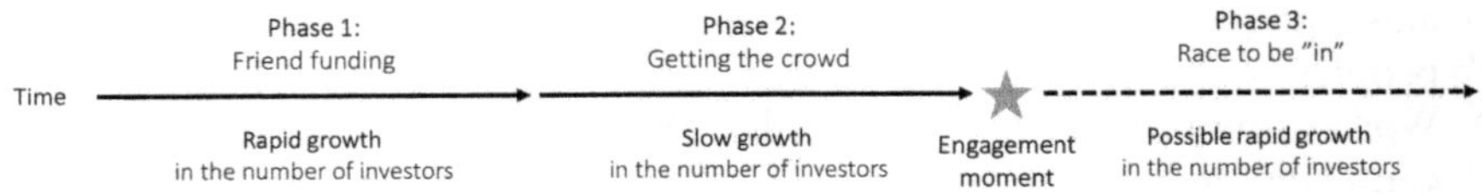


*Figure 2.4* Lifecycle of a crowdfunding campaign in terms of the behaviour of its participants

Source: Based on Ordanini et al. (2011)

in-group effects of crowdfunding, e.g. when platform users, influenced by the behaviour of other participants, follow the crowd and support popular campaigns.

In-group effects can be indirectly influenced by the campaign initiator, including by taking advantage of marketing tools, which stimulate positive effects while limiting the occurrence of negative ones related to the diffusion of responsibility.

## 2.4 Marketing management of crowdfunding campaigns

### *2.4.1 Segmentation of crowdfunding campaign participants*

Crowdfunding has three major advantages over conventional sources of financing: lower costs of raising capital, rapid access to market data, and building brand awareness of the campaign initiator's products (Agrawal et al., 2013; Gerber, Hui, & Kuo, 2012). An additional advantage is that the participants are often the first ones to purchase given products later (Burtch, Ghose, & Wattal, 2013). Crowdfunding campaigns can thus be used not only as a means of financing but also as a marketing tool. At the same time, however, being an initiative aimed at raising funds from a large number of individual, amateur investors, it is itself the subject of marketing activities (Sayedi & Baghaie, 2017).

Crowdfunding marketing strategies can be analysed at two levels: crowdfunding platform strategies and specific campaign strategies (more on this subject: Belleflamme, Omrani, & Peitz, 2016; Troise, 2019). The existing research on the latter, however, does not address marketing strategies in a holistic way, but rather focuses on selected elements, starting from the identification of the benefits sought by campaign participants (Agrawal et al., 2013; Bagheri et al., 2019; Estrin et al., 2018; Gerber & Hui, 2013; Schwienbacher & Larralde, 2010), through segmentation of participants (Feola, Vesci, Marinato, & Parente, 2021; Ryu & Kim, 2016) (narrow definition of the marketing strategy), to the analysis of tactical solutions related to the different marketing-mix elements of the campaign (broad definition of the marketing strategy) (Hu, Li, & Shi, 2015). The behaviours of crowdfunding campaign participants were analysed in Section 2.3. Further deliberations will be based on a review of the literature with regard to the use of this information in the market segmentation process.

In the previous research, segments of crowdfunding campaign participants were identified for two models: reward-based and equity crowdfunding. Analysing six types of motivations for supporting crowdfunding campaigns, such as interest, enjoyment, philanthropy, reward, connection with the initiator or the subject of the campaign, and social recognition, Ryu and Kim (2016) identified four typical groups of campaign participants in the reward-based model. The first segment comprised people who supported campaign out of charitable motivations. The second one consisted of 'reward hunters', behaving in an analogous way to typical market investors. The third segment consisted of passionate participants of the brand in question. The fourth group was similar to the third one, but was characterised by lower intensity of extrinsic motivations.

In turn, based on the criteria for selecting projects, Feola et al. (2021) proposed segmentation of participants of equity crowdfunding campaigns. Taking into account six variables (confidence in team, confidence in venture, platform characteristics, financial pledge and project attractiveness, community driver, and societal driver), four segments were identified:

- 'Venture trustful' – mainly young people, highly proficient in the use of crowdfunding platforms, with at least an average propensity for taking risk and a high level of intrinsic motivation;
- 'Crowdfunding technicians' – characterised by an average proficiency in the use of crowdfunding platforms, an average propensity for taking risk via online channels, and the highest level of intrinsic motivation among the identified segments;
- 'Financial investors, talent scouters' – characterised by the lowest level of proficiency in the use of crowdfunding platforms, an average propensity for taking risk via online channels, and an average intrinsic motivation;
- 'Social dreamers' – characterised by a low level of proficiency in the use of crowdfunding platforms, the lowest propensity for taking risk via online channels, and the lowest internal motivation for supporting crowdfunding campaigns.

In order to deliver value to these groups of participants, three phases of the crowdfunding campaign are required: the passive phase (the basic presentation of the subject matter of the campaign), the active phase (undertaking promotional activities), and the interactive phase (interacting with potential participants) (Pomykalski, 2005). The exact way in which this process takes place results from the specific nature of the segments in question and is carried out with the use of marketing-mix tools: product, price, place (distribution), promotion, and people (according to the 5P framework adopted for service marketing).

### 2.4.2 *Product, price, and distribution in crowdfunding campaigns*

The product of crowdfunding is the campaign along with the project that can be implemented with the funds raised. Providing information about its subject matter, circumstances, and initiators, as well as its presentation in an appropriate way can, therefore, be considered a key element for the success of the campaign (Mollick, 2014). It has been shown that the transparency and form of the description of the subject matter of the campaign are closely related to the likelihood of achieving its target (Zhou, Lu, Fan, & Wang, 2018). However, the results of the existing studies do not provide a clear answer as to whether the length of the description also matters in this regard (Block, Hornuf, & Moritz, 2018; Zhou et al., 2018).

Information on the projects submitted for crowdfunding is important from the point of view of reducing information asymmetry between the initiator and potential participants. On the other hand, however, revealing too much information in the project description carries the risk of the submitted idea being copied (Hagedorn & Pinkwart, 2016). This problem can be solved by reducing the level of detail of the information provided. However, as reported by Hagedorn and Pinkwart (2016), the initiators do not see the need to do this. Crowdfunding campaigns are usually conducted for products at an advanced stage of development, so copying and introducing them on the market would require too much time to be profitable.

Some researchers argue that offering a large variety of rewards in return for support increases the likelihood of achieving the financial target of the campaign (Kunz, Bretschneider, Erler, & Leimeister, 2017), as it caters to the diverse interests and motivations of the participants. Those who criticise this approach point out (based on the results of empirical studies) that excessively wide choice of available rewards may actually have a negative impact on the decision whether to support a given campaign (Chen, Thomas, & Kohli, 2016; Du, Li, & Wang, 2019; Frydrych, Bock, Kinder, & Koeck, 2014). Nevertheless, since crowdfunding campaign participants constitute a group that is heterogeneous, the campaign initiator should offer a sufficient number of rewards, differentiated in terms of quality and price, so as to cover the largest possible share of the market of potential participants (Hu et al., 2015). This approach confirms the need for segmentation of crowdfunding campaign participants in order to maximise the value proposition by presenting a differentiated offer to different target groups.

Pricing decisions depend on the established commission (decided by the platform) and the prices of rewards and/or shares (decided by the campaign initiator). Results of empirical studies based on reward-based and equity crowdfunding models suggest that increasing the financial target negatively affects the likelihood of reaching it (Mollick, 2014; Vulkan, Åstebro, & Sierra, 2016). On the other hand, some participants are willing to offer a cash bonus when the target is higher, indicating that increasing it may also serve as a positive stimulus for mobilising participants (Hornuf & Neuenkirch, 2017). Ultimately, the financial threshold determining the success of a campaign may depend on the level of risk involved and the rewards offered by the initiator (Schwienbacher, 2018). The more attractive the potential rewards, the more likely the initiator is to take more risk by increasing the campaign target. At the same time, the nature of crowdfunding allows the entrepreneur to identify (and reward) the most committed and enthusiastic participants, applying the principle of price discrimination (Belleflamme et al., 2013).

A significant challenge in the case of equity crowdfunding is the accurate valuation of shares and the decision of how many shares should be issued. The smaller the proportion of the shares issued in the company's share capital, the greater the chance of success of the campaign (Vismara, 2016a). The amount of the capital offered is very important in terms of maintaining control of the company after subsequent rounds of crowdfunding. Offering too much capital to campaign participants reduces the share in future profits for existing investors (Ralcheva & Roosenboom, 2019).

The distribution channel is understood as the place where the crowdfunding campaign takes place. Usually, it is a crowdfunding platform, so it is crucial for the initiators to select the appropriate crowdfunding model under which the campaign is to be run. Based on the considerations presented in Section 2.1, a key factor taken into account in this regard is the stage of development of the company. Once a suitable model has been selected, the initiator makes a decision regarding the choice of the crowdfunding platform. In the case of equity crowdfunding, the choice may be limited by the legal form of the organisation, as some platforms only work with joint stock companies.

Another important decision is related to the length of the campaign, which typically ranges between 30 and 90 days. As for the optimal duration, there have been no conclusive research results in this regard (Salahaldin, Angerer, Kraus, & Trabelsi, 2019). An excessively long campaign duration can be perceived as a sign of doubt on the part of the initiator in its success, which may discourage potential participants (Clauss et al., 2018; Mollick, 2014). On the other hand, based on signalling theory, if a longer time frame is adopted, successive contributions may generate the interest of new participants. The longer the time frame, the stronger this effect will be (Cordova, Dolci, & Gianfrate, 2015).

### *2.4.3 Marketing communication in crowdfunding campaigns*

The aforementioned signalling theory is also applicable to the marketing communication in crowdfunding campaigns. It assumes that providing precise information (which would otherwise not be directly observable) reduces the information asymmetry between two parties to the transaction by sending qualitative signals from the better informed party to the less informed one (Connelly, Certo, Ireland, & Reutzel, 2011). Such a signal, however, must be (Spence, 1973):

- Observable (otherwise it would not be noticed by the recipient);
- Costly (otherwise it would be too easy to imitate).

In the case of crowdfunding, these signals take the form of updates published on both the campaign page and the initiator's own channels (Block et al., 2018). The key elements of signalling include the sender, the signal, the receiver, and the signalling environment (Figure 2.5). Signalling not only reduces information asymmetry but also helps to increase the openness of the participants and the credibility of the initiator (Moritz & Lutz, 2015), thereby also significantly increasing the likelihood of achieving the financial target (Block et al., 2018; Kuppuswamy & Bayus, 2017a; Mollick, 2014; Xu et al., 2014).

Signalling theory is applicable to both the reward-based and equity crowdfunding models. In order to be effective, the signals must be (Block et al., 2018):

- Consistent and communicated with sufficiently high frequency to increase the chance of them reaching the recipient;
- Clear and understandable to ensure that they are interpreted as intended by the sender;
- Delivered in an environment that facilitates their understanding.

Irregular updates and an average quality of information provided to potential investors reduce the participant retention rate in crowdfunding campaigns (Estrin et al., 2018).

In addition, the signals must have an appropriate content and must be transmitted at the appropriate time (Xu et al., 2014), as their effect is not immediate and the recipients need up to several days to process the information before making a payment to support a given campaign (Hornuf & Schwienbacher, 2015, 2018).

Among the six types of communication, which increase the likelihood of reaching the financial target of a campaign in the reward-based crowdfunding model, the most important one is campaign reminders (Xu et al., 2014), followed by progress reports, new reward announcements, social promotions, news, and responses to questions. In the case of equity crowdfunding campaigns, the most important types of communication are information on new contributions, collaboration announcements, and progress reports (Block et al., 2018).

On the other hand, the equity crowdfunding community is not influenced by expert opinions, initiators' success stories, and information on

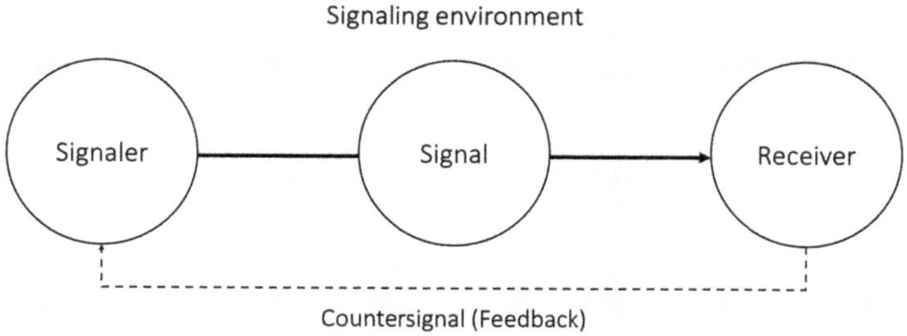


*Figure 2.5* Schematic representation of signalling theory
Source: Based on Block et al. (2018)

awards, patents, and success achieved (Block et al., 2018). In contrast to reward-based crowdfunding, the behaviour of investors in equity crowdfunding campaigns is not affected in any way by information concerning the team responsible for the organisation of the campaign (Ahlers et al., 2015; Block et al., 2018; Moritz & Lutz, 2015). As regards the impact of the use of multimedia (images or video files) for promotional purposes on investment decisions of campaign participants, the research results are inconclusive (Beier & Wagner, 2015; Clauss et al., 2018; Colombo et al., 2015; Mollick, 2014).

The marketing activity carried out for the purpose of a given equity crowdfunding campaign is positively correlated with the activity of initiators of other campaigns (Dorfleitner, Hornuf, & Weber, 2018), suggesting that initiators are, in a way, competing for the attention of potential participants. However, as observed by Hornuf and Schwienbacher (2015), the more active campaigns there are on an equity crowdfunding platform, the more investments are made as part of individual initiatives. Competition for the limited resources of participants is, therefore, not exclusionary in nature.

The initiator promoting the campaign through their own social media channels significantly increases the likelihood of reaching its financial target through building awareness of the campaign and generating interest in it among potential participants (Colombo et al., 2015; Hui & Gerber, 2015; Kopera, 2016). Social network outreach plays a crucial role in terms of attracting potential participants in the initial days of the campaign (in both the reward-based and donation-based models), which helps to achieve its financial target (Colombo et al., 2015; Mollick, 2014; Ordanini et al., 2011). Vismara (2016b) argues that initiators of equity crowdfunding campaigns are more likely to reach their financial targets if they have accumulated larger social capital (as measured by the number of contacts on LinkedIn). Promotion of the campaign on Twitter may also positively affect the likelihood of it reaching its financial target (Lu, Xie, Kong, & Yu, 2014).

In addition to the communication from the initiator, another type of content is messages from the participants themselves in the form of feedback to the sender and other members of the community. Feedback has a significant impact on the development of the crowdfunding campaign by providing relevant information to the initiator (Hornuf & Schwienbacher, 2018), as well as on the number of future contributions. As a rule, the more signals exchanged by the initiator and the participants, the higher the amount of contributions per participant (Kromidha & Robson, 2016).

Individuals who identify themselves as members of the initiator's social network tend to make larger payments than others (Kromidha & Robson, 2016). Social media also help initiators make new contacts, some of whom may become participants of the campaign (Beier & Wagner, 2015). It has been observed that campaigns which achieve their financial targets are predominantly supported by participants who are not personally known to the initiators (Borst, Moser, & Ferguson, 2018). Participants are guided in their actions by information gained from others in online discussion groups, mainly on social media (Estrin et al., 2018). Recommendations from third parties (including other participants) reduce information asymmetry and the importance of communication by the campaign organiser (Moritz & Lutz, 2015).

It is possible to identify two ways of functioning of crowdfunding campaign accounts in social media (Liao, Zhu, & Liao, 2015):

- Campaign initiators can link the project with their personal accounts, where they post information about the fundraising campaign;
- Campaigns can have their separate social media accounts.

In the first case, accounts linked to the campaign initiator are likely to include his or her personal contacts, which is beneficial in terms of providing a number of potential participants with information about the project.

Posting a large amount of similar content on multiple social media platforms has a negative impact on the campaign, as participants are likely to use multiple platforms as well and may see duplicate content as uninteresting and useless (Clauss, Niemand, Kraus, Schnetzer, & Brem, 2019). A good strategy for promoting a crowdfunding campaign on social media is to communicate, via selected channels, content that is not duplicated, which increases its validity and improves the effectiveness of using multiple social media platforms simultaneously.

## Notes

1 The term 'long tail' refers to a retail strategy that involves selling a large number of unique products in small quantities. The total sales of each, however, generates turnover that often surpasses that of the most popular, mass-marketed goods or services.

2 There are, of course, exceptions to these most common solutions. One example is the HelloAsso platform, which operates as a not-for-profit organisation, and whose revenues are made up of voluntary contributions and revenue from advertising.
3 See more on this subject in Section 2.2.
4 Due diligence is an in-depth analysis of a business project in the form of an audit prepared for potential investors.
5 Understanding the behaviour of participants of crowdfunding campaigns is crucial for developing a marketing strategy. This issue is discussed in detail in Section 2.3.
6 Campaigns that provide a return in the form of a share in the profits are sometimes identified as a separate subgroup of the equity crowdfunding model and referred to as royalty-based crowdfunding (Belleflamme, Omrani, & Peitz, 2015).
7 Bootstrapping is a practice of an entrepreneur financing a venture at an early stage from his or her own savings, the company's operating income, or other sources, without external financing (Fedorowski, 2013).
8 The 'silent partner' status is a special arrangement under German law, which denotes a minority investor in a company that does not carry the risk of claims from creditors if the company fails to meet its obligations.
9 As reported by Kędzierska-Szczepaniak (2017), back in 2014, the European Commission even discouraged EU member states from passing restrictive legislation with respect to crowdfunding. Instead, it was suggested to wait for the further development of this market and only then determine which areas of it require regulation. It was feared that excessively restrictive legislation would hinder the development of crowdfunding in Europe. Ultimately, by 2017, eleven countries (Austria, Belgium, Finland, France, Germany, Italy, Lithuania, the UK, the Netherlands, Portugal, and Spain) had introduced separate legislation to regulate the crowdfunding market.
10 The number of people familiarising themselves with the information concerning a given financial project under the crowdfunding model tends to be much higher than in the case where conventional sources of financing are used. The scale and variation in the adopted perspectives of analysis provides an opportunity to identify potential shortcomings of the subject matter of a given campaign.
11 The theory of signalling is closely related to the communication carried out by campaign initiators and is discussed in more detail in Section 2.4 on the elements of the marketing strategy of a crowdfunding campaign.
12 In a study by Hornuf and Schwienbacher (2018), these were payments over €5,000.

## References

Adamska-Mieruszewska, J., & Mrzygłód, U. (2014). Wykorzystanie finansowania społecznościowego w Polsce w latach 2011–2014. *Zeszyty Naukowe Uniwersytetu Szczecińskiego. Finanse, Rynki Finansowe, Ubezpieczenia*, *804*(67), 761–774.

Adamska-Mieruszewska, J., & Mrzygłód, U. (2017). Success and failures of crowdfunded projects in Poland Success and failures of crowdfunded projects in Poland. *Finanse, Rynki Finansowe, Ubezpieczenia*, *89*(2), 415–426. https://doi.org/10.18276/frfu.2017.89/2-34

Agrawal, A., Catalini, C., & Goldfarb, A. (2013). Some simple economics of crowdfunding. *Natural Bureau of Economic Research* (Vol. 19133). Retrieved from http://www.nber.org/papers/w19133

Agrawal, A., Catalini, C., & Goldfarb, A. (2015). Crowdfunding: Geography, social networks, and the timing of investment decisions. *Journal of Economics & Management Strategy*, *24*(2), 253–274. https://doi.org/10.1111/jems.12093
Ahlers, G. K. C., Cumming, D., Gunter, C., & Schweizer, D. (2015). Signaling in equity crowdfunding. *Entrepreneurship Theory and Practice*, *39*(4), 955–980. https://doi.org/10.1111/etap.12157
Armstrong, A., & Volkov, D. (2018). *Principles of Marketing*. Melbourne: Pearson Australia.
Arndt, J. (1967). Role of product-related conversations in the diffusion of a new product. *Journal of Marketing Research*, *4*(3), 291. https://doi.org/10.2307/3149462
Bagheri, A., Chitsazan, H., & Ebrahimi, A. (2019b). Crowdfunding motivations: A focus on donors' perspectives. *Technological Forecasting and Social Change*, *146*, 218–232. https://doi.org/10.1016/j.techfore.2019.05.002
Baran, G. (2013). *Marketing współtworzenia wartości z klientem*. Kraków: Instytut Spraw Publicznych Uniwersytetu Jagiellońskiego.
Baumgardner, T., Neufeld, C., Huang, P. C. T., Sondhi, T., Carlos, F., & Talha, M. A. (2017). Crowdfunding as a fast-expanding market for the creation of capital and shared value. *Thunderbird International Business Review*, *59*(1), 115–126. https://doi.org/10.1002/tie.21766
Bederson, B. B., & Quinn, A. J. (2011). Web workers unite! addressing challenges of online laborers. *CHI'11 Extended Abstracts on Human Factors in Computing Systems*, 97–105.
Beier, M., & Wagner, K. (2015). Crowdfunding success: A perspective from social media and e-commerce. *2015 International Conference on Information Systems: Exploring the Information Frontier, ICIS 2015*, 1–22.
Belleflamme, P., Lambert, T., & Schwienbacher, A. (2014). Crowdfunding: Tapping the right crowd. *Journal of Business Venturing*, *29*(5), 585–609. https://doi.org/10.1016/j.jbusvent.2013.07.003
Belleflamme, P., Lambert, T., Schwienbacher, A., Belleflamme, P., Lambert, T., & Individual, A. S. (2013). Individual crowdfunding practices. *Venture Capital*, *15*, 313–333. https://doi.org/10.1080/13691066.2013.785151
Belleflamme, P., Omrani, N., & Peitz, M. (2015). The economics of crowdfunding platforms. *Information Economics and Policy*, *33*, 11–28. https://doi.org/10.1016/j.infoecopol.2015.08.003
Belleflamme, P., Omrani, N., & Peitz, M. (2016). Understanding the strategies of crowdfunding platforms. In *CESifo DICE Report* (Vol. 14).
Berger, A. N., & Udell, G. F. (1998). The economics of small business finance: The roles of private equity and debt markets in the financial growth cycle. *Journal of Banking & Finance*, *22*(6–8), 613–673.
Bikhchandani, S., Hirshleifer, D., & Welch, I. (1998). Learning from the behavior of others: Conformity, fads, and informational cascades. *Journal of Economic Perspectives*, *12*(3), 151–170. https://doi.org/10.1257/jep.12.3.151
Block, J., Hornuf, L., & Moritz, A. (2018). Which updates during an equity crowdfunding campaign increase crowd participation? *Small Business Economics*, *50*(1), 3–27. https://doi.org/10.1007/s11187-017-9876-4
Blohm, I., Leimeister, J. M., & Kremar, H. (2013). Crowdsourcing: How to benefit from (too) many great ideas. *MIS Quarterly Executive*, *4*(12), 199–211.

Borst, I., Moser, C., & Ferguson, J. (2018). From friendfunding to crowdfunding: Relevance of relationships, social media, and platform activities to crowdfunding performance. *New Media and Society*, *20*(4), 1396–1414. https://doi.org/10.1177/1461444817694599

Brabham, D. C. (2008). Crowdsourcing as a model for problem solving: An introduction and cases. *Convergence*, *14*(1), 75–90. https://doi.org/10.1177/1354856507084420

Brabham, D. C. (2013). *Crowdsourcing*. Cambridge: Mit Press.

Bradford, C. S. (2012). Crowdfunding and the federal securities laws. *Columbia Business Law Review*, *119*, 1–150.

Bretschneider, U., & Leimeister, J. M. (2017). Not just an ego trip: Exploring backers' motivation for funding in incentive-based crowdfunding. *Journal of Strategic Information Systems (JSIS)*, *26*(4), 246–260. https://doi.org/10.1016/j.jsis.2017.02.002

Bruton, G., Khavul, S., Siegel, D., & Wright, M. (2015). New financial alternatives in seeding entrepreneurship: Microfinance, crowdfunding, and peer-to-peer innovations. *Entrepreneurship: Theory and Practice*, *39*(1), 9–26. https://doi.org/10.1111/etap.12143

Buecheler, T., Sieg, J. H., Füchslin, R. M., & Pfeifer, R. (2010). Crowdsourcing, open innovation and collective intelligence in the scientific method: A research agenda and operational framework. *Artificial Life XII: Proceedings of the 12th International Conference on the Synthesis and Simulation of Living Systems, ALIFE 2010*, 679–686. https://doi.org/10.21256/zhaw-4094

Burtch, G., Ghose, A., & Wattal, S. (2013). An empirical examination of the antecedents and consequences of investment patterns in crowd- funded markets. *Information Systems Research*, *24*(3), 499–519. http://dx.doi.org/10/1287/isre.1120.0468

Burtch, G., Ghose, A., & Wattal, S. (2015). The hidden cost of accommodating crowdfunder privacy preferences: A randomized field experiment. *Management Science*, *61*(5), 949–962. https://doi.org/10.1287/mnsc.2014.2069

Chanal, V., & Caron-Fasan, M.-L. (2008). How to invent a new business model based on crowdsourcing: The Crowdspirit® case. *Conference de l'Association Internationale de Man- Agement Strategique*, 1–27.

Chen, S., Thomas, S., & Kohli, C. (2016). What really makes a promotional campaign succeed on a crowdfunding platform?: Guilt, utilitarian products, emotional messaging, and fewer but meaningful rewards drive donations. *Journal of Advertising Research*, *56*(1), 81–94. https://doi.org/10.2501/JAR-2016-002

Cholakova, M., & Clarysse, B. (2015). Does the possibility to make equity investments in crowdfunding projects crowd out reward-based investments? *Entrepreneurship Theory and Practice*, *39*(1), 145–172. https://doi.org/10.1111/etap.12139

Choy, K., & Schlagwein, D. (2016). Crowdsourcing for a better world. On the relation between IT affordances and donor motivations in charitable crowdfunding. *Information Technology & People*, *29*(1), 221–247. https://doi.org/10.1108/ITP-09-2014-0215

Clauss, T., Breitenecker, R. J., Kraus, S., Brem, A., & Richter, C. (2018). Directing the wisdom of the crowd: The importance of social interaction among founders and the crowd during crowdfunding campaigns. *Economics of Innovation and New Technology*, *27*(8), 731–751. https://doi.org/10.1080/10438599.2018.1396660

Clauss, T., Niemand, T., Kraus, S., Schnetzer, P., & Brem, A. (2019). Increasing crowdfunding success through social media: The importance of reach and utilisation in reward-based crowdfunding. *International Journal of Innovation Management, 2050026*(May 2019), 1–30. https://doi.org/10.1142/S1363919620500267

Collins, L., & Pierrakis, Y. (2012). *The Venture Crowd. Crowdfunding Equity Investment into Business*. London: NESTA.

Colombo, M. G., Franzoni, C., & Rossi-Lamastra, C. (2015). Internal social capital and the attraction of early contributions in crowdfunding. *Entrepreneurship Theory and Practice*, *39*(1), 75–100. https://doi.org/10.1111/etap.12118

Colombo, M., & Shafi, K. (2016). Does reward-based crowdfunding help firms obtain venture capital and angel finance? Available at SSRN 2785538.

Connelly, B. L., Certo, S. T., Ireland, R. D., & Reutzel, C. R. (2011). Signaling theory: A review and assessment. *Journal of Management*, *37*(1), 39–67. https://doi.org/10.1177/0149206310388419

Cordova, A., Dolci, J., & Gianfrate, G. (2015). The determinants of crowdfunding success: Evidence from technology projects. *Procedia - Social and Behavioral Sciences*, *181*, 115–124. https://doi.org/10.1016/j.sbspro.2015.04.872

Cox, J., Nguyen, T., & Kang, S. M. (2018). The kindness of strangers? An investigation into the interaction of funder motivations in online crowdfunding campaigns. *Kyklos*, *71*(2), 187–212. https://doi.org/10.1111/kykl.12167

Cumming, D., & Hornuf, L. (2018). Introduction. In D. Cumming & L. Hornuf (Eds.), *The Economics of Crowdfunding* (pp. 1–8). Cham: Palgrave Macmillan.

Cumming, D. J., Leboeuf, G., & Schwienbacher, A. (2020). Crowdfunding models: Keep-it-all vs. all-or-nothing. *Financial Management*, *49*(2), 331–360. https://doi.org/10.1111/fima.12262

Deci, E. L., & Ryan, R. M. (1985). Cognitive evaluation theory. In *Intrinsic Motivation and Self-Determination in Human Behavior* (pp. 43–85). Cham: Springer.

Deci, E. L., & Ryan, R. M. (2008). Self-determination theory: A macrotheory of human motivation, development, and health. *Canadian Psychology*, *49*(3), 182–185. https://doi.org/10.1037/a0012801

DiPalantino, D., & Vojnovic, M. (2009). Crowdsourcing and all-pay auctions. *Proceedings of the 10th ACM Conference on Electronic Commerce*, 119–128.

Doan, A., Ramakrishnan, R., & Halevy, A. Y. (2011). Crowdsourcing systems on the world-wide web. *Communications of the ACM*, *54*(4), 86–96.

Dorfleitner, G., Hornuf, L., & Weber, M. (2018). Dynamics of investor communication in equity crowdfunding. *Electronic Markets*, *28*(4), 523–540. https://doi.org/10.1007/s12525-018-0294-5

Du, Z., Li, M., & Wang, K. (2019). "The more options, the better?" Investigating the impact of the number of options on backers' decisions in reward-based crowdfunding projects. *Information and Management*, *56*(3), 429–444. https://doi.org/10.1016/j.im.2018.08.003

Dziuba, Dariusz T. (2012). Rozwój systemów crowdfundingu – modele, oczekiwania i uwarunkowania. *Problemy Zarządzania*, *10*(3), 83–103.

Dziuba, Dariusz Tadeusz. (2015). *Ekonomika crowdfundingu. Zarys problematyki badawczej*. Warszawa: Difin.

Estellés-Arolas, E., & González-Ladrón-De-Guevara, F. (2012). Towards an integrated crowdsourcing definition. *Journal of Information Science*, *38*(2), 189–200. https://doi.org/10.1177/0165551512437638

Estellés-Arolas, E., Navarro-Giner, R., & González-Ladrón-de-Guevara, F. (2015). Crowdsourcing fundamentals: Definition and typology. In *Advances in Crowdsourcing* (pp. 33–48). Cham: Springer.

Estrin, S., Gozman, D., & Khavul, S. (2018). The evolution and adoption of equity crowdfunding: Entrepreneur and investor entry into a new market. *Small Business Economics*, *51*(2), 425–439. https://doi.org/10.1007/s11187-018-0009-5

Fedorowski, P. A. (2013). Finansowanie zaradne młodych przedsiębiorstw. *Kwartalnik Nauk o Przedsiębiorstwie*, *26*(1), 75–83. Retrieved from http://www.przedsiebiorstwo.waw.pl/

Feola, R., Vesci, M., Marinato, E., & Parente, R. (2021). Segmenting "digital investors": Evidence from the Italian equity crowdfunding market. *Small Business Economics*, *Small Business Economics*, *56*, 1235–1250. https://doi.org/10.1007/s11187-019-00265-3

Frydrych, D., Bock, A. J., Kinder, T., & Koeck, B. (2014). Exploring entrepreneurial legitimacy in reward-based crowdfunding. *Venture Capital*, *16*(3), 247–269. https://doi.org/10.1080/13691066.2014.916512

Füller, J. (2010). Refining virtual co-creation from a consumer perspective. *California Management Review*, *52*(2), 98–122.

Gafni, H., Marom, D., & Sade, O. (2018). Are the life and death of an early-stage venture indeed in the power of the tongue ? Lessons from online crowdfunding pitches. *Strategic Management Society*, *13*, 3–23. https://doi.org/10.1002/sej.1293

Geiger, D., Fielt, E., Rosemann, M., & Schader, M. (2012). Crowdsourcing information systems - definition, typology, and design. *International Conference on Information Systems, ICIS 2012*, *4*, 3562–3572.

Geiger, D., & Schader, M. (2014). Personalized task recommendation in crowdsourcing information systems—Current state of the art. *Decision Support Systems*, *65*, 3–16. https://doi.org/10.1016/j.dss.2014.05.007

Gerber, E. M., & Hui, J. (2013). Crowdfunding: Motivations and Deterrents for Participation. *ACM Transactions on Computer-Human Interaction (TOCHI)*, *20*(6), 34:1–32. https://doi.org/10.1145/2530540

Gerber, E. M., Hui, J. S., & Kuo, P. (2012). Crowdfunding : Why people are motivated to post and fund projects on crowdfunding platforms. *Proceedings of the International Workshop on Design, Influence, and Social Technologies: Techniques, Impacts and Ethics*, 2(11), 10.

Gierczak, M. M., Bretschneider, U., Haas, P., Blohm, I., & Leimeister, J. M. (2016). Crowdfunding: Outlining the new era of fundraising. In D. Brüntje & O. Gajda (Eds.), *Crowdfunding in Europe* (pp. 7–23). Cham: Springer.

Giudici, G., Guerini, M., & Rossi-Lamastra, C. (2018). Reward-based crowdfunding of entrepreneurial projects: The effect of local altruism and localized social capital on proponents' success. *Small Business Economics*, *50*(2), 307–324. https://doi.org/10.1007/s11187-016-9830-x

Greenberg, J., & Mollick, E. (2017). Activist choice homophily and the crowdfunding of female founders. *Administrative Science Quarterly*, *62*(2), 341–374. https://doi.org/10.1177/0001839216678847

Haas, P., Blohm, I., & Leimeister, J. M. (2014). An empirical taxonomy of crowdfunding intermediaries. *Thirty Fifth International Conference on Information Systems*, 1–18.

Hagedorn, A., & Pinkwart, A. (2016). The financing process of equity-based crowdfunding: An empirical analysis. In D. Brüntje & O. Gajda (Eds.), *Crowdfunding in Europe* (pp. 71–85). Cham: Springer.

Hemer, J. (2011). *A snapshot on crowdfunding*. Karlsruhe: Fraunhofer ISI.

Hollensen, S. (2010). *Marketing Management: A Relationship Approach*. Essex: Pearson Education.
Hornuf, L., & Neuenkirch, M. (2017). Pricing shares in equity crowdfunding. *Small Business Economics*, *48*(4), 795–811. https://doi.org/10.1007/s11187-016-9807-9
Hornuf, L., & Schwienbacher, A. (2015). Funding dynamics in crowdinvesting. *Eiträge Zur Jahrestagung Des Vereins Für Socialpolitik 2015: ÖkonomischeEntwicklung - Theorie Und Politik - Session: Financial Economics II*, 1–46.
Hornuf, L., & Schwienbacher, A. (2018). Market mechanisms and funding dynamics in equity crowdfunding. *Journal of Corporate Finance*, *50*, 556–574. https://doi.org/10.1016/j.jcorpfin.2017.08.009
Hossain, M., & Gospel, O. O. (2017). Crowdfunding: Motives, definitions, typology and ethical challenges. *Entrepreneurship Research Journal*, *7*. Retrieved from https://ssrn.com/abstract=2674532,
Hosseini, M., Phalp, K., Taylor, J., & Ali, R. (2014). The four pillars of crowdsourcing: A reference model. *Proceedings - International Conference on Research Challenges in Information Science*, 1–12. https://doi.org/10.1109/RCIS.2014.6861072
Howe, J. (2006). The rise of crowdsourcing. *Wired Magazine*, *14*(6), 1–4.
Hu, M., Li, X., & Shi, M. (2015). Product and pricing decisions in crowdfunding. *Marketing Science*, *34*(3), 331–345. https://doi.org/10.1287/mksc.2014.0900
Hui, J. S., & Gerber, E. M. (2015). Crowdfunding science : Sharing research with an extended audience. *Proceedings of the 18th ACM Conference on Computer Supported Cooperative Work & Social Computing*, 31–43.
Huili, Y., Zhenzhen, W., & Tao, Z. (2016). Study on the investors' participation motivations in award-based crowdfunding. *International Business and Management*, *12*(2), 29–33.
Iwankiewicz-Rak, B., & Mróz-Gorgoń, B. (2015). Crowdfunding-nowe zachowania internautów. *Marketing i Rynek*, (8 (CD)), 196–204.
Jedlińska, M. (2013). Zachowania klienta - istota, uwarunkowania, etapy. In A. Panasiuk (Ed.), *Marketing w turystyce i rekreacji* (pp. 61–80). Warszawa: Wydawnictwo Naukowe PWN.
Kaufmann, N., & Veit, D. (2011). More than fun and money. Worker motivation in crowdsourcing – a study on mechanical turk. *Proceedings of the Seventeenth Americas Conference on Information Systems*, (11), 1–11.
Kazai, G. (2011). In search of quality in crowdsourcing for search engine evaluation. *European Conference on Information Retrieval* (pp. 165–176). Cham: Springer.
Kędzierska-Szczepaniak, A. (2017). Perspektywy rozwoju crowdfundingu udziałowego w Polsce. *Zarządzanie i Finanse Journal of Management and Finance*, *15*(4), 211–224.
Kędzierska-Szczepaniak, A., Szopik-Depczyńska, K., & Łazorko, K. (2016). *Innowacje w organizacjach*. Warszawa: Texter.
Kleemann, F., Voß, G. G., & Rieder, K. (2008). Un(der)paid innovators: The commercial utilization of consumer work through crowdsourcing. *Science, Technology & Innovation Studies*, *4*(1), 5–26.
Kopera, S. (2016). Social media challenges. In T. Byers (Ed.), *Contemporary Issues in Sport Management: A Critical Introduction* (pp. 349–362). Sage Publications.
Kopera, S. (2019). Crowdsourcing jako narzędzie wsparcia e-przedsiębiorczości. In M. Bednarczyk, M. Najda-Janoszka, & S. Kopera (Eds.), *E-przedsiębiorczość. Zasady i praktyka* (pp. 229–242). Kraków: Wydawnictwo Uniwersytetu Jagiellońskiego.

Kotler, P., & Keller, K. L. (2016). *A Framework for Marketing Management*. Essex: Pearson Education.

Kozioł-Nadolna, K. (2015). Crowdfunding jako źródło finansowania innowacyjnych projektów. *Zeszyty Naukowe Uniwersytetu Szczecińskiego*, *854*, 671–683.

Kromidha, E., & Robson, P. (2016). Social identity and signalling success factors in online crowdfunding. *Entrepreneurship and Regional Development*, *28*(9–10), 605–629. https://doi.org/10.1080/08985626.2016.1198425

Krupa, D., & Żołądkiewicz, A. (2017). Equity crowdfunding as a form of financing projects in Poland. *Entrepreneurship and Management*, *XVIII*(June), 181–197.

Kunz, M. M., Bretschneider, U., Erler, M., & Leimeister, J. M. (2017). An empirical investigation of signaling in reward-based crowdfunding. *Electronic Commerce Research*, *17*(3), 425–461. https://doi.org/10.1007/s10660-016-9249-0

Kuppuswamy, V., & Bayus, B. L. (2017a). Crowdfunding creative ideas: The dynamics of project backers in Kickstarter. In L. Hornuf & D. Cumming (Eds.), *The Economics of Crowdfunding: Startups, Portals, and Investor Behavior* (pp. 151–182). Cham: Palgrave Macmillan.

Kuppuswamy, V., & Bayus, B. L. (2017b). Does my contribution to your crowdfunding project matter? *Journal of Business Venturing*, *32*(1), 72–89. https://doi.org/10.1016/j.jbusvent.2016.10.004

Kuti, M., & Madarasz, G. (2014). Crowdfunding. *Public Finance Quarterly*, *3*, 355–366.

Lasrado, L. A., & Lugmayr, A. (2013). Crowdfunding in Finland: A new alternative disruptive funding instrument for businesses. *Proceedings of International Conference on Making Sense of Converging Media*, 194–201.

Leboeuf, G., & Schwienbacher, A. (2018). Crowdfunding as a new financing tool. In D. Cumming & L. Hornuf (Eds.), *The Economics of Crowdfunding: Startups, Portals, and Investor Behavior* (pp. 11–28). Cham: Springer.

Lenart-Gansiniec, R. (2017). Crowdsourcing — systematyczny przegląd literatury. *Przegląd Organizacji*, *3*(926), 25–34.

Lenart-Gansiniec, R., & Sulkowski, L. (2018). Crowdsourcing - A new paradigm of organizational learning of public organizations. *Sustainability*, *10*(3359), 1–14. https://doi.org/10.3390/su10103359

Li, Y.-Z., He, T.-L., Song, Y.-R., Yang, Z., & Zhou, R.-T. (2018). Factors impacting donors ' intention to donate to charitable crowd-funding projects in China: A UTAUT-based model. *Information, Communication & Society*, *21*(3), 404–415. https://doi.org/10.1080/1369118X.2017.1282530

Liao, C., Zhu, Y., & Liao, X. (2015). The role of internal and external social capital in crowdfunding: Evidence from China. *Revista de Cercetare Si Interventie Socialâ*, *49*, 187–204.

Lissowska, M. (2018a). Crowdfunding – the interplay between evolving organization and embedding institutions. *Accounting, Economics, and Law: A Convivium*, *11*(3), 1–20. https://doi.org/10.1515/ael-2017-0032

Lissowska, M. (2018b). Crowdfunding – zjawisko, problemy, regulacja. *Gospodarka Narodowa*, *1*(293), 59–86. https://doi.org/10.33119/GN/100568

Lu, C.-T., Xie, S., Kong, X., & Yu, P. S. (2014). Inferring the impacts of social media on crowdfunding. *Proceedings of the 7th ACM International Conference on Web Search and Data Mining*, 573–582.

Lukkarinen, A., Wallenius, J., & Seppälä, T. (2018). Investor motivations and decision criteria in equity crowdfunding. *SSRN Electronic Journal*, *11*, 1–44. https://doi.org/10.2139/ssrn.3263434
Maslow, A. H. (1954). *Motivation and Personality*. New York: Harper&Row.
Medina-Molina, C., Rey-Moreno, M., Felício, J. A., & Romano Paguillo, I. (2019). Participation in crowdfunding among users of collaborative platforms: The role of innovativeness and social capital. *Review of Managerial Science*, *13*(3), 529–543. https://doi.org/10.1007/s11846-019-00329-4
Mollick, E. (2014). The dynamics of crowdfunding: An exploratory study. *Journal of Business Venturing*, *29*(1), 1–16. https://doi.org/10.1016/j.jbusvent.2013.06.005
Moritz, A., & Lutz, E. (2015). Investor communication in equity-based crowdfunding: A qualitative-empirical study. *Qualitative Research in Financial Markets*, *7*(5), 309–342. Retrieved from http://dx.doi.org/10.1108/QRFM-07-2014-0021%0A
Motylska-Kuźma, A. (2018). Equity crowdfunding - doświadczenia polskie. *Prace Naukowe Uniwersytetu Ekonomicznego We Wrocławiu*, (530), 118–126. https://doi.org/10.15611/pn.2018.530.11
Mruk, H. (2015). Zachowania konsumentów. In H. Mruk, B. Pilarczyk, & M. Sławińska (Eds.), *Marketing. Koncepcje - strategie - trendy* (pp. 103–125). Poznań: Wydawnictwo Uniwersytetu Ekonomicznego w Poznaniu.
Oliveira, F., Ramos, I., & Santos, L. (2010). Definition of a crowdsourcing innovation service for the European SMEs. *Lecture Notes in Computer Science (Including Subseries Lecture Notes in Artificial Intelligence and Lecture Notes in Bioinformatics)*, *6385 LNCS*, 412–416. https://doi.org/10.1007/978-3-642-16985-4_37
Ordanini, A., Miceli, L., & Pizzetti, M. (2011). Crowd-funding: Transforming customers into investors through innovative service platforms. *Journal of Service Management*, *22*(4), 443–470. https://doi.org/10.1108/09564231111155079
Pluszyńska, A. (2018). Crowdfunding - historia i definiowanie. In A. Pluszyńska & A. Szopa (Eds.), *Crowdfunding w Polsce* (pp. 13–32). Krakow: Wydawnictwo Uniwersytetu Jagiellońskiego.
Poetz, M. K., & Schreier, M. (2012). The value of crowdsourcing: Can users really compete with professionals in generating new product ideas? *Journal of Product Innovation Management*, *29*(2), 245–256. https://doi.org/10.1111/j.1540-5885.2011.00893.x
Pomykalski, A. (2005). *Zarządzanie i planowanie marketingowe*. Warszawa: Wydawnictwo Naukowe PWN.
Ralcheva, A., & Roosenboom, P. (2019). Forecasting success in equity crowdfunding. *Small Business Economics*, (February). https://doi.org/10.1007/s11187-019-00144-x
Rochet, J.-C., & Tirole, J. (2004). Two-sided markets: An overview. In *Institut d'Economie Industrielle*. https://doi.org/10.1007/10_2008_30
Rossi, A., & Vismara, S. (2018). What do crowdfunding platforms do? A comparison between investment-based platforms in Europe. *Eurasian Business Review*, *8*(1), 93–118. https://doi.org/10.1007/s40821-017-0092-6
Ryan, R. M., & Deci, E. L. (2000). Self-determination theory and the facilitation of intrinsic motivation, social development, and well-being. *American Psychologist*, *55*(1), 68–78. https://doi.org/10.1037110003-066X.55.1.68
Ryu, S., & Kim, Y. (2016). Electronic Commerce Research and Applications A typology of crowdfunding sponsors : Birds of a feather flock together ? *Electronic*

*Commerce Research and Applications*, *16*, 43–54. https://doi.org/10.1016/j.elerap.2016.01.006

Sadzius, L., & Sadzius, T. (2017). Existing Legal Issues for Crowdfunding Regulation in European Union Member. *International Journal of Business, Humanities and Technology*, *7*(3), 52–62.

Salahaldin, L., Angerer, M., Kraus, S., & Trabelsi, D. (2019). A duration-based model of crowdfunding project choice. *Finance Research Letters*, *29*, 404–410. https://doi.org/10.1016/j.frl.2018.11.005

Sánchez, D. Á., Gimilio, D. P., & Altamirano, J. I. (2015). Crowdsourcing: A new way to citizen empowerment. In F. J. Estelles-Miguel, I. Garrigos-Simon, & S. Gil-Pechuán (Eds.), *Advances in Crowdsourcing* (pp. 73–86). Cham: Springer.

Sayedi, A., & Baghaie, M. (2017). Crowdfunding as a marketing tool. Retrieved from https://ssrn.com/abstract=2938183

Schenk, E., & Guittard, C. (2011). Towards a characterization of crowdsourcing practices. *Journal of Innovation Economics*, *7*(1), 93–107. https://doi.org/10.3917/jie.007.0093

Schwienbacher, A. (2018). Entrepreneurial risk-taking in crowdfunding campaigns. *Small Business Economics*, *51*(4), 843–859. https://doi.org/10.1007/s11187-017-9965-4

Schwienbacher, A., & Larralde, B. (2010). Crowdfunding of small entrepreneurial ventures. In D. Cumming (Ed.), *The Oxford Handbook of Entrepreneurial Finance* (pp. 369–391). Oxford: Oxford University Press.

Sloane, P. (2011). The brave new world of open innovation. *Strategic Direction*, *27*(5), 3–4. https://doi.org/10.1108/02580541111125725

Smoleń, T. (2012). Zarządzanie marketingiem w firmie usługowej. In A. Czubała, A. Jonas, T. Smoleń, & J. W. Wiktor (Eds.), *Marketing usług* (pp. 42–80). Warszawa: Oficyna Ekonomiczna Grupa Wolters Kluwer.

Spence, M. (1973). Job market signaling. *The Quarterly Journal of Economics, 87*(3), 355–374.

Troise, C. (2019). Marketing strategies in equity crowdfunding: A comparative study of italian platforms. *International Journal of Marketing Studies*, *11*(4), 16–29. https://doi.org/10.5539/ijms.v11n4p16

Viotto, J. (2015). Competition and regulation of crowdfunding platforms: A two-sided market approach. *Communications and Strategies*, *99*, 33–50.

Vismara, S. (2016a). Equity retention and social network theory in equity crowdfunding. *Small Business Economics*, *46*(4), 579–590. https://doi.org/10.1007/s11187-016-9710-4

Vismara, S. (2016b). Information cascades among investors in equity crowdfunding. *Entrepreneurship Theory and Practice*, *42*(3), 467–497. https://doi.org/10.1111/etap.12261

Vulkan, N., Åstebro, T., & Sierra, M. F. (2016). Equity crowdfunding: A new phenomena. *Journal of Business Venturing Insights*, *5*, 37–49. https://doi.org/10.1016/j.jbvi.2016.02.001

Xu, A., Yang, X., Rao, H., Fu, W. T., Huang, S. W., & Bailey, B. P. (2014). Show me the money! An analysis of project updates during crowdfunding campaigns. *Conference on Human Factors in Computing Systems - Proceedings*, 591–600. https://doi.org/10.1145/2556288.2557045

Zhang, H., & Chen, W. (2018). Crowdfunding technological innovations: Interaction between consumer benefits and rewards. *Technovation*, *84*, 11–20. https://doi.org/10.1016/j.technovation.2018.05.001

Zhang, H., & Chen, W. (2019). Backer motivation in crowdfunding new product ideas: Is it about you or is it about me? *Journal of Product Innovation Management*, *36*(2), 241–262. https://doi.org/10.1111/jpim.12477

Zhao, Y. C., & Zhu, Q. (2014). Effects of extrinsic and intrinsic motivation on participation in crowdsourcing contest a perspective of self-determination theory. (71403119). https://doi.org/10.1108/OIR-08-2014-0188

Zhao, Y., & Zhu, Q. (2014). Evaluation on crowdsourcing research: Current status and future direction. *Information Systems Frontiers*, *16*, 417–434. https://doi.org/10.1007/s10796-012-9350-4

Zhou, M. J., Lu, B., Fan, W. P., & Wang, G. A. (2018). Project description and crowdfunding success: An exploratory study. *Information Systems Frontiers*, *20*(2), 259–274. https://doi.org/10.1007/s10796-016-9723-1

Chapter 3

# Sports clubs

## 3.1 Basis of the functioning and financing of sports clubs

### *3.1.1 Organisational and legal basis*

Sports organisations, depending on the approach to the product they offer, can be defined in narrow or broad terms. In narrow terms, these are entities whose offer consists of sports or physical activities (Tomanek, 2019). Waśkowski (2007), however, postulates to include in this group various supporting entities, such as sports equipment manufacturers, sports media, and consulting firms (broad definition). According to these two concepts, sports organisations can be divided into those that create appropriate conditions for practising sports and those that support it. Sports clubs, as organisations offering their members the opportunity to engage in physical activity and organising sports events, are an example of the former.

From the point of view of market structure, there are three types of organisations that create conditions for practising sports (Kościółek & Nessel, 2016; Pedersen & Thibault, 2019; Vos, Wicker, Breuer, & Scheerder, 2013):

- Public organisations – national and local government agencies or entities responsible for the implementation of sports programmes and the maintenance of sports infrastructure;
- Non-profit organisations – associations and foundations implementing statutory tasks to promote sports and physical activity, as well as sports associations and sports discipline management bodies;
- Commercial organisations – which, by definition, are profit-making entities; these include professional sports clubs, organisations offering sports or sports-related services, and companies owning or managing sports facilities or organising sports events.

Sports clubs are regarded as a key link in the functioning of the contemporary European sports market (Petry, Steinbach, & Tokarski, 2004). They can operate on both a non-profit and a for-profit basis (Downward,

DOI: 10.4324/9781003320623-4

Dawson, & Dejonghe, 2009). Non-profit sports clubs differ from the professional clubs in terms of the social, rather than business nature of their activity, their sources of financing (public instead of private), and main forms of hiring and remunerating staff (volunteering combined with civil law contracts vs. full-time employment contracts) (Cieśliński & Perechuda, 2015). In both cases, one is dealing with a dualism of organisational goals where, in addition to promoting and disseminating physical culture (amateur clubs) and maximising financial profits (professional clubs), there is also an objective related to maximising the sporting results.[1]

The formal criterion distinguishing the two types is their legal form adopted (Table 3.1). Professional sports clubs operate as joint-stock companies, while amateur (non-profit) ones most often function as associations (Kurleto, 2016). Non-profit clubs can be further subdivided into single- and multi-sports clubs,[2] depending on whether they offer one or more sports sections. In Europe (except for in Germany), single-sports clubs are the predominant form (Breuer et al., 2017). Moreover, the majority of European sports clubs have long traditions, and their age positively correlates with the number of fans and members.

According to Panfil (2004), the transition from amateur to professional club level can be described by a three-phase development process: from social through public to market level. The first phase, which starts once a sports club is established by a group of sports enthusiasts, is characterised by a spontaneous and informal mode of functioning. The activities undertaken are aimed at meeting the needs of the members. Hence, the organisation's activity is financed primarily from membership fees (and occasionally received

*Table 3.1* Comparison of amateur and professional sports clubs in organisational and financial terms

| | *Amateur sports clubs* | *Professional sports clubs* |
|---|---|---|
| Purpose of activity | Social and sports | Sports and business |
| Legal form (in Poland) | Associations, student sports clubs | Joint-stock companies |
| Main sources of revenue | Subsidies, membership fees, donations, economic activity | Matchday revenues, commercial revenues from the sale of TV rights and transfers |
| Main forms of employment | Volunteering, scholarships, civil law contracts | Employment and other contracts |
| Key challenges | Acquisition of basic financial, human and other resources | Choice between maximising sporting and financial results |
| Marketing orientation | Attempts at implementation | Basis for the organisation's activity |

Source: Based on Cieśliński and Perechuda (2015); Kurleto (2016); Waśkowski (2007)

grants). As the club grows, its organisational structures become increasingly formalised. Sports club are regarded to have transitioned to the second phase of development (public) once they start to receive public grants on a regular basis. In this stage, not only the needs of the members of the organisation have to be taken into account, but also those of the local community it directly affects. Sports clubs managed by individuals with no aspirations for further development or operating with limited development opportunities remain at this stage. Others move on to the market phase, in which their activities, as professional sports clubs, are based on the principles of free market.

The process described by Panfil (2004) is the result of the transformation of a sports organisation from an informal club that brings together sports enthusiasts to a publicly subsidised entity pursuing social objectives, and finally to a commercial venture. The emergence of a division into professional and amateur sports clubs was related to the increasing popularity of the sports events organised and, consequently, to the growing commercialisation potential of passive participation in sports events (Downward et al., 2009). Some of the clubs, originally for amateur athletes, have evolved from small organisations with a local ownership structure into publicly listed corporations, business consortia, or companies owned by individuals (often foreign investors) (Andreff & Staudohar, 2000). The aforementioned transformations have led to the emergence of professional sports in the modern understanding of the term, with dedicated stadiums, admission fees to sporting events, and a transfer market for players.

However, the development opportunities for sports clubs differ depending on whether they operate within the European or American sports organisation system (Andreff & Staudohar, 2000; Sloane, 2006). The European sports model has a hierarchical organisation and league tournaments are open. This means that both professional and amateur clubs compete within a single system consisting of several levels based on promotion and relegation (Andreff & Staudohar, 2000). In the case of the most popular sports, professional sports clubs are competing at the highest level, while other levels are open to amateur clubs. As non-profit sports clubs can offer scholarships to the best athletes, the transition from the amateur to the professional level is very smooth, for both the athletes and the clubs themselves (Radke, 2018).

In contrast, in the American model, there is a strict division between profit-oriented professional sports clubs and amateur clubs pursuing social goals (Foster, 2005). Under this model, university competitions provide the link between amateur and professional sports levels. Although amateur in nature, they ensure a steady supply of young athletes who can be recruited to professional league clubs. Such competitions are closed and limited only to those organisations that meet specific formal requirements (Radke, 2018). There is no relegation under this system, and through the mechanisms of draft[3] and salary cap,[4] the competitive balance is ensured to make the sports events as attractive as possible to the audience. Due to the geographical area covered by the analysis of the empirical data presented, Section 3.1.2 focuses on the basics of functioning of sports clubs in the European system.

In Europe, sports traditionally adopts a hierarchical organisation similar to a pyramid structure (Figure 3.1), with sports clubs forming the basis of the entire system (European Commission, 1999). The top level of this hierarchy is the European federations, which are responsible for establishing technical regulations, competition rules, organising competitions at the European level, and cooperation with national federations aimed at promoting sports. The entities responsible for organising and running sports competitions in various disciplines at the national level are sports associations (otherwise known as national federations). Their competences depend on the general administrative arrangements adopted by individual countries.

In some countries, under certain conditions (such as in Poland, when more than half of the teams entering a given competition are joint-stock companies), the national federation is obliged to establish a professional league.[5] This entails the need for the establishment of a new joint-stock company responsible for the organisation of such a league and its exclusion from the jurisdiction of the sports association responsible for the management of the sports discipline in question (Grabska-Luberacka, Piechota, & Radke, 2018).

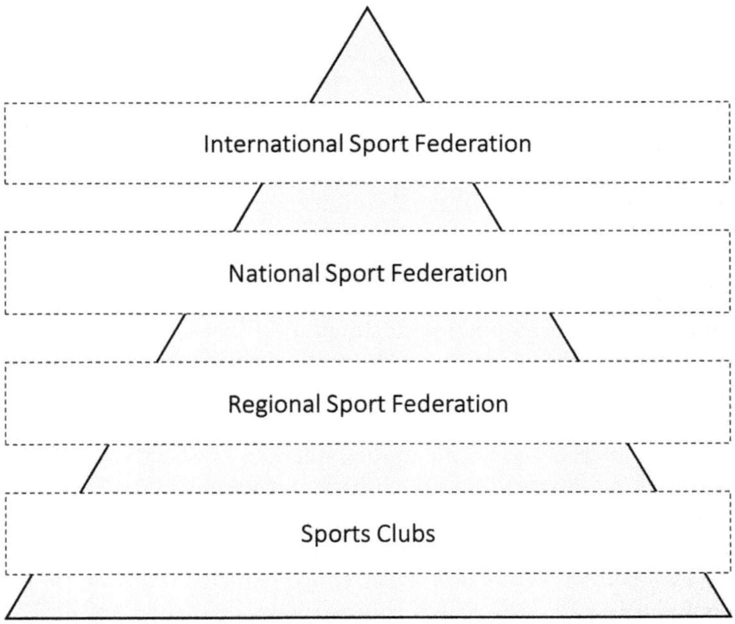


*Figure 3.1* European model of sports organisation

Source: Radke (2018); Tomanek (2019)

The aforementioned company is independent of the sports association. However, in practice, the latter may own its shares (including as a majority shareholder).

### 3.1.2 *Amateur sports clubs funding*

In the European system, non-profit sports clubs pursue sports policy objectives at the grassroots level (Vos et al., 2011). One of the two main objectives of sports policy, in addition to increasing the competitiveness of professional sports at the international level, is promoting active forms of sports in the society (Green, 2006). Initiatives based on the principle 'sports for all' are offered by all three types of entities (non-profit sports clubs, state, and commercial entities). While part of the offer is provided primarily by sports clubs (e.g. team sports), other areas are dominated by commercial providers (e.g. gyms, fitness clubs). They are, therefore, substitutive in nature (Hallmann, Feiler, & Breuer, 2015). Unlike commercial undertakings, amateur sports clubs also perform other important functions related to social integration through sports (Ulseth, 2004).

The role of non-profit sports clubs in terms of implementation of sports policy objectives explains why their functioning is largely dependent on public sources of financing (Kościółek, 2018; Vos et al., 2011). In most European countries, sports clubs are subsidised mainly from local government funds. However, the scale of financing differs significantly from country to country. The average for European countries is 16% (Breuer et al., 2017). Although in some cases the share of subsidies is relatively small (5% in the Netherlands, 6% in England, 9% in Germany), the literature emphasises their importance in the revenue structure of amateur sports clubs (Breuer et al., 2017; Kościółek, 2018; Wicker & Breuer, 2011), mostly because of the crowd-in effect of other revenues resulting from public support (Wicker, Breuer, & Hennigs, 2012). The amount of subsidiary can be based on the number of members, members at a certain age, or the number of licenced coaches (Feiler, Wicker & Breuer, 2019). However, some sports clubs do not even apply for public funding, mainly due to a lack of knowledge in this regard or failure to fulfil the administrative requirements of the application procedure (Sotiriadou & Wicker, 2013).

Sports clubs rely heavily on membership fees as a source of funding compared to other non-profit organisations (Table 3.1) (Kościółek, 2019). The amount of membership fees depends on various factors such as the sports discipline, range of services, costs of training staff and maintaining facilities, and age group (Huth & Kurscheidt, 2019; Nagel, 2008; Wicker, 2011). Discounts are often provided to families and socially disadvantaged groups. According to Wicker (2011), members are willing to pay higher fees than the actual amount incurred by them, indicating that the perceived benefits of membership outweigh the costs. Additionally, if a club faces financial difficulties, members are willing to pay even more, demonstrating their commitment to the club (Swierzy et al., 2018). Feiler et al. (2019) noted that the existing membership fees are influenced by costs, competition, demand, and non-profit sector-specific issues. Coaches and sports facilities costs are among the factors that affect the fees, while the costs of sports equipment are typically covered from other sources.

In addition to subsidies and membership fees, other typical sources of funding for amateur sports clubs include proceeds from federations, sponsorship, patronage and private donations, sales of food, beverages and services (training, facility rental), sales of goods and services at sports events, sales of sporting goods, and other proceeds (including from lotteries, foundations, etc.) (Eurostrategies, 2011). The internal variation in funding sources differs to a large extent depending on the country and a given sports club (Breuer et al., 2017; Kościółek, 2018).

Empirical evidence has shown that increasing revenue diversification has a positive impact on a club's financial situation, revenue volatility, and governing body investment (Cordery, Sim, & Baskerville, 2018; Wicker & Breuer, 2014). The recommended diversified structure for financial stability is when most expenses are covered by membership fees, as this is the most stable source of income (Wicker, Longley, & Breuer, 2015).

As shown, non-profit sports clubs have the ability to generate revenues from multiple sources. However, their financial capacity is somewhat discussed. On the one hand, more than three out of four European non-profit sports clubs report positive financial balance, but, on the other hand, only one in three declares no financial problems (Breuer et al., 2017). Feiler et al. (2023) found that three factors have a significant impact on the subjective perception of financial problems in non-profit sports clubs: operating margin, revenue diversity, and a ratio specifically created for the non-profit sports club context reflecting proportional sports facility expenses. Furthermore, they also suggest that an increase in administrative expenses in relation to total revenues is negatively associated with a decrease in perceived financial problems over time. This means that as the club spends more on administrative costs, such as salaries or rent for office space, the perception of its financial situation is less likely to improve.

Overall, amateur sports clubs are typically funded through the SSSL model, which stands for spectator (S), subsidy (S), and local sponsor (S) funding, with support coming primarily from local (L) organisations. This model is still prevalent for professional sports teams with less sporting and marketing potential, leading to low media coverage and limited influx of foreign capital. However, well-developed clubs are typically funded through the MCMMG model, which includes funding from media (M), corporations (C), merchandising (M), and markets (M) on a global (G) scale (Andreff & Staudohar, 2000).

### 3.1.3 *Professional sports clubs funding*

The MCMMG model covers the three categories of professional sports clubs revenues (Deloitte, 2019b, 2019a; Sports Business Group, 2019; Wyszyński, 2014):

- Matchday revenues (corresponding to the 'S' from the SSSL model), i.e. revenues generated from tickets sold and ancillary consumption during sports events (e.g. catering services);
- Commercial revenues – primarily from sponsorship agreements and merchandising, with the potential scale of sponsorship depending on the sports discipline (football clubs being most attractive to advertisers) and the league (the higher the league a team plays in, the more sponsors it has) (Jedel & Kończak, 2019; Wyszyński, 2014);
- Sale of broadcasting rights – in addition to the sale of rights to broadcast matches at the domestic level on the TV and radio, this category also includes bonus proceeds for participation in national and international cups.

Some propose an additional, fourth category of revenue – proceeds from player transfers (Deloitte, 2019b, 2019a). However, this category is treated as optional, as it involves a transfer of funds between clubs without generating additional value for the discipline as such. In addition, transfers are typically one-off cases and do not reflect the organisation's ability to generate sustainable revenues.

The matchday revenues are mainly dependent on the level of the number of fans attending the game. According to the review paper of Schreyer and Ansari (2022), there are a variety of factors that explain match attendance. These factors include (i) customer preferences, such as exogenous shocks, club characteristics, and habit formation; (ii) economic factors, such as availability of substitutes, market composition and size, economic impact, ticket price, and travel cost; (iii) quality of viewing, such as quality of stadium and timing of the contest; (iv) quality of seating; and (v) characteristics of the sporting contest, such as uncertainty of outcome, quality of the contest, success of competing teams, and significance of the game.

The main stream of commercial revenues for sports clubs comes from sponsors, which may be local companies investing in the club for corporate social responsibility (CSR) or historical reasons, or global brands aiming to promote themselves through sports. Demirel (2020) provides evidence that sponsorship fit influences consumers' perceptions of a brand's CSR, which in turn affects their behavioural intentions towards the sponsoring brand. In the global market, sponsorship decisions are primarily driven by sport team factors, such as media exposure opportunities, sponsorship fit, team image, fan base strength, star coach and/or player, team on-field performance, and hospitality opportunities. Country factors, including interest level in sport and political and economic states, and environmental factors, including competitors, ambush marketing, and league authority over sponsorship, are of much less importance (Lee & Ross, 2012).

Given the importance of broadcasting rights, their sale and distribution of revenues constitute a separate topic of discussion. There are two basic models of broadcasting rights management (Andreff & Bourg, 2006):

- Commercial negotiations and marketing of broadcasting rights are conducted by the clubs acting as owners of such rights;
- The sale of broadcasting rights is negotiated and carried out by the league company as the owner of these rights.

When broadcasting rights are sold by the competition organiser as a package covering the entire competition, the problem of distribution of the funds arises. Decisions in this regard are most often based on algorithms that take into account current sporting performance (measured, e.g. by the place in the ranking at the end of the competition), past performance, and the marketing attractiveness of the participating teams (Andreff & Bourg, 2006).

The valuation of players, which corresponds to the revenues from transfers, has also been the issue widely explored in the literature. Franceschi et al. (2023) review the literature and integrate existing knowledge in this matter and provide six categories of football players' valuation drivers. They are (i) selling and buying clubs characteristics, including financial situation and sporting performance; (ii) time referrals, (iii) labour regroupings, related to player contract, market design, and other valuations; (iv) performance of players, including key performance indicators as goals, assists, or saves, and consequences of given performance such as minutes played and successes; (v) individual characteristics of players, including physical and demographical profiles and past career paths; and (vi) popularity.

In addition to external market conditions and the club's internal strategy, revenue structure is also influenced by the ownership status. Based on the example of football teams, they can be owned by an association[6] or individual investors (domestic or foreign, including public institutions), or operate in the form of a listed company (Dietl & Weingartner, 2011; Franck, 2010; Rohde & Breuer, 2017). Clubs owned by associations tend to maximise sponsorship revenues, while private investors receive higher matchday revenues and proceeds from TV broadcasts (Dietl & Weingartner, 2011). Foreign private investors have a positive impact on the level of remuneration and sports performance in the national league, but a negative impact on the level of revenues earned (Rohde & Breuer, 2016b; Wilson, 2013). While, in theory, it is possible to own a number of clubs, investors are not allowed to own shares in more than one of the teams participating in the Union of European Football Associations (UEFA) club competition at the same time.[7]

When it comes to expenditure and its importance for sporting performance, the most significant aspect is player salaries. Their optimal level is assumed at around 60% of the club's total revenues (Deloitte, 2019a). This factor is the key determinant explaining 75% of the variability in the sporting performance of football sports clubs (Sports Business Group, 2019). Using the example of football clubs, when planning expenditure, it is necessary to comply with UEFA financial fair play (FFP) regulations, which impose a number of financial requirements on clubs, the most important of which are the prohibition on incurring outstanding debts and the need to achieve a break-even point (Peeters & Szymanski, 2014). In case of the latter, a sports club must be able to demonstrate that the revenues (proceeds from ticket sales, merchandising, sponsorship, and the sale of broadcasting rights) do not exceed expenditures (player salaries and transfers), with an acceptable deviation of €5 million per year.

The choice whether to prioritise sporting results or focus on financial objectives is regarded as one of the key challenges for managing professional sports clubs. Both objectives are interconnected: on the one hand, domestic as well as international sporting achievements generate higher revenues, while, on the other, additional funding translates into improved sporting performance in the future (Dobson & Goddard, 1998; Rohde & Breuer, 2016a). As a rule, European sports clubs are result-oriented, whereas American sports clubs can be regarded as profit-oriented (Andreff & Staudohar, 2000; Garcia-del-Barrio & Szymanski, 2009). In Europe, the revenues generated are most often invested in improving the club's sporting performance, resulting in a negative correlation (to a moderate degree) between place in the ranking and the level of profit generated (Wilson, 2013).

The opportunities offered by equity crowdfunding are open to professional clubs operating as commercial companies, which is why the management of this type of sports clubs will be analysed in detail in subsequent sections.

## 3.2 Marketing management in sports clubs

### *3.2.1 Sports marketing and sports clubs*

Sports marketing is the application of theoretical marketing principles and processes to sports products and services, and the marketing of non-sports- and sports-related goods and services through their association with sports (Shank & Lyberger, 2015). This concept consists of two pillars: marketing of sports (by sports organisations) and marketing through sports (by non-sports organisations) (Grabińska & Nessel, 2016; Hoye, Smith, Nicholson, Stewart, & Westerbeek, 2009; Mullin, Hardy, & Sutton, 2014; Pedersen & Thibault, 2019; Smith, 2008). Sports clubs are active in both of these areas. In the case of the former, the club is the object of marketing activities (e.g. organising matches). An example of the latter is the use of a sports club by another organisation for marketing purposes, e.g. promotion through sponsorship.

Sports marketing is, at the same time, interconnected with other types of marketing activities, including personal marketing (e.g. of a given athlete) and organisational marketing (of a given sports organisations) (Klisiński & Szwaja, 2012). The activities of sports clubs, therefore, fall within the scope of both sports marketing and organisational marketing. However, regardless of the specific activities undertaken by a sports club, the development of an appropriate strategy is essential to ensure their effectiveness (Mackreth & Bond, 2020). The process of marketing management in a sports club is analogous to that of organisations with other profiles (Grabińska & Nessel, 2016; Hoye et al., 2009; Mullin et al., 2014; Shank & Lyberger, 2015). It consists of the following stages[8]:

- Analysis of the internal and external situation (macro- and micro-environment) of the organisation;
- Formulation of strategic objectives;
- Planning of a marketing strategy based on the identification of customers' needs, segmentation, and market positioning;
- Implementation of the strategy with the use of available marketing-mix elements;
- Evaluation and control of the results of strategy implementation.

The macro-environment is examined using the PESTEL (Political, Economic, Social, Technological, Environmental, Legal) analysis, well established in the literature on marketing management. The micro-environment, in turn, can be defined as including sports associations, companies managing professional leagues, fans (customers), sponsors, public sector entities, the media, competitive clubs, and, in the case of amateur sports clubs, also volunteers and members of the organisation (Pawlak & Smoleń, 2015; Waśkowski, 2007). Public sector entities (especially local authorities) along with sponsors, volunteers, and members form a homogeneous group of the so-called supporting entities (Waśkowski, 2007).

Sports clubs are in direct competition with one another both in terms of access to the customer and supplier base, but the rivalry-based nature of their activities essentially requires the existence of competitors. Clubs that are weaker make the sports events with their participation less attractive. On the other hand, sports clubs often have to directly cooperate with one another, e.g. when negotiating the sale of TV broadcasting rights for a given competition, which is referred to as so-called co-opetition, i.e. cooperation between entities in direct competition with each other (Czakon, 2013).

From the point of view of relations with the environment, the sports club market is characterised by double duality (Sznajder, 2007). The first level of duality results from the presented classification into marketing of sports and through sports, where the sports club operates simultaneously on:

- The sports market, co-creating a sports event with its competitor;
- The advertising and sponsorship market, when advertising or sponsorship services are provided to or through it.

At the second level of duality, one can identify:

- The primary market, consisting of the spectators watching the sports event live at the sports venue;
- The secondary market, consisting of spectators watching the broadcast of the sports event.

In addition to individuals, i.e. TV viewers (passive consumers) and in-game spectators (active consumers), an additional group is business customers of sports clubs, including sponsors and media including those which acquire broadcasting rights to sports events (Figure 3.2) (Schwarz & Hunter, 2008; Shank & Lyberger, 2015). Waśkowski (2007) refers to individual customers as receivers and business customers as donors. This complexity means that the development of sports products by sports clubs and the adoption of a customer-oriented marketing strategy require the different expectations and consumption patterns of each of these groups to be taken into account. Since the recipients of crowdfunding campaigns are mainly individual participants, the remaining part of this publication will focus on them.

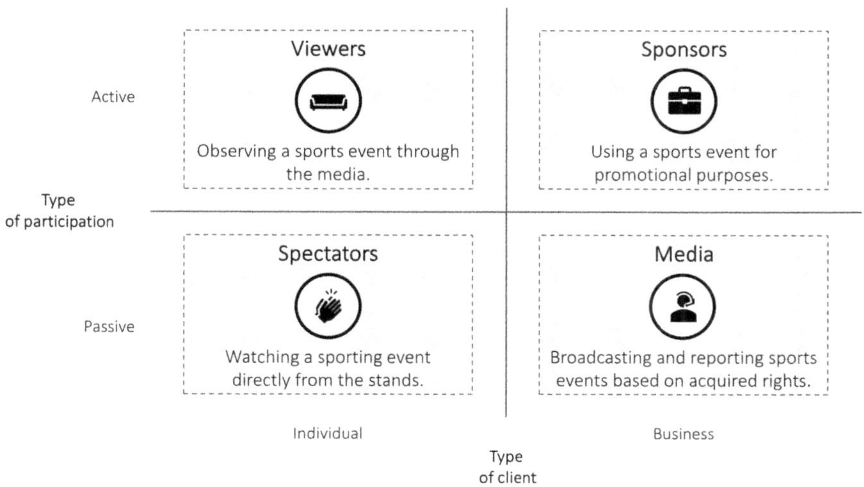


*Figure 3.2* Recipients of a sports event product

Source: Based on Schwarz and Hunter (2008); Shank and Lyberger (2015); Waśkowski (2007)

The vast majority of sports clubs adapt the STP approach when developing their marketing strategies, and their positioning on the market is mainly based on the benefits they can generate for the recipients (Brooksbank, Garland, & Werder, 2012). This means that sports clubs do not use market positioning based on price competition. This is due to the fact that highly loyal fans are a group that is extremely constant in their consumer choices (Bodet & Bernache-Assollant, 2011; Gladden & Funk, 2001; S. Lee, Shin, Park, & Kwon, 2010), and it would be difficult to expect these preferences to change under the influence of the price factor. The value proposition resulting from market positioning and delivered with the use of marketing-mix tools should, therefore, be oriented not so much towards attracting competitors' customers but towards gaining new fans without any preferences and activating the existing fan base. The following sections will discuss the key dilemmas in shaping the marketing-mix elements by sports clubs in order to achieve these goals.

### *3.2.2 Product, price, and distribution in the case of sports clubs*

A sports product is a good, a service, or any combination thereof that satisfies the needs of an individual or corporate customer (Nessel, 2016). In the case of a professional sports club, individual customers may be viewers or spectators of an event, while business customers may be sponsors, business partners, or buyers of broadcasting rights. Fullerton and Merz (2008) classify sports products into those intended for passive engagement in sports, active engagement in sports, and sports-related products (e.g. sportswear). Another classification of sports products is based on their nature and includes the following categories (Shank & Lyberger, 2015): sports events, sports merchandise, sports infrastructure, and sports news. Based on this classification, products offered by professional sports clubs can include (Sznajder, 2008): sports events with ancillary services, products bearing the club logo (produced by the organisation itself or by third parties based on a granted licence), rights to broadcast matches on TV (and other media), and promotion through sponsorship or advertising.

As presented in Table 3.1, each product consists of three levels: the product core (defining the actual benefit purchased by the customers), the actual product (taking into account its features), and the extended product (additional benefits) (Armstrong & Volkov, 2018). All of the aforementioned sports products should, therefore, be perceived as an extension of the sports event, which is the core of the basic product of sports clubs (Mullin et al., 2014). When the sporting competition itself forms the core product, the actual product consists of the tangible elements of the event (stadium facilities; quality of seating, quality of catering), while the extended product includes the associated intangible attributes (including atmosphere, experience, and quality of service) (Berbeka, 2004; Mackreth & Bond, 2020) (Table 3.2).

According to inverse joint product theory by Neale (1964), within professional team sports, two firms (sports teams), both with separate business functions, are required to produce one product (sports competition). In practical terms, fans purchase not the sports event as such, but all the emotions that accompany it (Grabińska & Nessel, 2016). The actual benefits include an opportunity to be part of a community that the club brings together to experience emotions together and to enjoy the benefits associated with the image of a given sports organisation (Rudawska, 2011). The more difficult it is to predict the final shape of the core (match result), the better the product evaluation *ex ante*. This is corroborated by empirical research, which shows that increasing the uncertainty of the final sporting outcome positively affects the interest in the product on the part of its audience (fans) (Coates & Humphreys, 2012; Pawlowski & Anders, 2012).

In order to shape the sports club product defined in such way (taking into account the complexity and intangible nature of the benefits that consumers acquire on this market), it seems necessary to adopt the service-dominant logic (S-D logic for short). According to Tsiotsou (2016), sports consumption, both as a spectator and as an active participant, satisfies three of the

*Table 3.2* Attributes of sports event products offered by professional sports clubs

| *Product level* | *Individual customer* | *Business customer* |
|---|---|---|
| Product core | Pleasure derived from participation in a sports event, opportunity to admire talented athletes, sense of belonging to a group | Opportunity to promote own products by associating them with the sports club |
| Actual product | Players, coaches, atmosphere, and venue (in the case of active participants) or quality of broadcasting (in the case of passive participants) | Advertising space available during the sports event |
| Extended product | Atmosphere, experience, quality of service | Display of the sponsor's brand logo on advertising spaces during the event and (optionally) during the TV broadcast |

Source: Based on Berbeka (2004); Grabińska and Nessel (2016); Hoye et al. (2009); Mackreth and Bond (2020); Panfil (2004)

five axioms of this logic postulating that service is the fundamental basis of the transaction, value is always co-created by multiple actors (including the beneficiary), and social and economic entities are resource integrators. An example of value co-created by fans and sports clubs is the atmosphere at sports events, affected by the fans themselves through their involvement in the tifo of the match (Chen, Lin, & Chiu, 2013). In terms of in-person participation in a sports event (not watching a TV broadcast), its atmosphere is also created by service providers, athletes, media, sponsors, etc., and a favourable outcome can only be achieved when all these actors integrate their individual resources.

Decisions concerning the pricing of sports clubs' products depend on the costs of organising the events and the resulting benefits as perceived by buyers. In addition to determining the price of tickets for a sports event, sports clubs also establish prices of player transfers, sale of broadcasting rights, sale of merchandise, sponsorship, and additional business activities (Waśkowski, 2007). In the case of sports events, determining the level of prices is a fairly complex issue, as it seems better to ensure that the stands are full even if this entails selling tickets below a level that ensures maximisation of revenue from this source (Grabińska & Nessel, 2016). This is due to the fact that an empty stadium or sports hall may negatively affect the perception of the event. In addition, low attendance results in a loss of opportunities for generating revenue from ancillary services offered during the event (e.g. sales of club products and catering services).

The level of prices for the opportunity to attend a sports event is determined by the venue (sector), the time of purchase (the earlier one makes a purchase, the cheaper the ticket), the sales channel (conventional or online), and the class of the opponent (in the case of the most attractive matches, the ticket prices are higher) (Pawlak & Smoleń, 2015). In addition, discounts are offered for certain customer groups (e.g. children, first-time match-goers).

Loyalty is also encouraged through the introduction of an offer of season passes[9] and discounts for pass renewals. From the point of view of the fans themselves, the price they are willing to pay for a sports event depends on four key factors: the presence of a recognisable sports star in the local team, the number of points scored in previous matches by the hosts, additional benefits (e.g. in the form of discount coupons) and the expected price of the product (Y. H. Lee & Kang, 2011).

European sports clubs follow a conventional approach to pricing (establishing specific amounts for specific services) without adopting a dynamic pricing approach.[10] The experience of US professional leagues and simulations carried out for one of the Bundesliga football clubs indicates that such a measure would increase matchday revenues (Kemper & Breuer, 2016; Shapiro & Drayer, 2012). Hence, Nufer and Fischer (2013) predict that it is only a matter of time until professional sports clubs in Europe also start using this approach.

According to basic marketing assumptions, the role of distribution is to enable the buyer to use the products he or she is interested in, in the right place and at the right time (Sławińska, 2015). The literature identifies two approaches to the issue of distribution by sports club managers. One of them is related to enabling safe and easy access to a sports event, as well as providing this service on the most favourable days, at the most convenient time (Waśkowski, 2007). It can, therefore, be called a process approach.

On the other hand, distribution is also understood in an instrumental way, as the process of selling tickets (and passes), club merchandise, and providing a catering service during matches (Pawlak & Smoleń, 2015). In the case of the latter, we are dealing with the phenomenon of distribution channel shortening through the shift of sales of club products online (Grabińska & Nessel, 2016). In terms of the potential to make use of crowdfunding by sports clubs, this seems to be desirable due to the fact that the campaign is conducted in a digital space which is already used for purchasing sports club products.

### 3.2.3 Communication, brand, and personnel in sports clubs

When it comes to promotional activities by sports clubs, a certain duality can be observed, much like in the case of distribution decisions. On one hand, clubs aim to promote specific sports events, while, on the other hand, they also aim to build and promote their brand identity (Grabińska & Nessel, 2016; Pawlak & Smoleń, 2015; Waśkowski, 2007). These activities can be divided into those of a strategic (brand building) and tactical nature (event promotion). What is crucial at the tactical level is fan engagement, which makes it possible to increase (or at least maintain) the existing consumption level (H. McDonald & Stavros, 2007).

The most important channels used by consumers to interact with brands are social media. The major factor determining the level of fan engagement on a sports club's social media channels is the level of identification of the fans with the club's brand and, to a lesser extent, the need for social integration (Vale & Fernandes, 2018). Fans who feel an emotional connection to their club's brand also display other non-transactional but desirable behaviours: generating positive word-of-mouth marketing, creating audiovisual materials concerning the club, communicating with other members of the fan community, and following media coverage of their team (Ahearne, Bhattacharya, & Gruen, 2005; De Beer & Stander, 2016).

The concept of sports club brand should be considered similar to the concept of the brand as such. It consists of a combination of elements allowing for its identification, including the name,[11] term, sign, symbol, or design (American Marketing Association, n.d.). Moreover, a sports brand is also defined by its reputation (Bednarczyk & Kurleto, 2016). Identification of fans with a club, considered to be the key factor explaining their consumer behaviour, is tantamount to their identification with the club brand (Ross, James, & Vargas, 2006).

The brand, thus, is the basis for a sports club to build a competitive advantage (Bednarczyk & Kurleto, 2016). The benefits of having a strong brand can be classified into three areas (Waśkowski, 2007):

- Prestige – resulting in increased interest in the organisation from the media, sponsors, and other entities;
- Sports-related – facilitating negotiation of contacts with players, as well as a more attractive atmosphere during sports events (strong club brands have a larger number of committed fans);
- Financial – an opportunity to use the brand to sell club merchandises, as well as to sell licences for the use of the brand logo.

These three areas are interrelated to one another.

Typically, football clubs have used elements of brand associations in marketing communications (Anagnostopoulos, Parganas, Chadwick, & Fenton, 2018; Maderer, Parganas, & Anagnostopoulos, 2018; Parganas, Anagnostopoulos, & Chadwick, 2015). As far as the attributes of football club brands are concerned, the literature proposes two alternative concepts. According to the Team Association Model (TAM), sports club brands consist of attributes related to the sports product (team successes, star players, head coaches, and team management) and unrelated to the sports product (logos, stadium, traditions, and values) (Gladden & Funk, 2002). The other option is the Team Brand Association Scale (TBAS), which includes such aspects as success, history, stadium, team characteristics, logo, concessions, social integration, rivalry, commitment, organisational attributes, and non-sports personnel (Ross et al., 2006). The most commonly used brand attributes are those related to the product, such as team success and players and, to a lesser extent, club history and tradition, fans, and events (Anagnostopoulos et al., 2018; Maderer et al., 2018). In the area of communication via social media, what is observable is the contextualisation of the number of interactions under posts with specific thematic categories. For example, among Liverpool FC fans, the posts with the most interactions on Instagram are those concerning the head coach, while on Twitter, those are related to the club's sponsor.

The visual and tangible elements of a brand make up what is referred to as the physical evidence of the service offered by an organisation. In the case of a sports club, these include the quality of the infrastructure and facilities, access to sports equipment, amenities, additional benefits offered to participants, and club merchandises (Grabińska & Nessel, 2016). The role of sports infrastructure for professional sports clubs is highlighted by the so-called 'new stadium effect', i.e. a sharp rise in match attendance in the case of clubs that have recently acquired new facilities (Clapp & Hakes, 2005).

These facilities often provide the opportunity to generate additional revenue by serving as tourist attractions (Berbeka, 2013).

Looking at sports clubs as service businesses, the quality of these services is strongly correlated with the performance of the staff. Waśkowski (2007) identifies three groups of sports club staff: players together with the training staff, administrative staff, and middle and senior management. Cewińska (2013) slightly modifies this classification suggesting the following: training staff, administrative staff (including upper and lower level management), and technical staff (storeroom managers, cloakroom attendants, paramedics, etc.). According to Sznajder (2007), the staff classification can be reduced to two basic dimensions:

- Sports-related, responsible for the management of the sports team;
- Business-related, responsible for the management of the marketing, financial, and operational aspects.

In practice, the roles described are often assigned to the same persons due to the limited human resources available to sports clubs (Wicker & Breuer, 2011). Persons managing these organisations are, therefore, required to possess a comprehensive set of competencies, knowledge, and skills, the most important of which are related to the aspects of public relations, self-management, basic sports knowledge, financing, budgeting, sponsorship, event management, and IT (Horch & Schütte, 2003). The competence of the staff in the aforementioned areas determines the extent to which the products offered by the sports club will meet the needs of its recipients (Hoye et al., 2009).

Klisiński and Szwaja (2012) question the possibility of developing a single strategy for all sports organisations since, as observed by Pomykalski (2005), this process requires taking into account organisational, economic, and social resources which are unique to every organisation. Research on the marketing strategies of sports clubs is, therefore, limited to a specific category of organisation, a specific product or market situation. Equity crowdfunding campaigns, therefore, require the development of a separate marketing strategy, as they constitute a separate area of the sports club's activity.

## 3.3 Consumer and investment behaviour of sports club fan communities

### *3.3.1 Specific nature of consumer behaviour of sports club fans*

The specific nature of consumer behaviour of sports club fans is related to the emotional aspect of their behaviour. Fans have a psychological connection with the club that gives them a sense of belonging and identification (Wann & Branscombe, 1990; Wann & Pierce, 2003). The level of identification is a key factor explaining consumer behaviour of most fans: from the frequency of going to matches, through buying licensed club merchandises, to making investments (e.g. Huth, 2020; Y. Kim, Magnusen, Kim, & Lee, 2019; Palau-Saumell, Matute, & Forgas-Coll, 2022; Swanson et al., 2003).

However, as indicated by Lock and Heere (2017), this identification may stem from an internal need to self-identify with a certain idea, individual, group members, and the values they hold. In terms of the need for self-identification, the theoretical framework for the study of the fan's emotional connection to a given club is the identification theory proposed by Stryker (1968), while when it comes to the sense of belonging to a given group, it is the social identification theory by Tajfel and Turner (1986). Research on fan identification used to be conducted without taking this classification into account (often without a clearly outlined theoretical framework at all). Hence, while the impact of the emotional connection with the club is fairly well established in the literature, there are certain inconsistencies in the precise understanding of the concepts.

Based on social identity theory, the construct of identification with a club has been expanded to a multidimensional concept, where emotional connection does not merely relate to the team or organisation but also covers the connection to the fan community and given sports discipline (Yoshida, Heere, & Gordon, 2015). On the other hand, an emotional connection to the location where a given club is based is not correlated with the level of identification. Nonetheless, the very fact of being a fan of a particular team is very often connected to one's place of residence, as fans tend to support their local sports clubs (Giulianotti, 2002). The globalisation of sports, accelerated by the development of the media, the progressing commercialisation of major sports events, and easier access to broadcasts of matches, has led to the development of the so-called distant fan segment, whose consumer behaviour differs from that of local fans, but who tend to identify just as strongly as the latter with their club (Lianopoulos, Theodorakis, Tsigilis, Gardikiotis, & Koustelios, 2020).

The increasing number of distant fans is, to some extent, related to the fact that people are more likely to identify with more successful clubs.[12] Cialdini et al. (1976) explained this phenomenon by the 'basking in reflected glory' (BIRG) mechanism, claiming that a person who identifies with a particular team attributes positive qualities of that team to himself or herself and perceives its successes as his or her own. The opposite phenomenon is 'cutting-off reflected failure' (CORF) which involves avoiding identification with a poorly performing team in order to protect one's good reputation (Snyder, Lassegard, & Ford, 1986).

Identification is a key, but not the only motivation for the consumption of sports and sports club products. A number of studies have analysed other factors that motivate fans to action. Many of these attempted to design psychometric scales – research tools that identify motivations and can be later used by other researchers to measure various variables. In the case of motivation to attend sports events, the first such tool is considered to be the Sport Fan Motivation Scale (SFMS) developed by Wann (1995) and Wann and Pierce (2003). Other tools that were developed in subsequent years include: Sport Consumption Motivation Scale (SCMS), Spectator Decision-Making Inventory (SDMI), Scale for Motivators and Constraints of Sport Consumption (SMCSC), and Consumer Orientation Towards Sporting Events (COTSE) (M. A. McDonald, Milne, & Hong, 2002; Pons, Mourali, & Nyeck, 2006; Trail & James, 2001; Zhang, Lam, Bennett, & Connaughton, 2003).

The identified motivations for the consumption of sports events primarily stem from (Table 3.3): the need for individual development (e.g. entertainment, eustress, escape from problems), social aspects (spending time with family and friends, sense of belonging to a group), and expectations regarding the attractiveness of the event itself (price, the class of players, competing teams, and the setting of the event).

Research has also been conducted to explore fan motivations in areas other than just sports events. These include:

- Purchase of merchandise with the club's logo – motivated by the pleasure of using these products, socialisation with other members of the fan community, aesthetics and attractiveness of the product, the display of one's association with the club, and the representation of a bond with the local community (Papadimitriou & Apostolopoulou, 2018);
- Word-of-mouth marketing of a favourite club – mainly being an expression of identification with the team, a manifestation of the desire to belong to the group, an example of eustress, and a means to enhance self-esteem;
- Engaging on social media profiles of the club – seeking information, entertainment, pastime, passion (strong affection towards the club), hope (desire to achieve a certain outcome), respect (expression of expectations, ambitions, and situational anticipation) and camaraderie (sharing experiences) (Stavros, Meng, Westberg, & Farrelly, 2014; Swanson et al., 2003; Witkemper, Lim, & Waldburger, 2012).

It is also known that interest in foreign baseball leagues is driven by general interest in this sports discipline, the players, and the quality of the games (Hong, McDonald, Yoon, & Fujimoto, 2005). In the case of passive participation in e-sports competitions, a unique motivation (not found in other sports consumer studies) was the desire to improve one's own skills (Hong et al., 2005; Qian, Wang, Zhang, & Lu, 2020).

These examples highlight the need for sectoral (focused on the object of the transaction) identification of the buying motivations of sports club fans. It is, therefore, necessary to expand the existing knowledge to include another area of their activity – their motivation to join equity crowdfunding campaigns, as well as to design a psychometric scale for this purpose.

*Table 3.3* Buying motivations of sports club fans

| *Authors and year* | *Analysed group of fans* | *Scale* | *Buying motivations* |
|---|---|---|---|
| Wann (1995) | Spectators of US college league games | Sport Fan Motivation Scale (SFMS) | Eight dimensions of sports fan motivations: positive stress (eustress), self-esteem, escape, entertainment, economics, aesthetics, sense of belonging to a group and family. |
| Trail and James (2001) | Major League Baseball (MLB) league game ticket holders (baseball, USA) | Motivation Scale for Sport Consumption (MSSC) | Taking into account the limitations of D.L. Wann's scale in terms of its relevance and applicability, G. Trail and J. James developed a scale including the following dimensions of sports spectators' motivations: team achievements, knowledge development, game aesthetics, drama, escape from everyday life, spending time with family, physical attractiveness and athletic ability of players, and social considerations. |
| Zhang et al. (2003) | Spectators of NBA games | Spectator Decision-Making Inventory (SDMI) | The decision whether to attend a given game is influenced by<br>host team (level of play, presence of sports stars, win/loss ratio, place in the ranking); opponent team (level of play, presence of sports stars); promotion of the match (discounts, advertising, reminders, prices, attractiveness of seating, additional attractions); date (day of the week, time of the match). |
| Pons et al. (2006) | Spectators and participants of hockey and baseball games | Consumer Orientation Toward Sporting Events | Three dimensions of orientation towards sports events: socialisation (an opportunity for discussion with other people), sensation seeking (positive feelings resulting from the consumption of the sports product), experience (development of knowledge, interest in sports and players). |

### 3.3.2 *Segmentation of sports club fans*

Sports club fans do not form a homogeneous group, in terms of neither socio-demographic characteristics nor consumer behaviour. Their diversity combined with the complexity of the sports club product (sports events, club merchandises, etc.) has attracted the interest of numerous researchers who attempted to identify and characterise the segments of this market.

Observation of consumer behaviour on the sports market has led to the formulation of the so-called 'escalator' model (Schwarz & Hunter, 2008; Mullin et al., 2014), which presents a basic typology of sports consumers. It is a graphical representation of the development of consumer engagement with sports as a fan or active amateur athlete. This concept identifies four market segments:

- Non-consumers – level at the bottom step of the staircase, representing people uninterested in a particular sports product (e.g. due to lack of awareness of its existence);
- Light and medium consumers – two customer segments that use the sports product irregularly; marketing activities towards this group are directed at increasing consumption intensity (e.g. by moving from the spectator level to being a participant in sports events);
- Heavy consumers – the most profitable group; the goal of marketing towards this group is to maintain their high level of engagement and to take corrective action when it shows a decrease.

The escalator concept provides a practical guideline for sports managers in terms of selection of a target group. It assumes that the needs of heavy consumers should be met first and that marketing activities should then be prioritised by 'walking down the staircase'. This is due to the fact that the acquisition of new customers is usually more cost-intensive than retaining the existing customers. However, such conceptual market segmentation is seriously limited in terms of its application and cognitive aspects. For example, it does not specify who the consumers belonging to each segment are and what they have in common.

The answer to the limitations of the presented model is empirical research, identifying and profiling segments of customers of sports club products. The theoretical framework for part of this research, which is, by design, similar to the 'escalator' model, is the psychological continuum model (PCM) developed by Funk and James (2001, 2006), according to which the development of the relationship between a fan and a sports club can be described by a four-stage process of passing through the subsequent phases of socio-psychological involvement: awareness, attraction, attachment, and allegiance (Figure 3.3). Based on an adaptation of the PCM model, four fan segments of Australian football teams and National Basketball Association (NBA) teams

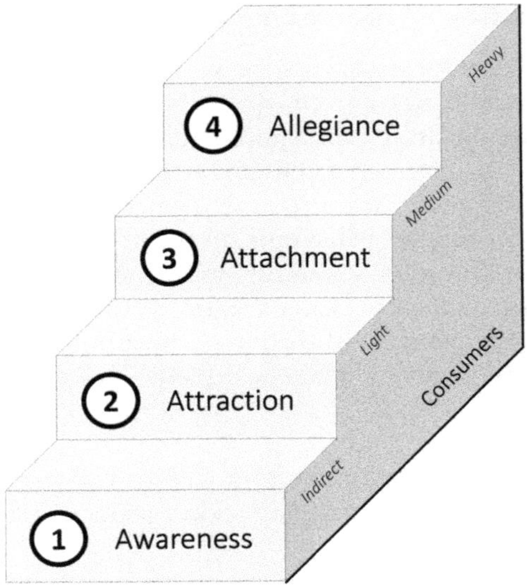


*Figure 3.3* The integration of PCM and escalator models

have been identified in empirical studies (Doyle, Kunkel, & Funk, 2013; Pu & James, 2017).

A similar theory to the two presented above, also being used for fan segmentation, is the concept of association with a sports club brand, based on which Ross (2007) identified two general segments of fans attending games of NBA league teams: with low and high club brand association. Based on the same criterion, Alexandris and Tsiotsou (2012) identified two segments of Greek football club fans. In two other studies, which based segmentation on the association with a club brand, three groups of English football club fans and four groups of fans of teams playing in the Champions League and Europa League were identified (Tapp & Clowes, 2002).

The segments identified on the basis of their association with the club brand differed from each other not only in psychographic terms but also in terms of socio-demographic aspects and the intensity of consumer behaviour. Among fans of Greek football clubs, the segment with high brand association included more men than women, between 22 and 26 years old, unmarried, with higher education (Alexandris & Tsiotsou, 2012). Fans following European football championship matches, on the other hand, can be classified into four segments: 'show-business lovers' (mostly men, regularly watching matches on TV but having almost no connection with the clubs); 'passionate fans' (women, with little involvement, hardly ever watching matches); 'admirers of celebrities and fair play' (highly involved, regularly watching European football matches on TV); and 'event followers' (very often watching matches on TV, very highly involved) (Bouzdine-Chameeva, Ferrand, Valette-Florence, & Chanavat, 2015). The aforementioned study, focusing on passive participants of sports events, makes it possible to identify an additional (according to the escalator and PCM models) group of customers of sports clubs: buyers of the product in the form of a sports event, who are not fans, in the strict sense of the word, of any of the teams playing. This category of non-fan customers is also mentioned in studies on market segmentation, using variables related to identification with the sports club.

As pointed out by Giulianotti (2002), based on identification with the club and attitude towards its product, one can identify four categories of individual customers of sports clubs: 'supporters' with a long-standing emotional commitment in the relationship with the club, 'fans' strongly identifying with the club but not too active in terms of consumption of club products, 'followers' interested in the club but not consuming the products offered by it, and 'flaneurs' watching broadcasts of matches without emotional attachment to the teams playing.

The classification proposed by Giulianotti (2002) has been corroborated by empirical research by H. McDonald, Leckie, Karg, Zubzevic, and Lock (2016), where, in addition to the aspect of identification with the club, attitudes towards changes and the CSR policy pursued by the club were included in the segmentation procedure. Five market segments were identified: 'instant fanatics' (very frequently attending matches and watching their broadcasts), 'community-focused fans' (identifying with the teams and engaged in CSR activities), 'independent triers' (with a high level of consumption but without an emotional connection with the team), 'social theatre-goers' (less engaged, with a relatively low level of identification with the club brand), and 'casuals' (rarely consuming club products, not feeling an emotional connection with the organisation, and perceiving the team as of little value).

There is also research classifying fans based on such factors as match attendance, accepted price levels, and benefits sought in sports events (Kaiser, Ströbel, Woratschek, & Durchholz, 2019; S. Kim, Yoo, & Pedersen, 2007; Y. H. Lee & Kang, 2011). In the case of classification based on benefits, four segments of basketball game spectators have been identified (Kaiser et al., 2019; S. Kim et al., 2007; Y. H. Lee & Kang, 2011): price-sensitive, price-oriented, quality-oriented, and game-oriented. With regard to the criteria determining consumption, three segments of Korean football club fans have been identified by (S. Kim et al., 2007) frequency of match attendance, mode of transport to matches, accompanying persons, source of information about matches, propensity to buy ancillary products, age, income, place of employment, and education. A parallel segmentation conducted for the same group of fans (Korean football clubs) based on price acceptance criteria also led to the identification of three market segments (Y. H. Lee & Kang, 2011).

The last group of the identified variables determining the segmentation of sports club fans are attitudes responsible for loyalty behaviour. Funk and

Pastore (2000) identified three market segments on this basis. This study was later expanded for the purpose of segmentation of Polish football fans. Two main attitudes explaining the loyalty behaviour of fans – identification with the club and satisfaction with the team's performance – were supplemented with the level of involvement on the club's social media profiles. This led to the identification of four fan segments (Kościółek & Nessel, 2019): (i) avid fans – with the highest intensity of all attitudes examined and a high frequency of all desired consumer behaviours (attending matches, following the organisation in the media, generating whisper marketing, and purchasing club products); (ii) die-hard fans – identifying, to a large extent, with their favourite team but showing lower engagement on the club's social media profiles and low satisfaction with the team's performance; this group is characterised by an average level of consumption, except for attending matches; (iii) casuals – similar to the group of 'die-hard' in terms of attitudes and behaviours, except that this group is more sensitive to the team's sporting performance; (iv) regulars – the least emotionally involved group, with the lowest level of consumption.

Summing up, in the existing studies, segmentation has been carried out for fans of basketball (participants and spectators of NBA league games), ice hockey, Australian football, football clubs, and newly formed sports clubs (Alexandris & Tsiotsou, 2012; Bouzdine-Chameeva et al., 2015; Doyle et al., 2013; Dwyer & Drayer, 2010; Funk, Mahony, & Ridinger, 2002; Giulianotti, 2002; Kaiser et al., 2019; S. Kim et al., 2007; Kościółek & Nessel, 2019; H. McDonald et al., 2016; Pu & James, 2017; Ross, 2007; Tapp & Clowes, 2002). In the vast majority of cases, psychological and behavioural variables related to customer needs and values were adopted as criteria for market segmentation. Taking into account the profiling stage, the researchers classified fan segments in terms of socio-demographic characteristics, evaluation of sports events, association with sports club brands, psychographic variables, level of commitment, consumer loyalty, identification with the team, buying motivations, and consumer behaviour (Table 3.2).

The research in question identified between two and five homogeneous groups of fans. Both *a priori* and *a posteriori* approaches were adopted. In the latter case, both methodological variants were applied: one-stage and two-stage segmentation. The most frequently used statistical method was cluster analysis, in particular the k-means method, usually preceded by Ward's method to determine the optimal number of segments. Other methodological procedures adopted for the purpose of segmentation of sports club fans include cross-tabulation, analysis of variance (ANOVA), and Analysis of Compositions of Microbiomes with Bias Correction 2 (ANCOM-2).

Due to the large number of perspectives adopted and configurations of variables used, it is difficult to synthesise the research based on a unified model of sports club fan market segments. However, regardless of the approach adopted, the results of the empirical research are in line with the concepts of the escalator and PCM models. While the part of the research focused on fans omitted the non-consumer segment, in each study, a group of fans was identified who were most engaged and identified, to the largest extent, with the club's brand and/or who were characterised by the highest consumption level of the club's product. In the case of global sports clubs (e.g. Champions League football and NBA basketball teams), researchers often identify segments of passive supporters, identifying with the club, consuming its products, but not participating in the sports events co-organised by the club (Table 3.4).

### *3.3.3 Fans as investors in sports clubs*

The fact of a sports club's company going public turns out to have only a short-term effect in terms of the increase in its revenues (Leach & Szymanski, 2015). What is observed is that many sports clubs are actually withdrawing from the stock market due to the failure to achieve the expected financial benefits (Benkraiem, Roy, & Louhichi, 2011; Leach & Szymanski, 2015). Indeed, the quotations of this type of organisations are prone to significant short-term fluctuations, which are highly correlated with the team's sporting performance (Benkraiem et al., 2011). An exception is a situation where the shares of a sports club are listed in a country with no tradition in the sports discipline represented by the company (e.g. football clubs in the US) (Majewski, 2014). Share prices of sports clubs are also affected by transfer rumours (Fűrész & Rappai, 2022). This leads to the perception of sports club shares as not overly profitable assets, resulting in a lack of interest among professional stock market investors.

Sports clubs primarily target their fans who are motivated to buy or sell shares based on their identification with the club, rather than conventional financial criteria, according to Huth (2020). Individual buyers of financial instruments for sports clubs do not expect or require a financial return on their investment; their decision is based on their desire to help the club achieve its sports-related goals, as indicated by Buchholz and Lopatta (2017). In the context of fan bongs, even if the fans consider the prospectus and risk hedging, these are fan attachment behaviours that explain investment decision to the greater extent (Weimar & Fox, 2021). Wicker et al. (2016) found that fans are willing to pay more for proactive goals, such as team promotion to a higher league, than for reactive goals like avoiding team relegation. In this context, the sporting success of the club is prioritised over financial benefits.

At the same time, the phenomenon of 'psychological ownership' stimulates an internal need to support an organisation that finds itself in difficulty rather than triggering a CORF mechanism (CORF) among some fans who strongly identify with a particular sports club (Cocieru, Delia, & Katz, 2019). This is a manifestation of what is referred to as fan activism, whereby

*Table 3.4* Overview of findings and research approaches to segmentation of sports club fans

| *Authors (year)* | *Study participants* | *Method* | *Criterion* | *Number of segments* | *Results* |
|---|---|---|---|---|---|
| Funk and Pastore (2000) | Sports club fans | *A priori* segmentation | Attitudes explaining loyalty behaviour | Three | Segments with different levels of intensity of loyalty behaviour: low, medium, and high. |
| Giulanotti (2002) | Football club fans | *A priori* segmentation | Identification with the club | Four | Segments: supporters, fans, followers, and flâneurs, derived from the matrix: hot–cool (attitude towards the club) and conventional–consumption-based (attitude towards the sports club's products). |
| Tapp and Clowes (2002) | Football club fans (England) | Cross-tabulation | Psychological variables | Three | Segments: professional wanders, carefree casuals, and repertoire fans, with each group holding different values and consumer needs. |
| Kim et al. (2007) | K-League football club fans (South Korea). | Cluster analysis (Ward's method and k-means) | Factors affecting participation in matches | Four | Segments interested in: promotion, venue, price, and undifferentiated. These groups have different demographic and consumption profiles. |
| Ross (2007) | NBA team fans | Cluster analysis (Ward's method and k-means) | Association with the club's brand | Two | With high and low associations with club brand. Segments differentiated by association with the brand and socio-demographic aspects. |
| Lee and Kang (2011) | Fans of Korean K-League clubs (South Korea) | *A priori* segmentation | Demographic groups | Three | Three fan segments ('general adults', 'college students', and 'middle and high school students') differentiated by the weight assigned to attributes determining ticket prices ('player', 'coupon', 'point', and 'expected price'). |
| Alexandris and Tsiotsou (2012) | Fans of Greek football clubs | Cluster analysis (k-means) | Attachment to the organisation | Two | Segments of fans with high and low attachments to the club. Fans with high attachment have higher scores in terms of the variables of self-expression and commitment to the team than fans with low attachment. |

| *Authors (year)* | *Study participants* | *Method* | *Criterion* | *Number of segments* | *Results* |
|---|---|---|---|---|---|
| Doyle et al. (2013) | Australian football club fans | Psychological continuum model | Psychological connection | Four | Segments identified based on the level of psychological connection with the sports club and sports league: aware, attracted, attached, and loyal. |
| Bouzdine-Chameeva et al. (2015) | Fans of Champions League and Europa League football clubs | ANCOM-2 | Association with the club's brand | Four | Segments: show-business lovers, passionate fans, admirers of celebrities, and event followers. These groups are also differentiated by frequency of media consumption and demographic aspects. |
| McDonald, et al. (2016) | Fans of newly established sports clubs | Cluster analysis (Ward's method and k-means) | Identification with the club, attitude to changes, and perceptions of CSR | Five | Instant fanatics, community-focused fans, independent triers, social theatre-goers, and casuals; further differentiated in terms of association with the club brand, satisfaction with sporting performance, identification, and engagement |
| Pu and James (2017) | NBA club fans (China) | Psychological continuum model | Psychological connection | Four | Changing buying motivations of individual segments (seeking to improve own skills, team success, or entertainment), resulting from the psychological continuum model: awareness, attraction, attachment, and allegiance. |
| Kaiser, et al. (2019) | Basketball club fans (Germany) | Conjoint analysis | Benefits vs. price | Four | Individual segments vary according to preferences with respect to opposing teams, seating categories, and willingness to pay. |
| Kościółek and Nessel (2019) | Football club fans (Poland) | Cluster analysis (k-means) | Attitudes explaining loyalty behaviour | Four | Segments differentiated according to the level of identification with the club, satisfaction with sporting results, engagement on social media, and demographic aspects. |
| Park et al. (2023) | Fans of Korean K-League clubs | Cluster analysis (k-means) | Psychological connection | Three | Segments differentiated hierarchically by all four dimensions of ambassadorial activities for the benefit of the club. |

fans organise themselves to act together for the good of 'their team' and their level of emotional connection to the club increases in times of crisis.

According to Prigge and Tegtmeier (2020), trading in sports club shares differs from trading in shares of other entities so much that the former can even be considered a separate asset class, with fundamental internal economic similarities and characteristics that distinguish them from other assets that are not part of that class. Given that investments in sports club shares are made primarily by the most committed fans, they can be considered as an example of collectors' assets, which yield intangible benefits to their buyers (e.g. pleasure from owning them, aesthetic sensations, prestige, satisfaction from belonging to a narrow group of holders) (Adamska, 2015). Shareholders of sports clubs prioritise intangible benefits in the form of successes of the club in which they have invested over its financial performance (Buchholz & Lopatta, 2017).

## Notes

1 In the case of non-profit sports clubs, Nagel (2008) identified an additional objective that relates to the integration of the local community which the organisation brings together.
2 In all European countries, football clubs are the most common (20% of all sports clubs in Europe are football clubs). In Poland, next to Norway, their proportion in relation to all clubs is the highest (30%). Poland also has a relatively high number of volleyball clubs or sports clubs with a volleyball section (12.3% in comparison with the European average of 7.2%) (Breuer et al., 2017).
3 Draft is a process of allocating uncontracted players to teams playing in a professional league. Club representatives take turns (based on specific principles) in selecting players with whom they would like to sign a contract. When a team selects a player, the team receives exclusive rights to sign that player to a contract (thus depriving the other clubs of this right).
4 Salary cap is a rule that places a limit on the amount of money that a team can spend on players. It applies in American professional leagues, including the National Football League (NFL), National Basketball Association (NBA), and National Hockey League (NHL) (Blair, 2009).
5 *Act of 25 June 2010 on Sport*, Journal of Laws, item 1463 as amended.
6 Germany has solutions that are unique on the European scale in terms of the ownership structure of sports clubs, which bear the hallmarks of protectionism. In accordance with the 50+1 rule applicable there, whenever an amateur club (in the form of an association) decides to transform into a commercial company (professional club), it must retain 50% of voting shares plus one. An exception to this rule is companies that have continued to support the associations in question for more than 20 years (Grabowski, 2019).
7 UEFA, *Regulations of the UEFA Champions League 2018-21 Cycle. 2019/20 Season*, Retrieved from https://www.uefa.com/MultimediaFiles/Download/Regulations/uefaorg/Regulations/02/60/37/12/2603712_DOWNLOAD.pdf, p. 15. [accessed on: 11.08.2020]
8 The marketing management process in organisations is described in detail in Section 1.2.

9 Most often sold for half of the season, for autumn and spring round matches, respectively.

10 The dynamic pricing approach refers to the concept of revenue management and involves adjusting ticket prices according to the actual demand. This concept assumes that prices can change from day to day or even minute to minute (Drayer, Rascher, & McEvoy, 2012).

11 A common practice is to include the name of the club's sponsor in the club's name. However, the stronger the club's brand (this applies mainly to football clubs), the greater the potential resistance of fans to changes in the club's name (Sznajder, 2008).

12 Moreover, as has been empirically shown with the example of the Norwegian football league and its foreign competitors, the increase in accessibility to the TV offer of foreign games 'cannibalises' the demand for active participation in domestic sports events (Kringstad, Solberg, & Jakobsen, 2018).

## References

Adamska, A. (2015). Inwestowanie w aktywa emocjonalne. *Zeszyty Naukowe Uniwersytetu Szczecińskiego. Finanse, Rynki Finansowe, Ubezpieczenia, 73*(854), 295–302.

Ahearne, M., Bhattacharya, C. B., & Gruen, T. (2005). Antecedents and consequences of customer-company identification: Expanding the role of relationship marketing. *Journal of Applied Psychology, 90*(3), 574–585. https://doi.org/10.1037/0021-9010.90.3.574

Alexandris, K., & Tsiotsou, R. H. (2012). Segmenting soccer spectators by attachment levels: A psychographic profile based on team self-expression and involvement. *European Sport Management Quarterly, 12*(1), 65–81. https://doi.org/10.1080/16184742.2011.637174

American Marketing Association (n.d.), *Branding*, Retrieved from https://www.ama.org/topics/branding/.

Anagnostopoulos, C., Parganas, P., Chadwick, S., & Fenton, A. (2018). Branding in pictures: using Instagram as a brand management tool in professional team sport organisations. *European Sport Management Quarterly, 18*(4), 413–438. https://doi.org/10.1080/16184742.2017.1410202

Andreff, W., & Bourg, J.-F. (2006). Broadcasting rights and competition in European football. In C. Jeanrenaud & S. Késenne (Eds.), *The Economics of Sport and the Media* (pp. 37–70). Cheltenham: Edward Elgar.

Andreff, W., & Staudohar, P. D. (2000). The evolving European model of professional sports finance. *Journal of Sports Economics, 1*(3), 257–276. https://doi.org/10.1177/152700250000100304

Armstrong, A., & Volkov, D. (2018). *Principles of Marketing*. Melbourne: Pearson Australia.

Bednarczyk, M., & Kurleto, M. (2016). Marka sportowa. In M. Bednarczyk & K. Nessel (Eds.), *Przedsiębiorczość w sporcie. Zasady i praktyka* (pp. 331–354). Warszawa: Wydawnictwo CeDeWu.

Benkraiem, R., Roy, F. Le, & Louhichi, W. (2011). Sporting performances and the volatility of listed football clubs. *International Journal of Sport Finance, 6*(4), 283–297.

Berbeka, J. (2004). *Marketing w sporcie*. Kraków: Wydawnictwo Akademii Ekonomicznej w Krakowie.
Berbeka, J. (2013). Ewolucja form i roli obiektów sportowych w turystyce miejskiej. *Studia Ekonomiczne, 147*, 9-20
Blair, R. D. (2009). Sports economics. *Australian Economic Review, 42*. https://doi.org/10.1111/j.1467-8462.2009.00562.x
Bodet, G., & Bernache-Assollant, I. (2011). Consumer loyalty in sport spectatorship services: The relationships with consumer satisfaction and team identification. *Psychology & Marketing, 28*(8), 781–802. https://doi.org/10.1002/mar.20412
Bouzdine-Chameeva, T., Ferrand, A., Valette-Florence, P., & Chanavat, N. (2015). Measurement and segmentation of sport fans using brand association networks: Application to Union of European Football Associations (UEFA) Champions League (UCL). *Sport Management Review, 18*(3), 407–420. https://doi.org/10.1016/j.smr.2014.11.002
Breuer, C., Feiler, S., Lopis-Goig, R., Elmose-Osterlund, K., Bürgi, R., & Claes, E. (2017). *Characteristics of European Sports Clubs. A Comparison of the Structure, Management, Voluntary Work and Social Integration among Sports Clubs Across Ten European Countries*. Odense: University of Southern Denmark.
Brooksbank, R., Garland, R., & Werder, W. (2012). Strategic marketing practices as drivers of successful business performance in British, Australian and New Zealand golf clubs. *European Sport Management Quarterly, 12*(5), 457–475. https://doi.org/10.1080/16184742.2012.688755
Buchholz, F., & Lopatta, K. (2017). Stakeholder salience of economic investors on professional football clubs in Europe. *European Sport Management Quarterly, 17*(4), 506–530. https://doi.org/10.1080/16184742.2017.1306870
Cewińska, J. (2013). *Zarządzanie zasobami ludzkimi w klubach sportowych non-profit w Polsce*. https://doi.org/10.1017/CBO9781107415324.004
Chen, C. Y., Lin, Y. H., & Chiu, H. T. (2013). Development and psychometric evaluation of sport stadium atmosphere scale in spectator sport events. *European Sport Management Quarterly, 13*(2), 200–215. https://doi.org/10.1080/16184742.2012.759602
Cialdini, R. B., Borden, R. J., Thorne, A., Walker, M. R., Freeman, S., & Sloan, L. R. (1976). Basking in reflected glory: Three (football) field studies. *Journal of Personality and Social Psychology, 34*(3), 366. https://doi.org/10.1037/0022-3514.34.3.366
Cieśliński, W. B., & Perechuda, I. (2015). Profit and nonprofit sports clubs : Financial and organizational comparison in Poland. *International Journal of Social, Behavioral, Educational, Economic and Management Engineering, 9*(6), 3502–3506.
Clapp, C. M., & Hakes, J. K. (2005). How long a honeymoon? The effect of new stadiums on attendance in major league baseball. *Journal of Sports Economics, 6*(3), 237–263. https://doi.org/10.1177/1527002504265957
Coates, D., & Humphreys, B. R. (2012). Game attendance and outcome uncertainty in the national hockey league. *Journal of Sports Economics, 13*(4), 364–377. https://doi.org/10.1177/1527002512450260
Cocieru, O. C., Delia, E. B., & Katz, M. (2019). It's our club! From supporter psychological ownership to supporter formal ownership. *Sport Management Review, 22*(3), 322–334. https://doi.org/10.1016/j.smr.2018.04.005
Cordery, C., Sim, D., & Baskerville, R. (2018). Financial vulnerability in football clubs: Learning from resource dependency and club theories. *Third Sector Review, 24*(1), 49–70.

Czakon, W. (2013). Strategia koopetycji w rozwoju organizacji. *Organizacja i Zarządzanie*, *52*(1147), 127–134.

De Beer, L. T., & Stander, F. W. (2016). For the "like" of the game: Assessing the role of social media engagement in football consumer outcomes. *African Journal of Hospitality, Tourism and Leisure*, *5*(2), 1–14. Retrieved from www.ajhtl.com

Deloitte. (2019a). *Pieniądze leżą na boisku. Ranking przychodów klubów piłkarskich. Raport "Piłkarska liga finansowa - rok 2018."* Retrievered from https://www2.deloitte.com/content/dam/Deloitte/pl/Documents/Reports/PL__Liga_finansowa_2018.pdf

Deloitte. (2019b). *Raport 1 Liga finansowa. Finansowe zaplecze Ekstraklasy*. Retrievered from https://upload.1liga.org/files/Raport_1_Liga_finansowa_-_2018__edycja_2019_1569252301.pdf

Demirel, A. (2020). CSR in sport sponsorship consumers' perceptions of a sponsoring brand's CSR. *International Journal of Sports Marketing and Sponsorship*, *21*(2), 371–388. https://doi.org/10.1108/IJSMS-09-2019-0108

Dietl, H. M., & Weingartner, C. (2011). *The Effect of Professional Football Clubs' Legal Structure on Sponsoring Revenue*. Retrieved from https://papers.ssrn.com/sol3/papers.cfm?abstract_id=2493130.

Dobson, S. M., & Goddard, J. A. (1998). Performance and revenue in professional league football: evidence from Granger causality tests. *Applied Economics*, *30*(12), 1641–1651. https://doi.org/10.1080/000368498324715

Downward, P., Dawson, A., & Dejonghe, T. (2009). *Sports economics: Theory, evidence and policy*. London and New York: Routledge.

Doyle, J. P., Kunkel, T., & Funk, D. C. (2013). Sports spectator segmentation: Examining the differing psychological connections among spectators of leagues and teams. *International Journal of Sports Marketing and Sponsorship*, *15*, 95–111. https://doi.org/10.1108/IJSMS-14-02-2013-B003

Drayer, J., Rascher, D. A., & McEvoy, C. D. (2012). An examination of underlying consumer demand and sport pricing using secondary market data. *Sport Management Review*, *15*(4), 448–460. https://doi.org/10.1016/j.smr.2012.03.005

Dwyer, B., & Drayer, J. (2010). Fantasy sport consumer segmentation: An investigation into the differing consumption modes of fantasy football participants. *Sport Marketing Quarterly*, *19*(4), 207–216.

European Commission (1999). Opinion of the Committee of the Regions on "The European Model of Sport", *Official Journal of the European Communities*, https://eur-lex.europa.eu/legal-content/EN/TXT/PDF/?uri=CELEX:51999IR0037&from=ES

Eurostrategies. (2011). *Study on the Funding of Grassroots Sports in the EU. With a Focus on the Internal Market Aspects Concerning Legislative Frameworks and Systems of Financing*. Brussels.

Feiler, S., Coates, D., Wicker, P., & Breuer, C. (2023). The perceived financial situation of nonprofit sports clubs explained by objective financial measures. *Sport Management Review*, *26*(4), 607–627. https://doi.org/10.1080/14413523.2022.2152936

Feiler, S., Wicker, P., & Breuer, C. (2019). Nonprofit pricing: Determinants of membership fee levels in nonprofit sports clubs in Germany. *International Journal of Sport Finance*, *14*(4), 262–277.

Foster, K. (2005). Alternative models for the regulation of global sport. In L. Allison (Ed.), *The Global Politics of Sport. The Role of Global Institutions in Sport* (pp. 57–78). London and New York: Routledge.

Franceschi, M., Brocard, J. F., Follert, F., & Gouguet, J. J. (2023). Determinants of football players' valuation: A systematic review. *Journal of Economic Surveys*, 1–24. https://doi.org/10.1111/joes.12552

Franck, E. (2010). Private firm, public corporation or member's association governance structures in European football. *International Journal of Sport Finance*, *5*(2), 108–127.

Fullerton, S., & Merz, G. R. (2008). The four domains of sports marketing: A conceptual framework. *Sport Marketing Quarterly*, *17*(2), 90–108.

Funk, D. C., & James, J. (2001). The psychological continuum model: A conceptual framework for understanding an individual's psychological connection to sport. *Sport Management Review*, *4*(2), 119–150. https://doi.org/10.1016/S1441-3523(01)70072-1

Funk, D. C., & James, J. D. (2006). Consumer loyalty: The meaning of attachment in the development of sport team allegiance. *Journal of Sport Management*, *20*(2), 189–217. https://doi.org/10.1123/jsm.20.2.189

Funk, D. C., Mahony, D. F., & Ridinger, L. (2002). Characterizing consumer motivation as individual difference factors: Augmenting the sport interest inventory (SII) to explain level of spectator support. *Sport Marketing Quarterly*, *11*(1), 33–43.

Funk, D. C., & Pastore, D. L. (2000). Equating attitudes to allegiance: The usefulness of selected attitudinal information in segmenting loyalty to professional sports teams. *Sport Marketing Quarterly*, *9*(4), 175–184.

Fűrész, D. I., & Rappai, G. (2022). Information leakage in the football transfer market. *European Sport Management Quarterly*, *22*(3), 419–439. https://doi.org/10.1080/16184742.2020.1797847

Garcia-del-Barrio, P., & Szymanski, S. (2009). Goal! Profit maximization versus win maximization in soccer. *Review of Industrial Organization*, *34*(1), 45–68. https://doi.org/10.1007/s11151-009-9203-6

Giulianotti, R. (2002). Supporters, followers, fans, and flaneurs. *Journal of Sport & Social Issues*, *26*(1), 25–46.

Gladden, J. M., & Funk, D. C. (2001). Understanding brand loyalty in professional sport: Examining the link between brand associations and brand loyalty. *International Journal of Sports Marketing and Sponsorship*, *3*(1), 54–81. https://doi.org/10.1108/IJSMS-03-01-2001-B006

Gladden, J. M., & Funk, D. C. (2002). Developing an understanding of brand associations in team sport : Empirical evidence from consumers of professional sport. *Journal of Sport Management*, *16*, 54–81. https://doi.org/10.1123/jsm.16.1.54

Grabińska, E., & Nessel, K. (2016). Zarządzanie marketingowe w organizacji sportowej. In M. Bednarczyk & K. Nessel (Eds.), *Przedsiębiorczość w sporcie. Zasady i praktyka* (pp. 303–329). Krakow: CeDeWu.

Grabowski, A. (2019). *Ekonomia sportu. Zagadnienia metodologiczne i wybrane doświadczenia*. Warszawa: Wydawnictwo Naukowe PWN.

Grabska-Luberacka, K., Piechota, R., & Radke, H. (2018). Pozarządowa organizacja sportu. In M. Leciak (Ed.), *Prawo sportowe* (pp. 83–126). Warszawa: C.H. Beck.

Green, M. (2006). From 'sport for all'to not about 'sport'at all?: Interrogating sport policy interventions in the United Kingdom. *European Sport Management Quarterly*, *6*(3), 217–238. https://doi.org/10.1080/16184740601094936

Hallmann, K., Feiler, S., & Breuer, C. (2015). Design and delivery of sport for all programmes: should it be market, non-profit, or state-run? *International Journal of Sport Policy and Politics*, *7*(4), 565–585. https://doi.org/10.1080/19406940.2015.1088051

Hong, J., McDonald, M. A., Yoon, C., & Fujimoto, J. (2005). Motivation for Japanese baseball fans' interest in Major League Baseball. *Management*, *1*, 141–154. https://doi.org/10.1504/IJSMM.2005.007126

Horch, H. D., & Schütte, N. (2003). Competencies of sport managers in German sport clubs and sport federations. *Managing Leisure*, *8*(2), 70–84. https://doi.org/10.1080/1360671032000085684

Hoye, R., Smith, A., Nicholson, M., Stewart, B., & Westerbeek, H. (2009). *Sport Management. Principles and Applications. Second edition.* London and New York: Routledge. https://doi.org/10.1017/CBO9781107415324.004

Huth, C. (2020). Who invests in financial instruments of sport clubs ? An empirical analysis of actual and potential individual investors of professional European football clubs. *European Sport Management Quarterly*, *20*(4), 500–519. https://doi.org/10.1080/16184742.2019.1684539

Huth, C., & Kurscheidt, M. (2019). Membership versus green fee pricing for golf courses: the impact of market and golf club determinants. *European Sport Management Quarterly*, *19*(3), 331–352. https://doi.org/10.1080/16184742.2018.1527380

Jedel, J., & Kończak, J. (2019). *Rynek sportu i sponsoringu sportowego w Polsce.* Gdańsk: Wydawnictwo Uczelniane Akademii Wychowania Fizycznego i Sportu.

Kaiser, M., Ströbel, T., Woratschek, H., & Durchholz, C. (2019). How well do you know your spectators? A study on spectator segmentation based on preference analysis and willingness to pay for tickets. *European Sport Management Quarterly*, *19*(2), 178–200. https://doi.org/10.1080/16184742.2018.1499790

Kemper, C., & Breuer, C. (2016). How efficient is dynamic pricing for sport events? Designing a dynamic pricing model for Bayern Munich. *International Journal of Sport Finance*, *11*(1), 4–25.

Kim, S., Yoo, E., & Pedersen, P. M. (2007). Market segmentation in the K-League: An analysis of spectators of the Korean Professional Soccer League. *International Journal of Sports Marketing and Sponsorship*, *8*(2), 26–43. https://doi.org/10.1108/ijsms-08-02-2007-b005

Kim, Y., Magnusen, M., Kim, M., & Lee, H.-W. (2019). Meta-analytic review of sport consumption: factors affecting attendance to sporting events. *Sport Marketing Quarterly*, *28*(3), 117–134. https://doi.org/10.32731/smq.283.092019.01

Klisiński, M., & Szwaja, M. (2012). Wybrane aspekty zarządzaniem klubem sportowym jako przedsiębiorstwem. *Finanse, Rynki Finansowe, Ubezpieczenia*, *55*(736), 79–88.

Kościółek, S. (2018). Rola dotacji przedmiotowej w funkcjonowaniu polskich klubów sportowych o statusie organizacji pożytku publicznego. *Annales Universitatis Mariae Curie-Skłodowska, Sectio H, Oeconomia*, *51*(4), 153–162. https://doi.org/10.17951/h.2017.51.4.153

Kościółek, S. (2019). Do sports clubs differ from other non-governmental organizations in terms of revenue sources? The case of Poland. *Ekonomia i Prawo*, *18*(3), 283–294. https://doi.org/10.12775/eip.2019.020

Kościółek, S., & Nessel, K. (2016). Podaż na rynku sportu. In M. Bednarczyk & K. Nessel (Eds.), *Przedsiębiorczość w sporcie. Zasady i praktyka* (pp. 97–112). Warszawa: Wydawnictwo CeDeWu.

Kościółek, S., & Nessel, K. (2019). Market segmentation of football fans in Poland. In J. J. Zhang & B. G. Pitts (Eds.), *Globalized Sport Management in Diverse Cultural Contexts* (pp. 154–176). London and New York: Routledge.

Kringstad, M., Solberg, H. A., & Jakobsen, T. G. (2018). Does live broadcasting reduce stadium attendance? The case of Norwegian football. *Sport, Business and Management: An International Journal*, *8*(1), 67–81. https://doi.org/10.1108/SBM-11-2016-0071

Kurleto, M. (2016). Przedsiębiorstwa i organizacje sportowe – uwarunkowania prawne. In M. Bednarczyk & K. Nessel (Eds.), *Przedsiębiorczość w sporcie. Zasady i praktyka* (pp. 113–133). Warszawa: Wydawnictwo CeDeWu.

Leach, S., & Szymanski, S. (2015). Making money out of football. *Scottish Journal of Political Economy*, *62*(1), 25–50. https://doi.org/10.1111/sjpe.12065

Lee, S., & Ross, S. D. (2012). Sport sponsorship decision making in a global market. *Sport, Business and Management: An International Journal*, *2*(2), 156–168. https://doi.org/10.1108/20426781211243999

Lee, S., Shin, H., Park, J.-J., & Kwon, O.-R. (2010). A brand loyalty model utilitizing team identification and customer satisfaction in the licensed sports product industry. *Journal of Research*, *5*(1), 60–67.

Lee, Y. H., & Kang, J. H. (2011). Designing ticket price strategies for professional sports teams using conjoint analysis. *International Journal of Sports Marketing and Sponsorship*, *12*(2), 124–137. https://doi.org/10.1108/ijsms-12-02-2011-b004

Lianopoulos, Y., Theodorakis, N. D., Tsigilis, N., Gardikiotis, A., & Koustelios, A. (2020). Elevating self-esteem through sport team identification: A study about local and distant sport fans. *International Journal of Sports Marketing and Sponsorship*, *21*(4), 695–718. https://doi.org/10.1108/IJSMS-10-2019-0115

Lock, D., & Heere, B. (2017). Identity crisis: a theoretical analysis of 'team identification' research. *European Sport Management Quarterly*, *17*(4), 413–435. https://doi.org/10.1080/16184742.2017.1306872

Mackreth, K., & Bond, A. J. (2020). Changing the sport product: Marketing implications for championship rugby league clubs in the United Kingdom. *Managing Sport and Leisure*, *0*(0), 1–16. https://doi.org/10.1080/23750472.2020.1773298

Maderer, D., Parganas, P., & Anagnostopoulos, C. (2018). Brand-image communication through social media: The case of European professional football clubs. *International Journal of Sport Communication*, *11*(3), 319–338. https://doi.org/10.1123/ijsc.2018-0086

Majewski, S. (2014). Modelling of football companies' rates of return according to sport results and bookmakers' expectations on the example of serie A. *Business and Economic Horizons*, *10*(3), 214–222. https://doi.org/10.15208/beh.2014.18

McDonald, H., Leckie, C., Karg, A., Zubzevic, N., & Lock, D. (2016). Segmenting initial fans of a new team: A taxonomy of sport early adopters. *Journal of Consumer Behaviour*, *15*(2), 136–148. https://doi.org/10.1002/cb.1558

McDonald, H., & Stavros, C. (2007). A defection analysis of lapsed season ticket holders: a consumer and organizational study. *Sport Marketing Quarterly*, *16*(4), 218–229.

McDonald, M. A., Milne, G. R., & Hong, J. (2002). Motivational factors for evaluating sport spectator and participant markets. *Sport Marketing Quarterly*, *11*(2), 100–113.

Mullin, B. J., Hardy, S., & Sutton, W. (2014). *Sport Marketing 4th Edition*. Champaign: Human Kinetics.

Nagel, S. (2008). Goals of sports clubs. *European Journal for Sport and Society*, *5*(2), 121–141. https://doi.org/10.1080/16138171.2008.11687815

Neale, W. C. (1964). The peculiar economics of professional sports. *The Quarterly Journal of Economics*, *78*(1), 1–14. https://doi.org/10.2307/1880543

Nessel, K. (2016). Rynek i produkt sportowy. In M. Bednarczyk & K. Nessel (Eds.), *Przedsiębiorczość w sporcie. Zasady i praktyka* (pp. 65–76). Kraków: Wydawnictwo CeDeWu.

Nufer, G., & Fischer, J. (2013). Ticket pricing in European football-analysis and implications. *Sport and Art*, *1*(2), 49–60. https://doi.org/10.13189/saj.2013.010205

Palau-Saumell, R., Matute, J., & Forgas-Coll, S. (2022). The roles of team identification and psychological ownership in fans' intentions to purchase team-licensed and a sponsor's products: the case of FC Barcelona members. *Sport Management Review*, *25*(5), 791–819. https://doi.org/10.1080/14413523.2021.1991676

Panfil, R. (2004). *Zarządzanie produktem klubu sportowego*. https://doi.org/10.1017/CBO9781107415324.004

Papadimitriou, D., & Apostolopoulou, A. (2018). Capturing the meanings of sport licensed products. *Journal of Marketing Communications*, *24*(5), 433–449. https://doi.org/10.1080/13527266.2015.1065900

Parganas, P., Anagnostopoulos, C., & Chadwick, S. (2015). 'You'll never tweet alone': Managing sports brands through social media. *Journal of Brand Management*, *22*(7), 551–568. https://doi.org/10.1057/bm.2015.32

Park, S., Kim, S., & Chiu, W. (2023). Segmenting sport fans by eFANgelism: a cluster analysis of South Korean soccer fans. *Managing Sport and Leisure*, *28*(2), 182–196. https://doi.org/10.1080/23750472.2021.1873169

Pawlak, Z., & Smoleń, A. (2015). *Strategie zawodowych klubów sportowych w Polsce*. Warszawa: Szkoła Główna Handlowa-Oficyna Wydawnicza.

Pawlowski, T., & Anders, C. (2012). Stadium attendance in German professional football - the (un)importance of uncertainty of outcome reconsidered. *Applied Economics Letters*, *19*(16), 1553–1556. https://doi.org/10.1080/13504851.2011.639725

Pedersen, P. M., & Thibault, L. (2019). *Contemporary Sport Management. 6th Edition*. Champaign: Human Kinetics.

Peeters, T., & Szymanski, S. (2014). Financial fair play in European football. *Economic Policy*, *29*(78), 342–390. https://doi.org/10.1111/1468-0327.12031

Petry, K., Steinbach, D., & Tokarski, W. (2004). Sport systems in the countries of the European Union: similarities and differences. *European Journal for Sport and Society*, *1*(1), 15–21. https://doi.org/10.1080/16138171.2004.11687744

Pomykalski, A. (2005). *Zarządzanie i planowanie marketingowe*. Warszawa: Wydawnictwo Naukowe PWN.

Pons, F., Mourali, M., & Nyeck, S. (2006). Consumer orientation toward sporting events: Scale development and validation. *Journal of Service Research*, *8*(3), 276–287. https://doi.org/10.1177/1094670505283931

Prigge, S., & Tegtmeier, L. (2020). Football stocks: a new asset class attractive to institutional investors? Empirical results and impulses for researching investor motivations beyond return. *Sport, Business and Management: An International Journal*, *10*(4), 471–494. https://doi.org/10.1108/SBM-07-2019-0063

Pu, H., & James, J. (2017). The distant fan segment: Exploring motives and psychological connection of International National Basketball Association fans. *International Journal of Sports Marketing and Sponsorship*, *18*(4), 418–438. https://doi.org/10.1108/IJSMS-05-2016-0022

Schreyer, D., & Ansari, P. (2022). Stadium attendance demand research: A scoping review. *Journal of Sports Economics*, *23*(6), 749–788. https://doi.org/10.1177/15270025211000404

Qian, T. Y., Wang, J. J., Zhang, J. J., & Lu, L. Z. (2020). It is in the game: Dimensions of esports online spectator motivation and development of a scale. *European Sport Management Quarterly*, *20*(4), 458–479. https://doi.org/10.1080/16184742.2019.1630464

Radke, H. (2018). Modele organizacji sportu. In M. Leciak (Ed.), *Prawo sportowe* (pp. 75–82). Warszawa: Wydawnictwo C.H. Beck.

Rohde, M., & Breuer, C. (2016a). Europe's Elite football: Financial growth, sporting success, transfer investment, and private majority investors. *International Journal of Financial Studies*, *4*(2), 12–32. https://doi.org/10.3390/ijfs4020012

Rohde, M., & Breuer, C. (2016b). The financial impact of (foreign) private investors on team investments and profits in professional Football: Empirical evidence from the premier league. *Applied Economics and Finance*, *3*(2), 243–255. https://doi.org/10.11114/aef.v3i2.1366

Rohde, M., & Breuer, C. (2017). The market for football club investors: A review of theory and empirical evidence from professional European football. *European Sport Management Quarterly*, *17*(3), 265–289. https://doi.org/10.1080/16184742.2017.1279203

Ross, S. D. (2007). Segmenting sport fans using brand associations: A cluster analysis. *Sport Marketing Quarterly*, *16*(1), 15–24.

Ross, S. D., James, J. D., & Vargas, P. (2006). Development of a scale to measure team brand associations in professional sport. *Journal of Sport Management*, *20*(2), 260–279. https://doi.org/10.1123/jsm.20.2.260

Rudawska, E. (2011). Interesariusze w marketingu relacji na rynku usług sportowych. *Zeszyty Naukowe Uniwersytetu Szczecińskiego. Ekonomiczne Problemy Usług*, *79*, 153–165.

Schwarz, E. C., & Hunter, J. D. (2008). *Advanced Theory and Practice in Sport Marketing*. Oxford: Butterworth-Heinemann.

Shank, M. D., & Lyberger, M. R. (2015). *Sports Marketing. A Strategic Perspective* (5th ed.). London and New York: Routledge.

Shapiro, S. L., & Drayer, J. (2012). A new age of demand-based pricing: An examination of dynamic ticket pricing and secondary market prices in major league baseball. *Sport Management Review*, *26*, 532–546. https://doi.org/10.1016/j.smr.2013.05.002

Sławińska, M. (2015). Zarządzanie dystrybucją. In H. Mruk, B. Pilarczyk, & M. Sławińska (Eds.), *Marketing. Koncepcja - strategie - trendy* (pp. 235–263). Poznań: Wydawnictwo Uniwersytetu Ekonomicznego w Poznaniu.

Sloane, P. J. (2006). The European model of sport. In W. Andreff & S. Szymanski (Eds.), *Handbook on the Economics of Sport* (pp. 299–303). Cheltenham: Edward Elgar Publishing.
Smith, A. C. T. (2008). *Introduction to Sport Marketing*. Oxford: Butterworth-Heinemann.
Snyder, C. R., Lassegard, M., & Ford, C. E. (1986). Distancing after group success and failure: Basking in reflected glory and cutting off reflected failure. *Journal of Personality and Social Psychology*, *51*(2), 382. https://doi.org/10.1037/0022-3514.51.2.382
Sotiriadou, P., & Wicker, P. (2013). Community sports clubs' responses to institutional and resource dependence pressures for government grants. *Annals of Leisure Research*, *16*(4), 297–314. https://doi.org/10.1080/11745398.2013.853338
Sports Business Group. (2019). *World in Motion. Annual Review of Football Finance 2019*. Manchester.
Stavros, C., Meng, M. D., Westberg, K., & Farrelly, F. (2014). Understanding fan motivation for interacting on social media. *Sport Management Review*, *17*(4), 455–469. https://doi.org/10.1016/j.smr.2013.11.004
Stryker, S. (1968). Identity salience and role performance: The relevance of symbolic interaction theory for family research. *Journal of Marriage and the Family*, *30*(4), 558–564.
Swanson, S. R., Gwinner, K. P., Larson, B. V., & Janda, S. (2003). Motivations of college student game attendance and word-of-mouth behavior: The impact of gender differences. *Sport Marketing Quarterly*, *12*(3), 151–162.
Swierzy, P., Wicker, P., & Breuer, C. (2018). Willingness-to-pay for memberships in nonprofit sports clubs: The role of organizational capacity. *International Journal of Sport Finance, 13*(3), 261–278
Sznajder, A. (2007). Charakterystyka rynku sportu profesjonalnego. *Gospodarka Narodowa*, (10), 45–65.
Sznajder, A. (2008). *Marketing sportu*. Warszawa: Polskie Wydawnictwo Ekonomiczne.
Tajfel, H., & Turner, J. C. (1986). The social identity theory of intergroup behaviour. In S. Worchel & W. G. Austin (Eds.), *Psychology of Intergroup Relations* (pp. 7–24). Chicago: Nelson-Hall.
Tapp, A., & Clowes, J. (2002). From "carefree casuals" to "professional wanderers" supporters. *European Journal of Marketing*, *36*(11/12), 1248–1269. https://doi.org/10.1108/03090560210445164
Tomanek, M. (2019). *Zarządzanie jakością w klubie sportowym*. Wydawnictwo Naukowe Uniwersytetu Mikołaja Kopernika.
Trail, G. T., & James, J. D. (2001). The motivation scale for sport consumption: Assessment of the scale's psychometric properties. *Journal of Sport Behavior*, *24*(1), 108–127.
Tsiotsou, R. H. (2016). A service ecosystem experience-based framework for sport marketing. *Service Industries Journal*, *36*(11–12), 478–509. https://doi.org/10.1080/02642069.2016.1255731
Ulseth, A. B. (2004). Social integration in modern sport: Commercial fitness centres and voluntary sports clubs. *European Sport Management Quarterly*, *4*(2), 95–115. https://doi.org/10.1080/16184740408737471

Vale, L., & Fernandes, T. (2018). Social media and sports: Driving fan engagement with football clubs on Facebook. *Journal of Strategic Marketing*, *26*(1), 37–55. https://doi.org/10.1080/0965254X.2017.1359655

Vos, S., Breesch, D., Késenne, S., Van Hoecke, J., Vanreusel, B., & Scheerder, J. (2011). Governmental subsidies and coercive pressures. Evidence from sport clubs and their resource dependencies. *European Journal for Sport and Society*, *8*(4), 257–280. https://doi.org/10.1080/16138171.2011.11687882

Vos, S., Wicker, P., Breuer, C., & Scheerder, J. (2013). Sports policy systems in regulated Rhineland welfare states: Similarities and differences in financial structures of sports clubs. *International Journal of Sport Policy*, *5*(1), 55–71. https://doi.org/10.1080/19406940.2012.657665

Wann, D. L. (1995). Preliminary validation of the sport fan motivation scale. *Journal of Sport and Social Issues*, *19*(4), 377–396. https://doi.org/10.1177/019372395019004004

Wann, D. L., & Branscombe, N. R. (1990). Die-hard and fair-weather fans: Effects of identification on BIRGing and CORFing tendencies. *Journal of Sport and Social Issues*, *14*(2), 103–117. https://doi.org/10.1177/019372359001400203

Wann, D. L., & Pierce, S. (2003). Measuring sport team identification and commitment: An Empirical comparison of the sport spectator identification scale and the psychological commitment to team scale. *North American Journal of Psychology*, *5*(3), 365–372.

Waśkowski, Z. (2007). *Uwarunkowania i sposoby wdrażania orientacji marketingowej w klubach sportowych*. Poznań: Wydawnictwo Uniwersytetu Ekonomicznego w Poznaniu.

Weimar, D., & Fox, A. (2021). Fan involvement and unusual investor behavior: Evidence from a football fan bond. *International Journal of Sport Finance*, *16*(1), 16–32.

Wicker, P. (2011). Willingness-to-pay in non-profit sports clubs. *International Journal of Sport Finance*, *6*(2), 155–169.

Wicker, P., & Breuer, C. (2011). Scarcity of resources in German non-profit sport clubs. *Sport Management Review*, *14*(2), 188–201. https://doi.org/10.1016/j.smr.2010.09.001

Wicker, P., & Breuer, C. (2014). Examining the financial condition of sport governing bodies: The effects of revenue diversification and organizational success factors. *Voluntas*, *25*(4), 929–948. https://doi.org/10.1007/s11266-013-9387-0

Wicker, P., Longley, N., & Breuer, C. (2015). Revenue volatility in German nonprofit sports clubs. *Nonprofit and Voluntary Sector Quarterly*, *44*(1), 5–24. https://doi.org/10.1177/0899764013499072

Wicker, P., Whitehead, J. C., Johnson, B. K., & Mason, D. S. (2016). Willingness-to-pay for sporting success of football Bundesliga teams. *Contemporary Economic Policy*, *34*(3), 446–462. https://doi.org/10.1111/coep.12148

Wilson, R. (2013). The relationship between ownership structure and club performance in the English Premier League. *Sport, Business and Management: An International Journal*, *3*(1), 19–36. https://doi.org/10.1108/20426781311316889

Witkemper, C., Lim, C. H., & Waldburger, A. (2012). Social media and sports marketing: Examining the motivations and constraints of Twitter users. *Sport Marketing Quarterly*, *21*(3), 170–183.

Wyszyński, A. (2014). Sponsoring jako źródło przychodów klubów sportowych. *Marketing i Rynek*, *11*, 30–37.

Yoshida, M., Heere, B., & Gordon, B. (2015). Predicting behavioral loyalty through community: Why other fans are more important than our own intentions, our satisfaction, and the team itself. *Journal of Sport Management*, *29*(3), 318–333. https://doi.org/10.1123/jsm.2013-0306

Zhang, J. J., Lam, E. T. C., Bennett, G., & Connaughton, D. P. (2003). Measurement in physical education and exercise science confirmatory factor analysis of the spectator decision-making inventory (SDMI). *Measurement in Physical Education and Exercise Science*, *7*(2), 57–70. https://doi.org/10.1207/S15327841MPEE0702

Chapter 4

# Strategic marketing management of sports club equity crowdfunding campaigns

## 4.1 Equity crowdfunding campaigns of sports clubs

### *4.1.1 Sports club campaigns as an area of sports crowdfunding*

The existing research has presented three distinct terminological approaches to the relationship linking crowdfunding to sports. These include sports-related crowdfunding (Adam, 2018), crowdfunding of sports (Leroux-Sostenes & Bayle, 2019), and sports crowdfunding (Brochado, 2017). These studies were developed in parallel with separate thematic scopes. Adam (2018) analysed all campaigns conducted with the aims of supporting sports or physical activity (promoting sports, supporting sports clubs, creating sports infrastructure or sports equipment), while Leroux-Sostenes and Bayle (2019) included in their study only those campaigns that were initiated by sports clubs.

Adopting the classification used in the case of sports marketing, distinguishing between marketing of sports and marketing through sports, an analogous classification can be proposed with respect to crowdfunding and sports (Figure 4.1), with two separate branches:

- Crowdfunding of sports – when the initiator of the campaign is the entity responsible for the provision of the sports products;
- Sports-related crowdfunding – when the subject of the campaign is a product thematically related to sports, regardless of the nature of its initiator.

Adopting this approach, the issues related to strategic marketing management of crowdfunding campaigns should be classified under sports crowdfunding.

Initiators of sports-related crowdfunding campaigns can include individuals not related to sports (or whole groups of people), individual athletes (both amateurs and those known to the wider public), sports managers, sports clubs, members of amateur sports clubs, and sports associations or private companies organising sports events (Leroux-Sostenes & Bayle, 2019).

DOI: 10.4324/9781003320623-5

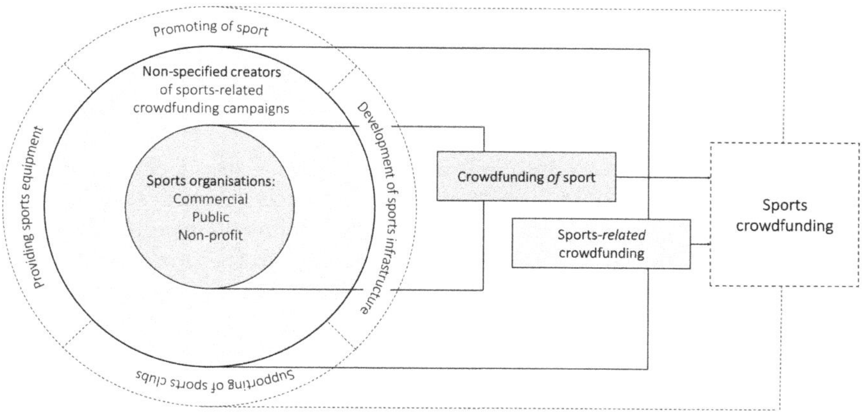


*Figure 4.1* Components of sports crowdfunding

Source: Based on Kościółek (2021)

Thematically, sports-related crowdfunding campaigns, which were created on the world's most popular reward-based crowdfunding platform (Kickstarer), were involved in (Adam, 2018):

- financing specific sports events and individual initiatives, including infrastructure for physical activity;
- sports equipment innovations;
- purchase of equipment for practising sport or improving sports performance for individual athletes or entire sports organisations;
- sports-themed creative works, including audiovisual materials, books on sports, and sports media;
- women in sports – the production of videos promoting physical activity among women and documenting their achievements, as well as providing them with sports equipment.

Each of the potential initiators can use general-purpose platforms or the special platforms specialising in the sector of sports initiatives. The latter (i.e. Make a Champ, Sport Funder, Pleadge Sport) are the exemplification of what is referred to as hyper-specialisation of the internet economy, which, in the context of crowdfunding, has resulted in the emergence of platforms oriented towards specific niches, not only industry-specific but also focusing on projects with a specific nature (Gierczak, Bretschneider, Haas, Blohm, & Leimeister, 2016; Malone, Laubacher, & Johns, 2011). On the most popular sports crowdfunding platform, Make a Champ (2022), alone, nearly 44,000 campaigns have been implemented so far (as of the end of 2022). Some of the sports-oriented platforms narrow their scope geographically to specific countries (e.g. in Germany there are four such entities – fairplaid, crowdFANding, KAM on!, and FUSSBALL CROWD; in Poland, fans4club was such a platform). However, based on the data available in The Crowdspace (2022) database, none of the platforms specialising in sports operate in the equity or loan-based model.

When it comes to crowdfunding in the context of sports clubs, an additional form of support has evolved, referred to as 'shared sponsorship', although it has not been very popular so far (Leroux-Sostenes & Bayle, 2019). It consists in involving institutional partners in the campaign in question. In addition to the selected prize, the supporters also receive a form of return from the sponsor (e.g. a shopping voucher of a certain amount). What we are dealing with in this case is a modification of the typical three-way relationship involved in the crowdfunding process between the initiator, the platform, and the supporter. The sponsor, although materially supporting only the latter, affects the other links in the process and the process itself through his or her involvement.

The involvement of companies in crowdfunding campaigns is aimed at the achievement of three categories of objectives: civic, communicative, and commercial (Leroux-Sostenes & Bayle, 2019). The first category refers to contributing to the promotion of specific values. The second one can target internal or external communication, highlighting, in the latter case, shared values with supporters and thus building a bond with the target group. The third, commercial objective is the activation of sponsorship rights.[1] No empirical evidence has been found that running a crowdfunding campaign and the associated increased media presence has a direct impact on attracting new commercial sponsors by a sports club (Abdourazakou & Leroux-Sostenes, 2016).

The existing analyses of factors determining the success of sports crowdfunding campaigns are somewhat limited. It has been demonstrated that the likelihood of reaching the financial goal of a campaign increases with an increasing number of participants and the application of the keep-it-all settlement model. In turn, no correlation between the duration of a campaign and its financial outcome has been found (Brochado, 2017). In the case of campaigns reaching their financial target, those with a lower completion threshold and a higher number of supporters are more likely to record surpluses. On the example of sports channels on YouTube, Ciechan-Kujawa and Górnowicz (2020) showed that campaigns tend to receive a higher number of contributions via donation-based crowdfunding if they have a large number of subscribers, views per video, and banners with links to campaigns.

In the context of sports clubs, Huth (2018) referred to crowdfunding as a supporter-based instrument. Indeed, participants in sports club reward-based crowdfunding campaigns are often fans or members of the club who support the project (Huth, 2018; Kościółek, 2021). If someone has supported a club financially before, they are more likely to back the club again via crowdfunding (Huth, 2018). The motivations of the backers include emotional engagement with the club, altruism, collecting rewards, causative agency, helping family or friends, and belonging to the community (Kościółek, 2021). Similarly, crowdlending campaigns for sports clubs also attract supporters who want to help (Ratz, 2020). Their willingness to invest is also driven by the meaningfulness of the project and psychological factors such as trust and fan loyalty.

When it comes to equity crowdfunding, it should be considered as an instrument used to inject capital into professional sports club companies, but one which changes the ownership structure of these organisations only to a limited extent. Disregarding individual cases of sports start-ups focused on the establishment of a new club, it is difficult to expect private investors with the means to invest in a sports club to share a controlling stake with a large group of individual shareholders (such trends have not been observed on the regulated stock market either). The possibility of equity crowdfunding campaign shareholders acquiring a controlling stake in a sports club, thus, exists only with respect to relatively small organisations.

### *4.1.2 Use of equity crowdfunding by sports clubs*

In view of the lacking platforms specialising in equity crowdfunding of sports clubs, this type of campaigns are conducted on general-purpose platforms. Based on the data from the Polish and German markets, the number of implemented campaigns involving issuing shares or loans is limited to a few per year at most in each country (Table 4.1). This is due to the fact that the initiators of these campaigns may only be entities operating as commercial law companies, which makes this tool legally unavailable to typical amateur clubs (functioning as associations).

When comparing the Polish and the German market, it can be observed that the popularity of selected crowdfunding models differs between the two countries. In Poland, by the end of 2022, there were seven sports clubs making use of equity crowdfunding, while there were no organisations initiating campaigns under the lending-based crowdfunding model. In Germany, the situation was exactly the opposite, with seven lending-based crowdfunding campaigns launched by sports clubs by 2020, and none implemented in the equity crowdfunding model. Given that some lenders waive the return they are entitled to, crowdlending is a more convenient solution for the club, as it does not result in a permanent connection between the organisation and the fragmented shareholding structure.

When it comes to the specific objectives of such campaigns, they can be divided into two categories:

- Specific development projects related to infrastructure or equipment required by the team;
- General-purpose projects aimed at improving the club's financial situation.

*Table 4.1* Equity crowdfunding campaigns of sports clubs implemented in Poland and Germany (as at the end of 2022)

| | *Initiator* | *Sports discipline* | *Country* | *Level of competition* | *Financial target* | *Funding achieved* | *Model* | *Rate of return* | *Price per share* | *% of shares issued* | *Objective* |
|---|---|---|---|---|---|---|---|---|---|---|---|
| 1 | VfL Osnabruck | Football | Germany | Third division | €400,000 | €506,304 | Lending | 3% (+2% in case of promotion) | – | – | Liquidity for licensing |
| 2 | Hertha BSC Berlin | Football | Germany | First division | €1,000,000 | €1,000,000 | Lending | 4.50% | – | – | Digitalisation and technological advancements for training |
| 3 | Rot-Weiss Essen | Football | Germany | Third division | €50,000 | €21,882 | Lending | Minimum of 10% for a maximum of 10 years | – | – | Infrastructure for youth centre |
| 4 | Lokomotive Leipzig | Football | Germany | Fifth division | €15,000 | €77,260 | Lending | 1.50% | – | – | Infrastructure (stadium) |
| 5 | Hertha BSC Berlin | Football | Germany | First division | €1,500,000 | €1,500,000 | Lending | 4.0% | – | – | Youth development centre |
| 6 | 1. FC Kaiserslautern | Football | Germany | Third division | €500,000 | €1,075,800 | Lending | 5.0% | – | – | Financial re-structure process |
| 7 | Karlsruher S.C. | Football | Germany | Third division | €500,000 | €2,493,000 | Lending | 4.0% | – | – | Modernisation training facilities, youth development centre and infrastructure |
| 8 | Wisła Kraków | Football | Poland | First division | €25 | €941,176 | Equity | – | 25 | 5.1 | Avoidance of club's bankruptcy |

| | | | | | | | | | | | |
|---|---|---|---|---|---|---|---|---|---|---|---|
| 9 | Wisła Kraków | Football | Poland | First division | €25 | €727,294 | Equity | – | 25 | 5.2 | Increasing financial stability |
| 10 | Elana Torun | Football | Poland | Fourth division | €82,353 | €89,082 | Equity | – | 1 | 13.3 | Modernisation training facilities, youth development infrastructure |
| 11 | Start Gniezno | Speedway | Poland | Second division | €185,647 | €119,044 | Equity | – | 6 | 20 | Youth development infrastructure |
| 12 | Stomil Olsztyn | Football | Poland | Second division | €117,647 | €117,647 | Equity | – | 40 | 9.4 | Modernisation of training facilities, development of youth training system |
| 13 | KTS Weszło | Football | Poland | Sixth division | €40 | €1,000,000 | Equity | – | 40 | 20 | Development of a new club (managed by the crowdinvestors) |
| 14 | Skra Czestochowa | Football | Poland | Second division | €33,333 | In progress | Equity | – | 0.11 | 24.72 | Infrastructure (stadium modernisation) |

Source: Based on Beesfund.com, Emiteo.pl and Ratz (2020)

The third category represents the specific case of KTS Weszło, a club that is a start-up in which each investor is ultimately to gain real decision-making capacity in the organisation's structures.

The campaigns implemented in Poland illustrate well the considerable diversity of sports clubs running equity crowdfunding campaigns. Wisła Kraków is a football company with a team playing in the top league. The two campaigns implemented by it assumed the maximum legally permitted financial target at the time of 4 million PLN. The first share issue was completed in a record time for the Beesfund platform of one day. The fragmented shareholder base (including more than 9,000 investors) then acquired 5% of the shares of Wisła Kraków S.A. As part of the second issue, a further 5% of shares were placed on the market, at which time over 3 million PLN was raised, but the financial target was not achieved. However, the success threshold for the campaign was set at the level of 100 PLN, meaning that once this small amount was exceeded, the issue had to be considered as binding.

A similar solution, which yielded similar results, was adopted by KTS Weszło (a football club established in 2018, currently [as of the 2022/2023 season] playing in the sixth division). In this case, the success threshold was established at only 180 PLN, while the campaign managed to raise the maximum amount permitted by law (4.5 million PLN[2]). Due to the popularity of the journalist behind the project and the social network around the media projects managed by him, the campaign attracted 3471 participants, whose contributions reached the maximum financial target of the campaign on its second day.

Different decisions regarding the campaign's success thresholds were adopted by the other four Polish sports clubs. The financial target of Elana Toruń (a club playing in the second football league at the time of share issue) was planning to raise 1 million PLN, with a success threshold of 350,000 PLN, which was only reached on the last day of the campaign. Speedway sports club Start Gniezno (I league, second level of competition) announced an issue of shares for almost the same amount (999,000 PLN), with a success threshold of 30,000 PLN. If the financial target was reached (eventually 500,000 PLN was raised), the crowdfunding shareholders were to take up to 20% of the club's shares. Stomil Olsztyn (I football league) issued shares worth 2 million PLN, representing slightly over 9% of the club's total shares, with a success threshold of 500,000 PLN. In this case, however, the assumed success threshold was not reached (173,000 PLN was collected).

The price of a single share of Start Gniezno was estimated at 4 PLN, Stomil Olsztyn – 25 PLN, and Wisła and Elana – 100 PLN, while KTS Weszło was estimated at 180 PLN. The lack of transparency in terms of valuing shares issued over the counter means that these amounts do not necessarily reflect their real market value. However, the problem with the valuation of sports club shares also arises on the regulated market. When valuing sports club shares using standard methods, they end up being highly overvalued, with poor return on investment (Prigge & Tegtmeier, 2019, 2020). When it comes to equity crowdfunding, given that the main target of the campaign is non-professional investors, including sports club fans, the ethical challenges of crowdfunding due to the uncontrolled valuation of shares combined with market information asymmetry are further compounded (Hossain & Gospel, 2017; Kościółek, 2023).

### 4.1.3 Characteristics of equity crowdfunding campaigns of sports clubs – on the example of campaigns conducted in Poland

Based on the data presented in Section 4.1.2, Wisła Kraków used equity crowdfunding to raise capital twice (campaigns 'Moja Wisła' and '#NigdyNieZginie'), while the remaining sports club analysed: Elana Toruń ('Zainwestuj w Elanę'), Start Gniezno ('wySTARTuj z nami po sukces'), Stomil Olsztyn ('Najlepsze przed nami'), and KTS Weszło once (Elana Toruń, 2019; Start Gniezno, 2020; Wisła Kraków, 2019, 2020). Three more clubs such as Legionovia (women's volleyball), Dziki Warszawa (men's basketball), and Skra Częstochowa (football) were at the planning stage of share issue at the time of preparation of this publication (as of November 2022).

Four of the campaigns in question were conducted on the Beesfund platform, and only one (KTS Weszło) was run on the competitive platform Emiteo. The principle of operation of both platforms and the layout of the content presented were similar. Importantly, both of them are general-purpose platforms limited to equity crowdfunding.

Analysis of the content published on the campaign pages and the videos posted made it possible to identify four categories of unique selling propositions (USPs) used in the marketing communications: becoming a co-owner of a sports club, being part of a community, fun from participating in a unique project, and a promising return on investment.[3]

The USPs used differed between the football clubs analysed (Table 4.2). Stomil Olsztyn mainly communicated what benefits the campaign could generate for the club and highlighted only one USP – being part of the community. Similarly, Wisła Kraków (in the first campaign – I) and Elana Toruń communicated that possessing the club's shares symbolised being part of the community, or, as Stomil and Elana defined it, 'part of a family'. Only the campaign by KTS Weszło did not mention this benefit.

Wisła Kraków, Elana, and KTS Weszło highlighted that it would be fun for participants to take part in the campaign. Wisła and Elana did so contextually:

*It is the first campaign of this kind in Poland* [Wisła I];
*We invite you to participate in a historical event* [Elana].

In turn, KTS Weszło promoted its entire offer by emphasising the fun and satisfaction from reaching the financial target of the campaign. For this reason, the club's communication included such elements as '*it's like real life Football Manager*[4]', as well as claims that joining the project will allow one to enjoy the opportunity to manage the club together with other investors.

The post-campaign benefits for crowdinvestors also result from the status of being a co-owner of the club and the ability to influence the decisions of the club's board. Three of the four clubs examined (apart from Stomil) emphasised USPs related to co-owning the sports club:

> *From now on, fans of Wisła Kraków can have a say in what happens with the club they love* [Wisła I];
> *Anyone who has never owned a club can do so now!* [Wisła II];
> *We will do our best to involve you in making decisions related to the club* [Elana Toruń].

On the other hand, the typical investment-related USP (a return on investment) was mentioned only once. Wisła Kraków [II] undertook to buy back the issued shares over a period of three to five years in a manner profitable for the investors. In the case of the other campaigns, the investment-related aspect was not mentioned at all.

In addition to USPs, another aspect that was analysed concerned which brand associations were used by the sports clubs during their equity crowdfunding campaigns. As the textual content of all analysed campaigns conducted by Polish sports clubs was presented on standardised crowdfunding platform templates, the communication of each club was similar in this respect. The following brand associations were used: club logo, management, history, and tradition, club culture and values (Table 4.3).[5] An attribute that was not mentioned at all in the written communication on the campaign page was the stadium.

*Table 4.2* Unique value propositions used in the communication of equity crowdfunding campaigns of Polish sports clubs

| | *Wisła I* | *Wisła II* | *Elana* | *Stomil* | *KTS Weszło* |
|---|---|---|---|---|---|
| Becoming a co-owner of a sports club | ✔ | ✔ | ✔ | ⊗ | ✔ |
| Sense of belonging to a community | ✔ | ⊗ | ✔ | ✔ | ⊗ |
| Fun related to participating in a unique project | ✔ | ⊗ | ✔ | ⊗ | ✔ |
| Promising return on investment | ⊗ | ✔ | ⊗ | ⊗ | ⊗ |

✔ – element used; ⊗ – element not used

The use of the other brand associations identified based on the Team Association Model and Team Brand Association Scale (see Chapter 3), such as team success, star player(s), head coach, sponsors, and fans in the communication, varied depending on the club. Product-related associations (team success, star players, head coach) were not textually communicated by the semi-amateur club KTS Weszło, and the team success attribute was not present in Elana Toruń's campaign. Sponsors were only mentioned by Wisła Kraków (twice). When it comes to fans, only one club (KTS Weszło) did not use this association.

Even greater variation in terms of communication between the analysed clubs was observed in terms of the use of video materials. Only the video scripts of Stomil Olsztyn and KTS Weszło were similar to some extent, with the club owner explaining what the club would be able to achieve if the campaign was successful. Wisła Kraków's campaign focused on past successes and fan speeches (in the first campaign), as well as recent victories and the image of excited fans in the stadium (the second campaign), while Elana Toruń showed the senior and junior teams, as well as the club's stadium, while talking about the need for the expansion of infrastructure and investments in the club's junior teams.

*Table 4.3* Brand associations communicated by Polish football clubs as part of equity crowdfunding campaigns

| | *Wisla I* | | *Wisla II* | | *Elana* | | *Stomil* | | *KTS Weszło* | |
|---|---|---|---|---|---|---|---|---|---|---|
| | *T* | *V* | *T* | *V* | *T* | *V* | *T* | *V* | *T* | *V* |
| Product-related | | | | | | | | | | |
| Team success | ✔ | ✔ | ✔ | ✔ | ⊗ | ⊗ | ✔ | ⊗ | ⊗ | ⊗ |
| Star player(s) | ✔ | ✔ | ✔ | ✔ | ✔ | ✔ | ✔ | ⊗ | ⊗ | ⊗ |
| Head coach | ✔ | ✔ | ✔ | ⊗ | ✔ | ✔ | ✔ | ⊗ | ⊗ | ⊗ |
| Non-product-related | | | | | | | | | | |
| Brand mark | ✔ | ✔ | ✔ | ✔ | ✔ | ✔ | ✔ | ✔ | ✔ | ✔ |
| Management | ✔ | ⊗ | ✔ | ⊗ | ✔ | ✔ | ✔ | ✔ | ✔ | ✔ |
| Club history and tradition | ✔ | ✔ | ✔ | ⊗ | ✔ | ⊗ | ✔ | ⊗ | ✔ | ⊗ |
| Club culture and values | ✔ | ✔ | ✔ | ⊗ | ✔ | ✔ | ✔ | ✔ | ✔ | ✔ |
| Sponsor | ✔ | ⊗ | ✔ | ⊗ | ⊗ | ⊗ | ⊗ | ⊗ | ⊗ | ✔ |
| Fans | ✔ | ✔ | ✔ | ✔ | ✔ | ✔ | ⊗ | ⊗ | ⊗ | ✔ |
| Stadium | ⊗ | ✔ | ⊗ | ✔ | ⊗ | ✔ | ⊗ | ✔ | ⊗ | ⊗ |

T – text; V – video; ✔ – element used; ⊗ – element not used

Non-product-related associations were used in the videos of Stomil Olsztyn and KTS Weszło. Such associations were, however, used as standard in the three other campaigns with minor differences. Wisła Kraków's communication did not show the head coach in the video of the second campaign, and in Elana Toruń's video, the team's success was not mentioned in any way. Brand associations unrelated to the product depended on the video script, and it was not possible to identify a general pattern. The only common element for all videos was the logo of the club.

As far as the brand associations communicated by the clubs are concerned, there is no clear dominance of product-related or non-product-related associations. Each club used its logo in both forms of communication (video and text), as well as references to the club's history and traditions, culture and values, and management. Only KTS Weszło (the youngest club listed, with the lowest level of competition) did not make use of product-related associations at all. The communication mix includes elements containing social factors, tailored to the unique brand advantages of the individual clubs. This remains in close relationship with the idea of crowdfunding and the adopted USPs.

On the other hand, the results contradict the studies on the communication of football clubs on social media (Anagnostopoulos, Parganas, Chadwick, & Fenton, 2018; Parganas, Anagnostopoulos, & Chadwick, 2015), as brand associations related to the clubs' products used to be indicated as the dominant ones in the clubs' communication. It was noted, however, that different brand associations of clubs were used with different intensity depending on the context: the communication platform (Facebook and Twitter), the timing (during the season and off season) and even the team (Liverpool FC and Manchester United). In this regard, the analysis presented in this section corroborates that the communication mix of brand attributes depends on the context in which it is used.

## 4.2 Consumer behaviour of participants of sports club equity crowdfunding campaigns

### 4.2.1 *Motivations of campaign participants*

The existing research identifies three main investment motivations of participants of sports club equity crowdfunding campaigns: two intrinsic ones (achieving the goal of the campaign and becoming a co-owner of the club) and one extrinsic (rewards). An additional external motivation could be a return on investment, but this aspect is marginal and is only relevant to a small portion of the market (Kościółek, 2022, 2023). Equity crowdfunding campaigns conducted by sports clubs mainly attract their fans, which makes the level of identification with the club an additional intrinsic motivation that is a prerequisite for all other motivations. In the case of these types of campaigns, intrinsic motivations play the major role due to the importance attributed to them by the participants.

The motivations presented were identified using a research procedure, which made it possible to develop a psychometric scale, i.e. a tool that, just like other scales of the similar type (e.g. SERVQUAL for measuring service quality), can be used by sports managers, crowdfunding platform managers, and academics in subsequent studies of participants in sports club equity crowdfunding campaigns (Table 4.4). In practical terms, it requires including the presented items in a survey, where the respondents are asked to indicate the extent to which they agree with the statements presented on a Likert-type scale. In the analytical part, the results obtained should be subjected to a confirmatory factor analysis. Alternatively, a simplified version can be

*Table 4.4* Motivation scale for crowdinvesting in sports clubs

| *Motivation domains and items* |
|---|
| Intrinsic motivations |
| Status of being football club owner (STA) |
| **STA-1:** Owning a part of a football club is a lot of fun. |
| **STA-2:** Owning a part of a football club means that my dreams have come true. |
| **STA-3:** It feels nice to be a co-owner of the club. |
| **STA-4:** It gives me the right to be called a football club owner. |
| **STA-5:** I was aiming to obtain the status of a football club owner. |
| Fan identification (IDE) |
| **IDE-1:** I supported the club which is close to my heart. |
| **IDE-2:** Just because I am a fan of this club. |
| **IDE-3:** I identify myself with the club. |
| **IDE-4:** I care about what will happen with the club. |
| Supporting a cause, product and/or idea (SUP) |
| **SUP-1:** I like the effect that is expected as a result of the campaign. |
| **SUP-2:** I like the aim of the campaign. |
| **SUP-3:** I try to solve the club's problem. |
| Extrinsic motivations |
| Return on investment (ROI) |
| **ROI-1:** I can resell these shares for a higher price in the future. |
| **ROI-2:** My aim is to get a return on my investment. |
| **ROI-3:** I think I can earn on these shares someday. |
| **ROI-4:** This investment has the potential for a profitable return. |
| Rewards (REW) |
| **REW-1:** There was a chance to get a unique and attractive reward. |
| **REW-2:** There was a reward to get in return. |
| **REW-3:** I wanted to receive a tangible reward in return for my support. |

Source: Kościółek (2022)

adopted, with the results for individual items averaged within the individual motivation domains.

The identified motivations provide insight into why participants engage in crowdfunding campaigns. Conclusions from research presented in previous publications (for all models excluding donation-based model) are inconclusive in this respect:

- Cholakova and Clarysse (2015) attribute the most important role to extrinsic motivations indicating that non-material issues have little impact on consumer behaviour;
- Many researchers point out that intrinsic motivations are as important as extrinsic ones for crowdinvestment (Bretschneider & Leimeister, 2017; Estrin, Gozman, & Khavul, 2018; Gerber & Hui, 2013);
- There are, however, studies, like the one by Lukkarinen, Wallenius, and Seppälä (2018), which claim that rewards and potential return on investment are the least important factors among all motivations on this market.

The results of the research conducted in the area of sports support the latter perspective.

A possible explanation for the emerging discrepancies may be the assumption found in self-determination theory (SDT) that human motivations function at a global, contextual, and situational level (Vallerand, 1997). Hence, with the development of individual forms of crowdfunding, it was assumed (and later empirically proven) that the motivations for participating in campaigns under individual crowdfunding models may differ significantly (Schwienbacher & Larralde, 2010). In addition, Cholakova and Clarysse (2015) hypothesised that the motivations of crowdfunding campaign participants may also depend on the industry represented by the campaign initiator. Bürger and Kleinert (2021) confirmed this hypothesis by pointing out the unique nature of the behaviour of participants of crowdfunding campaigns conducted for the purpose of implementation of cultural projects (under a reward-based model). Research conducted in the field of sports also confirmed the correlation between the motivations of crowdfunding campaign participants and the industry represented by the initiator of the campaign – this time in the context of the equity crowdfunding model and sports organisations (Kościółek, 2023).

Moreover, the existing research has identified the feeling of liking the campaign initiator as one of the motivations for participating in crowdfunding campaigns (Agrawal, Catalini, & Goldfarb, 2013; Bretschneider & Leimeister, 2017; Estrin et al., 2018). When it comes to sports crowdfunding, the issue of emotional connection ranges from the level of simple affection to that of a stronger emotional bond, characterised by identification, attachment, and commitment. This bond has a broader conceptual meaning, as it also encompasses a motivation related to the desire to belong to the community of supporters (Cholakova & Clarysse, 2015; Gerber & Hui, 2013). The combination of both dimensions stems from the perception of a sports club as an organisation with a community it brings together (Biscaia et al., 2016; Kossakowski & Besta, 2018).

At the same time, research on the motivations for participating in crowdfunding campaigns among sports club fans corroborates the concept, according to which emotional commitment to the club (including fan identification, attachment, and commitment to the team) is a key factor explaining most consumer behaviour on this market (Lock & Heere, 2017). This factor has been shown to have an impact on such aspects as:

- Attendance at sports events (club matches) (Branscombe & Wann, 1992; Gwinner & Swanson, 2003; Laverie & Arnett, 2000; Matsuoka, Chelladurai, & Harada, 2003; Wann, Bayens, & Driver, 2004);
- Travelling to matches (Loewen & Wicker, 2021);
- Purchasing club merchandises (Gray & Wert-Gray, 2012; Kościółek, 2019; Trail, Fink, & Anderson, 2003);
- Following news about the club in the media (Gray & Wert-Gray, 2012; Hunt, Bristol, & Bashaw, 1999; Kościółek, 2019);
- Generating word-of-mouth marketing (Gray & Wert-Gray, 2012; Gwinner & Swanson, 2003; Kościółek, 2019; Madrigal, 1995; Madrigal & Chen, 2008; Trail et al., 2003);
- Investing in club financial instruments (Huth, 2020; Weimar & Fox, 2021).

Based on the observation of fan behaviour in terms of equity crowdfunding campaigns, this list can be extended with another area of fan activity determined by the level of fan identification, i.e. participation in equity crowdfunding campaigns (or simply crowdinvesting).

### *4.2.2 Segmentation of campaign participants*

The presented motivations for investing in crowdfunding campaigns were adapted to the market segmentation process (Kościółek, 2022). Individual segments were classified based on the motivations for crowdinvesting and then profiled using variables describing consumer behaviour towards the club, consumer attitudes towards the campaign, and socio-demographic aspects. The segmentation carried out was, thus, a two-stage segmentation, specific for a given product and based on unobservable variables (Tkaczynski, Rundle-Thiele, & Beaumont, 2010; Wedel & Kamakura, 2012). Such an approach is considered to be the most effective, as it makes it possible to conduct market segmentation not based on who buys a given product, but rather why he or she buys it. However, information concerning the characteristics of the crowdinvestors is also provided in the second stage of segmentation, i.e. profiling.

One can identify three segments of sports clubs crowdinvestors (Figure 4.2). Each of these groups can be characterised as follows (Kościółek, 2022):

1 Benefit-oriented crowdinvestors (*52% of total campaign participants*) – fans of the club (with high level of identification) who care about the objective of the campaign. In the case of this segment, what is also important for the participants is to obtain benefits in the form of co-ownership status of the club and, to a lesser extent, unique and attractive rewards. They accept the symbolic benefits, rather than assuming the possibility of having a real impact on the functioning of the club. This segment is made up of the club's most committed fans who are most likely to attend matches, buy official club merchandises, discuss the club with friends, engage on the club's social media profile, and look for information about the club. At the same time, it is the segment that is most determined to participate in campaigns. Meeting the needs of this group offers greater benefits than simply their contributions to the project. First of all, it is people from this segment who will be the campaign ambassadors, encouraging family and friends to get involved. They are also likely to crowdinvest again in future campaigns. In this respect, the only constraints are income (the lowest of all segments) and the need to meet the needs resulting from the club's co-ownership status.
2 Club-oriented crowdinvestors (*44%*) – similar to benefit-oriented segment, they are fans of the club and are supporting campaigns due to their identification to it and the desire to implement the project for the purpose of which the funds are raised. However, people in this segment do not expect any additional benefits in the form of prizes, return on investment, or co-owner status. They tend to support 'their' club unconditionally. It may come as a surprise, but this group is not the one that is most involved in direct consumption (attending matches, buying merchandises) nor in additional fan activities (discussions with friends and family, interactions on social media profiles, looking up information about the club). Fans in this segment are also less motivated than benefit-oriented crowdinvestors – they do not care as much about participating in the campaign and are less likely to encourage friends to donate or contribute larger amounts in the future. Out of all attitudes, they rate highest their readiness to participate in subsequent campaigns (if they are organised). So, on the one hand, people in this group do not need additional incentives to get involved in the campaign; on the other hand, they do not display additional initiative themselves.
3 Goal-oriented crowdinvestors (*4%*) – a niche market of participants who are not fans of the club nor are motivated by the desire to support the goal of the campaign. This segment includes individuals who see an

opportunity for a return on their investment. People in this group do not care about any additional benefits, such as rewards, or the mere fact of being in possession of the club's shares. As they are not fans of the club, they do not consume its products and their determination to participate in the campaign is rather low. While being a niche market, this segment can be profitable for the campaign initiator, as it attracts people with higher income (often living outside the city and area of the club's headquarters), relatively many of whom crowdinvest larger amounts than those in the other two segments.

The conducted segmentation was based on a unique set of motivations identified in the primary research. For this reason, it is not possible to refer to works dividing the market of recipients of sports organisation activities according to an analogous set of variables. In the area of sports management, segmentation is typically conducted on the basis of an emotional connection to the club, or at least taking into account this factor (Table 3.2). Most such studies (e.g. Doyle et al., 2013; Giulianotti, 2002; Park, Kim, & Chiu, 2023;

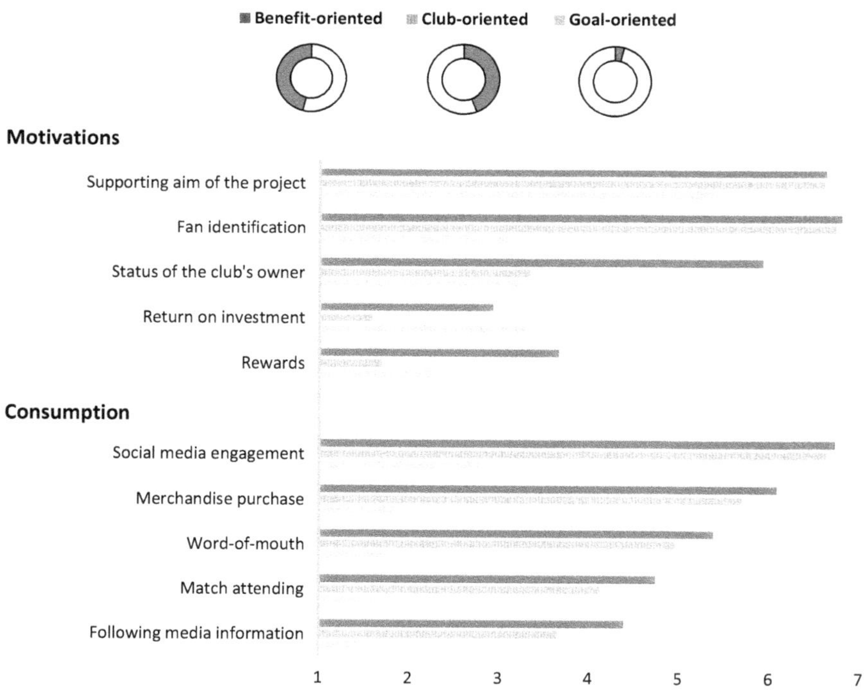


*Figure 4.2* Variation in the number of participants, motivations, and consumer behaviour between segments of sports club crowdinvestors

Source: Based on Kościółek (2022).

Pu & James, 2017) identify segments organised hierarchically according to the intensity of this variable. The theoretical framework of a large number of these studies has been the psychological continuum model (PCM) developed by Funk and James (2001), according to which recipients of sports club activities go through four successive stages in terms of the development of their commitment to a relationship with the club: awareness, attraction, attachment, and allegiance.

In the case of equity crowdfunding campaigns, the fan identification is an important motivation for making investments. Its level of intensity for the two largest segments is similar. This means that an adaptation of the PCM to the segmentation of sports club crowdfunding participants would not yield the most accurate results. Nevertheless, given a high level of identification intensity among the majority of crowdinvestors, it can be assumed that it is the recipients of sports club activities (fans) who are at the highest levels of the continuum – attachment and allegiance – that engage in equity crowdfunding campaigns.

The specific nature of the segmentation carried out in this way lies in the fact that the crowdinvestors segments are differentiated only by two socio-demographic variables:

- Place of residence – resulting from the over-representation of people living in the area of the club's location in the segments of crowdinvestors most identified with the campaign initiator;
- Income – resulting from the over-representation of people earning high income in the segment of crowdinvestors not highly identified with the club (goal-oriented).

Particular attention should be paid to place of residence. This variable significantly differentiates segments of sports club fans, on the one hand (Giulianotti, 2002; McDonald, Leckie, Karg, Zubzevic, & Lock, 2016), and is regarded as one of the key determinants of participation in crowdfunding campaigns, on the other (Giudici, Guerini, & Rossi Lamastra, 2013; Mollick, 2014). The latter is explained by the greater likelihood of personal connections (also in terms of sharing similar values) between the campaign initiator and the campaign participant when both are linked by the same location (Lin & Viswanathan, 2015). Most people crowdinvesting in a sports club live in either the city or at least the area where the supported organisation is based.

Nevertheless, participants of sports club equity crowdfunding campaigns are a relatively homogeneous group on account of its socio-demographic profile. This contradicts some of the previous research on the recipients of sports club activities and crowdfunding campaign participants. In the case of the segmentation of sports club fans (Polish, Korean, National Basketball Association (NBA) league teams, international football competitions), socio-demographic variables (including, in addition to place of residence, also gender, age, marital status, income, and education) were correlated with affiliation to the given market segments identified based on the fans' association with the club brand, factors determining attendance at club matches, and attitudes determining loyalty behaviour (Bouzdine-Chameeva, Ferrand, Valette-Florence, & Chanavat, 2015; Kim, Yoo, & Pedersen, 2007; Kościółek & Nessel, 2019; Lee & Kang, 2011; Ross, 2007).

### *4.2.3 Unique nature of behaviour of sports club campaign participants*

The distinctive nature of motivations of non-sports crowdfunding campaign participants (who are mainly motivated intrinsically) corroborate the concept developed based on the previous research that analysed individuals investing in sports clubs. At that time, it was assumed that these were investors driven by their identification with the club they supported, and that conventional investment-related motivations were of secondary importance to them (Huth, 2020; Wicker, Whitehead, Johnson, & Mason, 2016). For this reason, it is suggested to classify sports club shares as a separate class of assets, which are not attractive to typical investors seeking to maximise return on investment but attractive to those sympathising with the share issuer in question (Huth, 2020; Prigge & Tegtmeier, 2020).

What is equally important is that research on the motivations of people investing in sports club crowdfunding campaigns suggests that while shares may not be perceived as an attractive investment instrument, they still play a significant role in raising funds. The fact of owning this kind of security is important to crowdinvestors because of the status it gives them. This sheds new light on the role of share issue as a motivating factor for participation in equity crowdfunding campaigns (Bretschneider & Leimeister, 2017; Cholakova & Clarysse, 2015; Estrin et al., 2018; Lukkarinen et al., 2018). It has been shown that the opportunity to come into possession of shares of a given club can motivate campaign participants, even if they do not have expectations with regard to the potential return on their investment (Kościółek, 2023).

Despite the clear domination of intrinsic motivations of crowdinvestors, altruism, self-image, and recognition building were missing among the identified dimensions. The impact of these variables, originally identified as potential motivations of crowdinvestors, came to be disregarded in favour of other contextually adapted theoretical constructs (Kościółek, 2023). Elements of altruism can be observed in intrinsic motivations related to identification with the club (as a manifestation of a desire to selflessly support something important to the individual) and the implementation of the campaign goal (as a dimension entirely oriented towards the results that the funds may bring to the investor's immediate environment).

Image-related benefits, on the other hand, result directly from the status being a co-owner of the club. In addition to the decision-making capacity, changes in the way a given individual is perceived by other members of the community seem to be the main reason explaining this motivation. In this way, it has been possible to determine contextually the manner of building self-image among crowdinvestors of sports clubs. Bretschneider and Leimeister (2017) empirically proved that self-image is an important aspect for participants of equity crowdfunding campaigns. The research conducted in the area of sports crowdfunding has clarified how this process takes place within this particular community.

Similarly, in the case of segmentation, it can be assumed that equity crowdfunding campaigns are a specific form of sports club activity. Segmentations conducted with respect to the core activities of these organisations are not applicable in this regard. Crowdfunding campaigns, being a separate type of activity, thus require the development of a separate marketing strategy dedicated to this specific undertaking.

If one were to look for analogies to the well-established market segments of crowdfunding campaign participants, a potential point of reference could be the groups of supporters under the reward-based model. The four segments identified included (Ryu & Kim, 2016):

- 'Angelic backers' helping out of altruistic motivations, not expecting personal benefits from the provided support;
- 'Reward hunters' looking for attractive rewards; in the context of equity crowdfunding, these are individuals looking for investment opportunities;
- 'Avid fans' of specific initiators who are also oriented towards obtaining rewards and gaining an important position within the community;
- 'Tasteful hermits' who have a strong connection with the initiator (similar to avid fans), but who do not give high priority to other potential benefits of participating in a campaign (low level of external motivation).

Based on the presented characteristics, one can identify significant similarities between the pairs of segments of goal-oriented crowdinvestors and angelic backers, benefit-oriented crowdinvestors and avid fans, and club-oriented crowdinvestors and tasteful hermits (Table 4.5). What is lacking, however, is the segment equivalent to reward hunters, consisting of individuals looking for opportunities to obtain attractive rewards.

Goal-oriented crowdinvestors invested in the sports clubs because of their desire to implement the goal of the campaign, while the corresponding segment of angelic backers – because of their interest in the subject of the campaign and their philanthropic motivations. Benefit-oriented crowdinvestors manifested a high level of identification combined with the desire to become a co-owner of the club, while avid fans were interested in the subject of the campaign, derived satisfaction from providing support, but were also

*Table 4.5* Comparison of crowdinvestor segments of sports clubs and participants of reward-based crowdfunding campaigns

| *Segment* | | *Similarities* | *Differences* |
|---|---|---|---|
| *Participants in reward-based crowdfunding campaigns* | *Sports club crowdfunding investors* | | |
| Angelic backers | Goal-oriented | Selfless help | The segment of angelic backers differs in terms of the age structure from the goal-oriented crowdinvestors |
| Avid fans | Benefit-oriented | Highly motivated to help; feeling an emotional connection with the initiator, expecting certain benefits | Amount of provided support compared to other segments (high among avid fans) |
| Tasteful hermits | Club-oriented | Equally highly motivation to provide support as in the case of avid fans; lack of expectation of benefits | – |
| Reward hunters | – | Lack of a fourth segment among crowdinvestors of sports club shares – no group combining benefit-oriented approach and lack of connection with the initiator | |

Source: Based on Ryu and Kim (2016) and Kościółek (2023)

expecting attractive rewards, improving their own image and gaining recognition. Club-oriented investors, on the other hand, supported the club due to their identification with the initiator and a desire to achieve the goal of the campaign, similar to the segment of tasteful hermits, participating in crowdfunding campaigns because of their interest in a particular project, the pleasure derived from it, and philanthropic reasons.

Despite certain similarities with the participant segments of other crowdfunding campaigns (not initiated by sports clubs), the homogeneous groups of sports club crowdfunding investors are based on a contextually specialised set of motivations with a distinct conceptual framework. This corroborates the hypothesis of the specific nature of the functioning of the sports market in terms of consumer behaviour.

## 4.3 Developing marketing strategies for sports club equity crowdfunding campaigns – recommendations based on empirical research

### *4.3.1 Value propositions for the adopted target groups*

The recommendations are developed using the STP approach to marketing strategy development. According to this approach, market segmentation (S) is based on the values sought by customers. This is followed by the selection of a target group (targeting – T) and the creation of a desired brand or product perception (positioning – P) among the public. In customer-oriented marketing, the objective is not just to sell the product (attract crowdinvestors). Instead, it is about ensuring customer satisfaction by delivering the values that customers seek.

The identified motivations make it possible to draw inferences with regard to the values sought by crowdinvestors in sports clubs. These are related to the satisfaction of all three categories of human needs (Deci & Ryan, 2008):

- Competence – fulfilled by the status of co-owner of the club;
- Autonomous – manifested by the desire to implement the goal of their campaign (perceived as important to the crowdinvestor);
- Relatedness – fulfilled through an identification with the club and its community.

For crowdinvestors motivated by fan identification, any activity that has to do with the club's brand identity and integrates its fans is perceived as important. In its least engaging form, it is implemented through marketing communication highlighting these elements. In more complex forms, it involves increasing the level of interaction between the club, the fan, and other members of the community (e.g. on social media), and ultimately provides a space that allows supporters to co-create the values of the club (e.g. taking into account opinions posted by supporters on social media when making management decisions). Similarly, with regard to crowdinvestors who regard as important the aspect of being a co-owner of the club, the club's value proposition should include its commitment to organising general shareholders' meetings in order to give the crowdinvestors an opportunity to speak on issues of importance to the club.

Generating values related to the symbolic nature of the club's co-ownership status also involves ensuring the delivery of a share purchase certificate once a certain minimum value (determining the price per share) is exceeded. This may be combined with special thank-you notes or, in the case of smaller-scale campaigns, by tagging crowdinvestors on the club's social media profiles or even by presenting certificates to the crowdinvestors by the club's authorities or players.

When it comes to rewards, a common practice is to set specific contribution thresholds. Based on research on the motivations of fans participating in sports club's reward-based crowdfunding campaigns, in order to be considered valuable, they must be unavailable for regular sale (Kościółek, 2021). Therefore, the initiator has to design and produce attractive merchandises even before the campaign is launched.

If the manager of a sports club's crowdfunding campaign wants to reach out to a target group that includes people expecting a return on their investment, they are obliged to formulate an appropriate value proposition. In the case of low liquidity of shares issued over-the-counter (without organised stock market trading), potential return on investment can be expected:

- In the form of a share in the profits (paid as quasi-dividends);
- Through the sale of shares to other minority investors on one's own account;
- In the process of share buyback by the initiator.

Sports clubs that wish to offer value to their stakeholders can take various measures. For instance, they can organize a secondary market for trading shares or promise a share in the profits. Alternatively, they can present a plan to buy back shares within a fixed period with a specified rate of return. However, if the sports club does not expect any individuals seeking returns on their investment in the target group, they may not need to include such value propositions in their offer.

The initiator has the option to increase the share capital without informing about the specific purposes for which the additional funds are to be used. This, however, is not recommended, given that, based on the research conducted, the implementation of a specific goal is a key motivation for crowdinvestors. Even before the commencement of the campaign, the club's management should identify the investment areas acceptable to the fan community, which, based on past experience, is likely to be the most numerous group of campaign participants. If the goal to be implemented is to be financed entirely with the funds raised, it is necessary to take into account that its cost may not exceed 5 million EUR, the maximum legal amount allowed for share issues under equity crowdfunding campaigns in the European Union (Regulation [EU] 2020/1503 of the European Parliament and of the Council of 7 October 2020 on European crowdfunding service providers for business, and amending, 2019).

### 4.3.2 Delivery of value to the adopted target groups

What is important and directly results from the STP procedure for developing a marketing strategy is that value delivery must be differentiated based on the target group to which the specific value proposition is relevant.Taking into account the importance attributed to individual motivations, which – in this context – determines the values sought by campaigns participants, the following courses of action can be adopted with respect to each segment (Figure 4.3):

- Club-oriented crowdinvestors – formulation of a value proposition based on the collective action of the community for the benefit of the club, with a clearly defined campaign objective that is widely accepted by the given community, as well as emphasis on the possibility of moving higher in the internal hierarchy of the club after achieving the symbolic status of co-owner;
- Benefit-oriented crowdinvestors – the same value propositions as for club-oriented segment, plus information that being granted the status of co-owner of the club entitles one to receive confirmation in the form of a share certificate, a declaration of the intention to organise general meetings where crowdinvestors will have the opportunity to make decisions on club-related matters, as well as providing the option to choose unique, limited edition prizes with the club's logo, only available as part of the campaign (after exceeding predefined support thresholds);
- Goal-oriented crowdinvestors – value propositions stressing the importance of the goal pursued, not only for the club itself but also for its immediate environment (e.g. 'raison d'être' of a given competition, which the club, for historical reasons, is an important part of), as this segment largely consists of people who are not part of the fan community of the club; information should also be provided for this group on the possibility of becoming a co-owner of the club and (optionally) an opportunity to sell shares at a profit in the future.

Based on the selection of target groups and the indication of value propositions dedicated to them, the next element of the strategy under the STP approach is to determine the market positioning of the campaign for each segment. Based on the findings presented in the overview and theoretical part of this publication, market positioning is understood as the way in which a product is perceived by the consumer compared to competitive products. However, as shown by research, sports club equity crowdfunding campaigns are not in competition with other campaigns of a similar type available at the time. This is due to the fact that sports clubs, in their role as campaign initiators, attract their own community of fans, rather than people regularly involved in crowdfunding. This determines the way in which the campaign's market positioning process is conducted.

When determining the market positioning of a campaign, comparative methods of perceiving the product elements of brands available on the market (e.g. commonly used perception maps) do not apply (Kłeczek & Sagan, 2013).

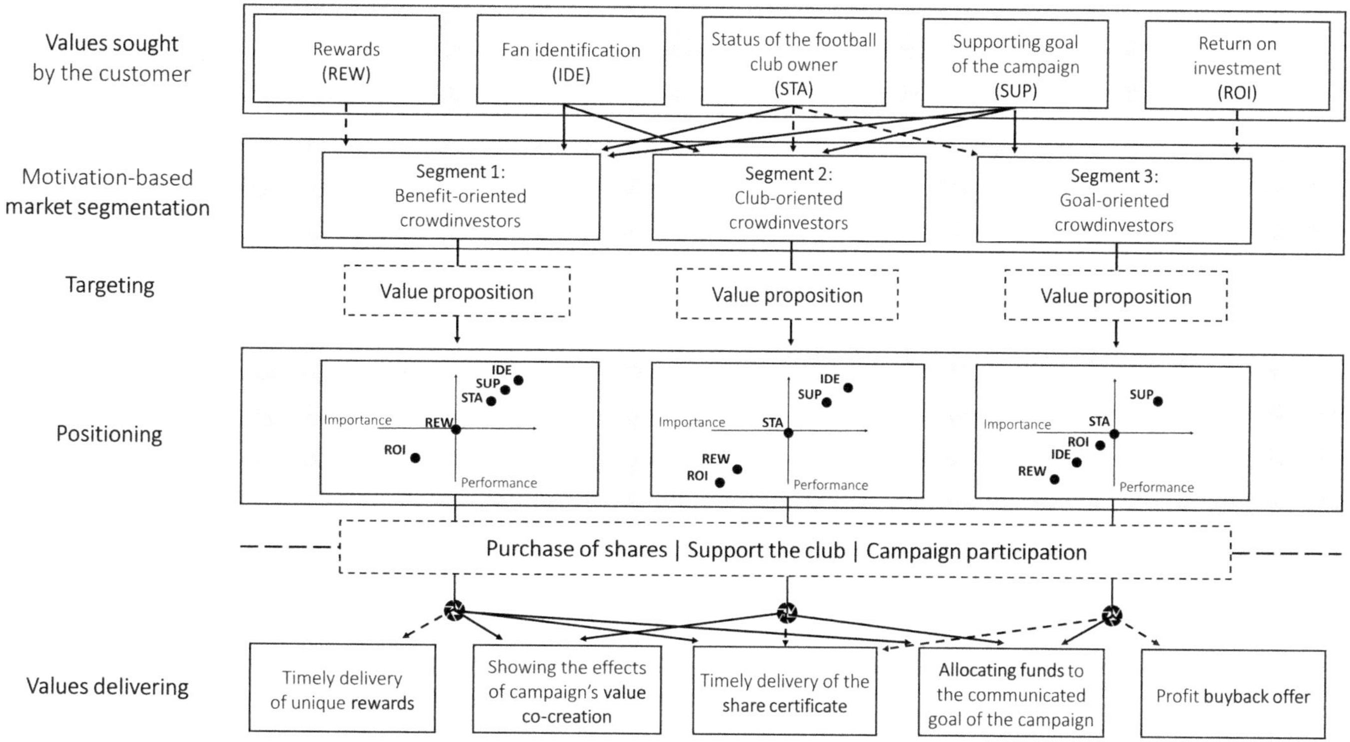


*Figure 4.3* Marketing strategy model of sports club equity crowdfunding campaigns taking into account crowdinvestor segmentation

The solid lines indicate the values prioritised by the given segments.

The dotted lines indicate the values that crowdinvestors in the given segments should be aware of.

A solution to this is changing the perspective of the analysis. If the organisation initiating the campaign has a large enough group of recipients to reach the financial target of the campaign, what is of crucial importance is an appropriate perceptual display of the key attributes of the product in question. A good solution to the challenges in market positioning under such conditions is to use the logic behind the Importance-Performance Analysis (IPA) matrix, which, in its basic application, is used to analyse customer satisfaction in terms of the importance and evaluation of the attributes of a given product (Martilla & James, 1977). However, the versatility of this method makes it possible to adapt it to solve other research problems, including those related to market positioning (Pike, 2017). It consists in juxtaposing the importance attributed by consumers to a given product attribute with its evaluation (Biesok & Wyród-Wróbel, 2015). Both components are typically measured with a Likert-type or similar scale. By determining the point of intersection at the midpoint of the weights and ratings, a four-element score matrix is created indicating:

- The product elements which should be focused on (high value of weights, low value of ratings);
- Efforts to be maintained at the current level (high value of both weights and ratings);
- The product elements which should be given low priority (low value of both weights and ratings);
- Efforts undertaken that may be excessive (low value of weights, high value of ratings).

In line with the above, when planning the market positioning of a campaign, the projected evaluation of each value proposition should correspond to the weights assigned to it by crowdinvestors. Based on the weights assigned to each of the value dimensions of sports club equity crowdfunding campaigns, the optimal situation for the venture in question is illustrated in the section concerning the positioning of the marketing strategy model (Figure 4.3). In the key top right corner of the positioning matrix, we have a range of product attributes of the equity crowdfunding campaign, from one attribute (goal-oriented crowdinvestors segment), through two (club-oriented crowdinvestors), to four (benefit-oriented crowdinvestors).

In the case of goal-oriented crowdinvestors, it is necessary to position the campaign in such a way that the effects of its objectives are perceived as highly relevant – preferably not only to the initiator of the project but also to its immediate environment. In the group of club-oriented crowdinvestors, in addition to the benefits presented to the earlier segment, the campaign should be perceived as an activity in which the club fans are obliged to engage. The aim is to give the impression of an obligation to take part in the campaign by anyone emotionally connected to the club who identifies with the initiator. In the case of benefit-oriented crowdinvestors, in addition to the benefits mentioned earlier, the value proposition must include elements related to the co-owner status of the club. Potential crowdinvestors from this segment should therefore see the campaign as an opportunity to make the dream of owning their own club come true, so as to be able to impress their friends, as well as to have an impact on the future functioning of the club.

In addition, for each segment, one or two attributes appear on the straight lines connecting boxes of the matrix – these are not key attributes but ones that the crowdinvestors should be aware of. They include:

- Rewards in the benefit-oriented segment;
- Club co-owner status in the club-oriented segment;
- Club co-owner status, and possible return on investment in the goal-oriented segment.

In the cases mentioned above, the values should be proposed and delivered, but do not have to be treated with high priority.

The role of managers who make use of the presented strategy is to make decisions concerning individual marketing-mix elements in such a way that they correspond to the values sought by the crowdinvestors, derived from the model, and position the attributes of the campaign according to its assumptions. For example, when considering decisions in terms of rewards, it is necessary to determine their type (product), the financial thresholds for the specific package (price), the form of their delivery (place), and the target group to which this benefit should be communicated (promotion). When developing a plan based on the strategy assumptions:

- The only segment for which it is worthwhile to carry out communication based on the delivery of values associated with the provision of attractive and unique rewards is benefit-oriented crowdinvestors;
- The product offered as a reward should be a good with limited availability, dedicated specifically to the campaign;
- Distribution is to be carried out within the area of residence of those who regularly attend matches (the option of collecting the prize at the stadium could also be offered);
- The reference point for pricing can be the products available in the official club shop (which crowdinvestors in this segment also use relatively frequently);
- Efforts of the management should focus on other attributes of the campaign product, since, as the positioning matrix shows, prizes are not a key aspect for potential crowdinvestors.

### 4.3.3 *Limitations with regard to the delivery of values to the adopted target groups*

The value proposition presented to the potential crowdinvestors within each segment is a form of commitment that the sports club initiating the campaign must fulfil after the conclusion of the campaign. The delivery of the value proposition presented results from adopting a customer orientation. The end result is customer satisfaction that helps to build a long-term relationship with the customer. While the equity crowdfunding campaign itself can be classified as a one-off product, it is targeted at the existing customer base of the core product (sports events). Gaining and maintaining the consumer loyalty of this group is highly important.

According to the adopted customer-oriented marketing approach, claims related to value proposition should only be included in the campaign if the initiator actually intends to deliver them. The risk of negative word-of-mouth marketing generated by recipients and the resulting negative consequences for the initiator's image appear to outweigh the opportunity to gain additional funds through equity crowdfunding. For this reason, all limitations and restrictions should be communicated to the crowdinvestors in advance and, as in the case analysed, they are not professional investors; the obligation to provide them with information[6] rests on the campaign initiator. For example, when it comes to share certificates (confirming co-ownership status of the club) and rewards in exchange for a certain level of support, the value proposition is fulfilled by their physical delivery to the campaign participants. However, this process can be time-consuming and generate dissatisfaction among crowdinvestors. Share certificates cannot be transferred to the crowdinvestors until the company has registered the new shareholders, and the speed of delivery of rewards is limited by the time it takes to ship up to several thousand packages.

At the same time, providing such information is related to an ethical issue campaign initiators are facing. It appears that the risk of information asymmetry, indicated as one of the ethical challenges of sports club equity crowdfunding campaigns, is even more important in this context (Kościółek, 2023). This is due to the fact that fans, who are the main target group of clubs' campaigns, are exposed to the risk of unfair practices to a greater extent than professional investors in other types of campaigns.

## Notes

1 Activation of sponsorship rights denotes taking measures pursuant to the provisions of the sponsorship agreement to achieve the objectives related to the acquisition of these rights (Bednarczyk et al., 2016).

2 The difference with respect to Wisła Kraków results from exchange rate differences between the PLN and EUR.

3 In order to determine the USPs, a content analysis of the materials was carried out using the open coding technique. Data was coded sentence by sentence and then

provided to a naive coder to repeat the procedure. The coding process consisted of three stages. In the first stage, both coders independently developed their own codes. In the second one, the differences in the code logs were discussed and integrated. In the third one, the coding procedures were carried out again. In the final stage, Cohen's Kappa coefficient was calculated to compare the results and assess the reliability of the analysis. Twenty-four sentences were found in which USPs were communicated (Cohen's Kappa = 0.821).

4 A computer game in which players take on the roles of coaches or managers of football clubs.

5 Deductive coding was used to analyse the communicated brand associations. Product-related brand attributes identified based on the TBAS and TAM models included: (i) team success, (ii) star player(s), (iii) head coach, while attributes not related to the product included: (iv) brand mark, (v) management, (vi) club history and tradition, (vii) club culture and values, (viii) event image, (ix) sponsors, (x) fans, and (xi) stadium. A code book for communicating brand associations was created based on the aforementioned attributes. Only the event perception attribute was omitted, as the crowdfunding campaign constitutes an event in itself.

6 This obligation does not stem from official regulations. The club is not obliged to provide information on the schedule of operations. From the perspective of relationship marketing, however, this may be necessary.

## References

Abdourazakou, Y., & Leroux-Sostenes, M.-J. (2016). Crowd funding : The New Frontier of sports sponsorship ? *International Journal of Kinesiology & Sports Science*, *4*(2), 18–26. https://doi.org/10.7575/aiac.ijkss.v.4n.2p.18

Adam, M. C. (2018). Reward or equity crowdfunding in sport related projects. *Journal of Sport and Kinetic Movement*, *I*(31), 19–26.

Agrawal, A., Catalini, C., & Goldfarb, A. (2013). Some simple economics of crowdfunding. *Natural Bureau of Economic Research*, *19133*. Retrieved from http://www.nber.org/papers/w19133

Anagnostopoulos, C., Parganas, P., Chadwick, S., & Fenton, A. (2018). Branding in pictures: Using Instagram as a brand management tool in professional team sport organisations. *European Sport Management Quarterly*, *18*(4), 413–438. https://doi.org/10.1080/16184742.2017.1410202

Bednarczyk, M., Kurleto, M., & Najda-Janoszka, M. (2016). Sponsoring sportu. In M. Bednarczyk & K. Nessel (Eds.), *Przedsiębiorczość w sporcie. Zasady i praktyka* (pp. 355–384). Warszawa: CeDeWu.

Biesok, G., & Wyród-Wróbel, J. (2015). Podejścia do analizy IPA w badaniach satysfakcji klienta. *Problemy Jakości*, *6*, 26–31. https://doi.org/10.15199/46.2015.6.5

Biscaia, R., Ross, S., Yoshida, M., Correia, A., Rosado, A., & Marôco, J. (2016). Investigating the role of fan club membership on perceptions of team brand equity in football. *Sport Management Review*, *19*(2), 157–170. https://doi.org/10.1016/j.smr.2015.02.001

Bouzdine-Chameeva, T., Ferrand, A., Valette-Florence, P., & Chanavat, N. (2015). Measurement and segmentation of sport fans using brand association networks: Application to Union of European Football Associations (UEFA) Champions League (UCL). *Sport Management Review*, *18*(3), 407–420. https://doi.org/10.1016/j.smr.2014.11.002

Branscombe, N. R., & Wann, D. L. (1992). Role of identification with a group, arousal, categorization processes, and self-esteem in sports spectator aggression. *Human Relations*, *45*(10), 1013–1033. https://doi.org/10.1177/001872679204501001

Bretschneider, U., & Leimeister, J. M. (2017). Not just an ego trip: Exploring backers' motivation for funding in incentive-based crowdfunding. *Journal of Strategic Information Systems (JSIS)*, *26*(4), 246–260. https://doi.org/10.1016/j.jsis.2017.02.002

Brochado, A. (2017). Success drivers of sports crowdfunding campaigns. Retrieved from https://repositorio.iscte-iul.pt/bitstream/10071/14881/5/Art4Cadernos MVM 57- VF.pdf

Bürger, T., & Kleinert, S. (2021). Crowdfunding cultural and commercial entrepreneurs: An empirical study on motivation in distinct backer communities. *Small Business Economics, 57*(2), 667–683. https://doi.org/10.1007/s11187-020-00419-8

Cholakova, M., & Clarysse, B. (2015). Does the possibility to make equity investments in crowdfunding projects crowd out reward-based investments? *Entrepreneurship Theory and Practice*, *39*(1), 145–172. https://doi.org/10.1111/etap.12139

Ciechan-Kujawa, M., & Górnowicz, J. (2020). Success determinants of sports projects financed with donation crowdfunding. *Journal of Physical Education and Sport*, *20*(5), 3046–3052. https://doi.org/10.7752/jpes.2020.s5414

Deci, E. L., & Ryan, R. M. (2008). Self-determination theory: A macrotheory of human motivation, development, and health. *Canadian Psychology*, *49*(3), 182–185. https://doi.org/10.1037/a0012801

Doyle, J. P., Kunkel, T., & Funk, D. C. (2013). Sports spectator segmentation: Examining the differing psychological connections among spectators of leagues and teams. *International Journal of Sports Marketing and Sponsorship*, *15*, 95–111. https://doi.org/10.1108/IJSMS-14-02-2013-B003

Elana Toruń. (2019). Zainwestuj w Elanę. Retrieved from Beesfund.com website: https://zainwestujwelane.pl/?_ga=2.202990609.1427656734.1596714360-644392426.1596714360&pk_vid=8c36d22773e960bd159678742098b3f9%0A

Estrin, S., Gozman, D., & Khavul, S. (2018). The evolution and adoption of equity crowdfunding: Entrepreneur and investor entry into a new market. *Small Business Economics*, *51*(2), 425–439. https://doi.org/10.1007/s11187-018-0009-5

Funk, D. C., & James, J. (2001). The psychological continuum model: A conceptual framework for understanding an individual's psychological connection to sport. *Sport Management Review*, *4*(2), 119–150. https://doi.org/10.1016/S1441-3523(01)70072-1

Gerber, E. M., & Hui, J. (2013). Crowdfunding: Motivations and deterrents for participation. *ACM Transactions on Computer-Human Interaction (TOCHI)*, *20*(6), 34:1–32. https://doi.org/10.1145/2530540

Gierczak, M. M., Bretschneider, U., Haas, P., Blohm, I., & Leimeister, J. M. (2016). Crowdfunding: Outlining the new era of fundraising. In D. Brüntje & O. Gajda (Eds.), *Crowdfunding in Europe* (pp. 7–23). Cham: Springer.

Giudici, G., Guerini, M., & Rossi Lamastra, C. (2013). Why crowdfunding projects can succeed: The role of proponents' individual and territorial social capital. Retrievered from https://papers.ssrn.com/sol3/papers.cfm?abstract_id=2255944

Giulianotti, R. (2002). Supporters, followers, fans, and flaneurs. *Journal of Sport & Social Issues*, *26*(1), 25–46.

Gray, G. T., & Wert-Gray, S. (2012). Customer retention in sports organization marketing: Examining the impact of team identification and satisfaction with team performance. *International Journal of Consumer Studies*, *36*(3), 275–281. https://doi.org/10.1111/j.1470-6431.2011.00999.x

Gwinner, K., & Swanson, S. R. (2003). A model of fan identification: Antecedents and sponsorship outcomes. *Journal of Services Marketing*, *17*(3), 275–294. https://doi.org/10.1108/08876040310474828

Hossain, M., & Gospel, O. O. (2017). Crowdfunding: Motives, definitions, typology and ethical challenges. *Entrepreneurship Research Journal*, *7*. Retrieved from https://ssrn.com/abstract=2674532,

Hunt, K. A., Bristol, T., & Bashaw, R. E. (1999). A conceptual approach to classifying sports fans. *Journal of Services Marketing*, *13*(6), 439–452. https://doi.org/10.1108/08876049910298720

Huth, C. (2018). Back to traditional stadium names: Fans' role in financing naming rights through crowdfunding. *Sport, Business and Management: An International Journal*, *8*(3), 214–234. https://doi.org/10.1108/SBM-05-2017-0027

Huth, C. (2020). Who invests in financial instruments of sport clubs ? An empirical analysis of actual and potential individual investors of professional European football clubs. *European Sport Management Quarterly*, *20*(4), 500–519. https://doi.org/10.1080/16184742.2019.1684539

Kim, S., Yoo, E., & Pedersen, P. M. (2007). Market segmentation in the K-League: An analysis of spectators of the Korean Professional Soccer League. *International Journal of Sports Marketing and Sponsorship*, *8*(2), 26–43. https://doi.org/10.1108/ijsms-08-02-2007-b005

Kłeczek, R., & Sagan, A. (2013). Badania ilościowe wizerunku marki. In J. Kall, R. Kłeczek, & A. Sagan (Eds.), *Zarządzanie marką* (pp. 71–120). Warszawa: Wolters Kluwer.

Kościółek, S. (2019). Consumer loyalty among fans of sports clubs: How much do they vary across disciplines? *Baltic Journal of Health and Physical Activity*, (Suppl. 1), 67–77. https://doi.org/10.29359/bjhpa.2019.suppl.1.06

Kościółek, S. (2021). Backers' motivations in sports clubs reward-based crowdfunding campaigns. *Journal of Physical Education and Sport*, *21*(Suppl. 2), 1165–1171. https://doi.org/10.7752/jpes.2021.s2147

Kościółek, S. (2022). Heterogeneity of motivations among crowdinvestors: Evidence from the football industry. *Journal of Enterprise Information Management*, *18*(4), 157–183. https://doi.org/10.7341/20221845

Kościółek, S. (2023). Motivations for Crowdinvesting in European Football Clubs. *Journal of Sport Management,* 1–13, https://doi.org/10.1123/jsm.2022-0080.

Kościółek, S., & Nessel, K. (2019). Market segmentation of Football Fans in Poland. In J. J. Zhang & B. G. Pitts (Eds.), *Globalized Sport Management in Diverse Cultural Contexts* (pp. 154–176). London and New York: Routledge.

Kossakowski, R., & Besta, T. (2018). Football, conservative values, and a feeling of oneness with the group: A study of Polish football fandom. *East European Politics and Societies*, *32*(4), 866–891. https://doi.org/10.1177/0888325418756991

Laverie, D. A., & Arnett, D. B. (2000). Factors affecting fan attendance: The influence of identity salience and satisfaction. *Journal of Leisure Research*, *32*(2), 225–246. https://doi.org/10.1080/00222216.2000.11949915

Lee, Y. H., & Kang, J. H. (2011). Designing ticket price strategies for professional sports teams using conjoint analysis. *International Journal of Sports Marketing and Sponsorship*, *12*(2), 124–137. https://doi.org/10.1108/ijsms-12-02-2011-b004

Leroux-Sostenes, M.-J., & Bayle, E. (2019). The crowdfunding of sport – paving the way to shared sponsorship ? *Current Issues in Sport Science*, *4*, 1–10. https://doi.org/10.15203/CISS

Lin, M., & Viswanathan, S. (2015). Home bias in online investments : An empirical study of an online crowd funding market. *Management Science*, *62*(5), 1393–1414. https://doi.org/10.1287/mnsc.2015.2206

Lock, D., & Heere, B. (2017). Identity crisis: A theoretical analysis of 'team identification' research. *European Sport Management Quarterly*, *17*(4), 413–435. https://doi.org/10.1080/16184742.2017.1306872

Loewen, C., & Wicker, P. (2021). Travelling to Bundesliga matches: The carbon footprint of football fans. *Journal of Sport & Tourism*, *25*(3), 253–272. https://doi.org/10.1080/14775085.2021.1932562

Lukkarinen, A., Wallenius, J., & Seppälä, T. (2018). Investor motivations and decision criteria in equity crowdfunding. *SSRN Electronic Journal*, *11*. https://doi.org/10.2139/ssrn.3263434

Madrigal, R. (1995). Cognitive and affective determinants of fan satisfaction with sporting event attendance. *Journal of Leisure Research*, *27*(3), 205–227. https://doi.org/10.1080/00222216.1995.11949745

Madrigal, R., & Chen, J. (2008). Moderating and mediating effects of team identification in regard to causal attributions and summary judgments following a game outcome. *Journal of Sport Management*, *22*(6), 717–733. https://doi.org/10.1123/jsm.22.6.717

Make a Champ (2022). *Crowdfunding your sport for free,* Retrieved from Makeachamp.com website: https://makeachamp.com/athletes.

Malone, T. W., Laubacher, R. J., & Johns, T. (2011). The age of hyperspecialization. *Harvard Business Review*, *89*(7–8), 56–65.

Martilla, J. A., & James, J. C. (1977). Importance-performance analysis. *Journal of Marketing*, *41*(1), 77–79. https://doi.org/10.1177/002224297704100112

Matsuoka, H., Chelladurai, P., & Harada, M. (2003). Direct and interaction effects of team identification and satisfaction on intention to attend games. *Sport Marketing Quarterly*, *12*, 244–253. https://doi.org/10.1126/science.1148310

McDonald, H., Leckie, C., Karg, A., Zubzevic, N., & Lock, D. (2016). Segmenting initial fans of a new team: A taxonomy of sport early adopters. *Journal of Consumer Behaviour*, *15*(2), 136–148. https://doi.org/10.1002/cb.1558

Mollick, E. (2014). The dynamics of crowdfunding: An exploratory study. *Journal of Business Venturing*, *29*(1), 1–16. https://doi.org/10.1016/j.jbusvent.2013.06.005

Parganas, P., Anagnostopoulos, C., & Chadwick, S. (2015). 'You'll never tweet alone': Managing sports brands through social media. *Journal of Brand Management*, *22*(7), 551–568. https://doi.org/10.1057/bm.2015.32

Park, S., Kim, S., & Chiu, W. (2023). Segmenting sport fans by eFANgelism: A cluster analysis of South Korean soccer fans. *Managing Sport and Leisure*, *8*(2), 182–196. https://doi.org/10.1080/23750472.2021.1873169

Pike, S. (2017). Destination positioning and temporality: Tracking relative strengths and weaknesses over time. *Journal of Hospitality and Tourism Management*, *31*, 126–133. https://doi.org/10.1016/j.jhtm.2016.11.005

Prigge, S., & Tegtmeier, L. (2019). Market valuation and risk profile of listed European football clubs. *Sport, Business and Management: An International Journal*, *9*(2), 146–163. https://doi.org/10.1108/SBM-04-2018-0033

Prigge, S., & Tegtmeier, L. (2020). Football stocks: A new asset class attractive to institutional investors? Empirical results and impulses for researching investor motivations beyond return. *Sport, Business and Management: An International Journal*, *10*(4), 471–494. https://doi.org/10.1108/SBM-07-2019-0063

Pu, H., & James, J. (2017). The distant fan segment: Exploring motives and psychological connection of International National Basketball Association fans. *International Journal of Sports Marketing and Sponsorship*, *18*(4), 418–438. https://doi.org/10.1108/IJSMS-05-2016-0022

Ratz, M. (2020). Crowdfunding in German association football clubs: Identifying supporters' drivers to invest. University of Northumbria at Newcastle (United Kingdom).

Regulation (EU) 2020/1503 of the European Parliament and of the Council of 7 October 2020 on European Crowdfunding service providers for business, and amending Regulation (EU) 2017/1129 and Directive (EU) 2019/1937

Ross, S. D. (2007). Segmenting sport fans using brand associations: A cluster analysis. *Sport Marketing Quarterly*, *16*(1), 15–24.

Ryu, S., & Kim, Y. (2016). Electronic commerce research and applications a typology of crowdfunding sponsors: Birds of a feather flock together ? *Electronic Commerce Research and Applications*, *16*, 43–54. https://doi.org/10.1016/j.elerap.2016.01.006

Schwienbacher, A., & Larralde, B. (2010). Crowdfunding of small entrepreneurial ventures. In D. Cumming (Ed.), *The Oxford Handbook of Entrepreneurial Finance* (pp. 369–391). Oxford: Oxford University Press.

Start Gniezno, S.A. (2020). wySTARTuj z nami. Strona inwestycji. Retrieved from Beesfund.com website: https://akcjastart.pl/?_ga=2.126558221.1427656734.1596714360-644392426.1596714360

The Crowdspace (2022). *Find and compare crowdfunding platforms*. Retrieved from The Crowdspace website: https://thecrowdspace.com/

Tkaczynski, A., Rundle-Thiele, S., & Beaumont, N. (2010). Destination segmentation: A recommended two-step approach. *Journal of Travel Research*, *49*(2), 139–152. https://doi.org/10.1177/0047287509336470

Trail, G. T., Fink, J. S., & Anderson, D. F. (2003). Sport spectator consumption behavior. *Sport Marketing Quarterly*, *12*, 8–17.

Vallerand, R. J. (1997). Toward a hierarchical model of intrinsic and extrinsic motivation. *Advances in Experimental Social Psychology*, *29*, 271–360. https://doi.org/10.1016/S0065-2601(08)60019-2

Wann, D., Bayens, C., & Driver, A. (2004). Likelihood of attending a sporting event as a function of ticket scarcity and team identification. *Sport Marketing Quarterly*, *13*(4), 209–215.

Wedel, M., & Kamakura, W. A. (2012). *Market Segmentation: Conceptual and Methodological Foundations* (Vol. 8). New York: Springer Science & Business Media.

Weimar, D., & Fox, A. (2021). Fan involvement and unusual investor behavior: Evidence from a football fan bond. *International Journal of Sport Finance*, *16*(2), 16–32. https://doi.org/10.32731/ijsf/161.022020.02

Wicker, P., Whitehead, J. C., Johnson, B. K., & Mason, D. S. (2016). Willingness-to-pay for sporting success of football bundesliga teams. *Contemporary Economic Policy*, *34*(3), 446–462. https://doi.org/10.1111/coep.12148

Wisła Kraków. (2019). Moja Wisła. Strona inwestycji. Retrieved from Beesfund.com website: https://wisla.beesfund.com/?_ga=2.202990609.1427656734.1596714360-644392426.1596714360&pk_vid=8c36d22773e960bd159678738698b3f9

Wisła Kraków. (2020). NigdyNieZginie. Strona inwestycji. Retrieved from Beesfund.com website: https://akcjewisla.pl/?__hstc=138250287.1bca93f690353ecbbbefb9b583b5558c.1596714360787.1596714360787.1596787180453.2&__hssc=138250287.4.1596787180453&__hsfp=2842042608&_ga=2.202990609.1427656734.1596714360-644392426.1596714360

# Conclusion

The main objectives of the monograph were to describe the specific nature of crowdfunding campaigns in the context of sports clubs, as well as to develop a model concept for the marketing strategy of sports club equity crowdfunding campaigns taking into account crowdinvestor segmentation. The conducted series of research (which is synthesised in this publication) made it possible to determine what kind of values crowdinvestors are looking for, which segments (and with what characteristics) they can be divided into, what the value proposition formulated for each segment should look like, how the campaign product should be positioned among crowdinvestors from the identified segments, and how to deliver value propositions to crowdinvestors with specific motivations and profiles.

The conceptual work and the analysis of empirical data provide a number of findings. At the conceptual level, the author defines a theoretical framework for sports crowdfunding, classifying it into crowdfunding of sports (when the campaign is initiated by a sports service provider) and sports-related crowdfunding (when the subject of the campaign is a sports project regardless of the nature of the primary activity of the campaign initiator). The presented analysis of sports club campaigns addresses the former.

The crowdinvestors' motivations identified are in line with the self-determination theory (Deci & Ryan, 2008; Ryan & Deci, 2000). Intrinsic motivations are dominant among sports club crowdfunding investors (which stands in contrast to most of the existing research available in the area of crowdfunding), and participants of sports club equity crowdfunding campaigns are a group unique in their consumer behaviour (which is in line with the concept of unique functioning of the sports market in terms of consumer behaviour). Out of all motivations, it is the level of identification with the club that plays a key role in the decision on whether to participate in crowdfunding campaigns (this variable is the main factor determining consumer behaviour of sports club products also in terms of other areas of club activity).

The segmentation carried out demonstrates the heterogeneity of motivations among sports club crowdinvestors, resulting in the need for a differentiated marketing approach by sports clubs initiating equity crowdfunding

DOI: 10.4324/9781003320623-6

campaigns. All the previously identified motivations (as well as the consumption variables and some of the socio-demographic variables) differentiate the adopted market segments, while the segmentation itself does not follow the psychological continuum model (Funk & James, 2001), since, as has been shown, sports club crowdinvestors are at the highest levels of the continuum of relationship with the club – attachment and allegiance.

On the basis of his previous research, the author of this monograph proposes a model concept of marketing strategy assumptions which includes the identification of the values sought by crowdinvestors in sports clubs, the formulation of value propositions that meet the needs of crowdinvestors, the definition of the positioning of the attributes of the campaign product, and the development of activities aimed at delivering the presented values to crowdinvestors. In addition to the theoretical contribution, the presented content also provides practical implications. The model concept of marketing strategy assumptions developed on the basis of the segmentation carried out can be directly adapted to business practice and provides a basis for the development of marketing strategies and plans for equity crowdfunding campaigns of sports clubs.

The main limitation of the presented research is its geographical scope and the number of campaigns included in the analysis. It is, therefore, recommended to verify the presented results in subsequent studies against other cultural contexts and include a larger number of campaigns in the analysis. It should also be determined to what extent the behaviour of participants of campaigns initiated by sports clubs differs depending on the crowdfunding model used. Furthermore, as research conducted among investors on the regulated stock market indicates, the ownership of shares in a given company has an impact on the subsequent consumer behaviour and attitudes of investors (Aspara, 2009). A logical extension of the research in question would be verification of whether this principle also applies to sports club crowdinvestors.

## References


Aspara (2009), Stock Ownership as a Motivation of Brand-Loyal and Brand-Supportive Behaviors. *Journal of Consumer Marketing*, 6, 427–436.

Deci, E. L., & Ryan, R. M. (2008). Self-determination theory: A macrotheory of human motivation, development, and health. *Canadian Psychology*, *49*(3), 182–185. https://doi.org/10.1037/a0012801

Funk, D. C., & James, J. (2001). The psychological continuum model: A conceptual framework for understanding an individual's psychological connection to sport. *Sport Management Review*, *4*(2), 119–150. https://doi.org/10.1016/S1441-3523(01)70072-1

Ryan, R. M., & Deci, E. L. (2000). Self-determination theory and the facilitation of intrinsic motivation, social development, and well-being. *American Psychologist*, *55*(1), 68–78. https://doi.org/10.1037110003-066X.55.1.68

# Index

Note: **Bold** page numbers refer to tables; *italic* page numbers refer to figures and page numbers followed by "n" denote endnotes.

For Product Safety Concerns and Information please contact our EU
representative GPSR@taylorandfrancis.com
Taylor & Francis Verlag GmbH, Kaufingerstraße 24, 80331 München, Germany

www.ingramcontent.com/pod-product-compliance
Ingram Content Group UK Ltd.
Pitfield, Milton Keynes, MK11 3LW, UK
UKHW020001200926
475702UK00015B/2415
* 9 7 8 1 0 3 2 3 4 1 1 7 0 *